Hugo Riemann's Theory of Harmony
and History of Music Theory, Book III

Hugo Riemann's Theory of Harmony

A Study by William C. Mickelsen

AND

History of Music Theory, Book III
by Hugo Riemann

Translated and edited by William C. Mickelsen

University of Nebraska Press
Lincoln and London

Publishers on the Plains

UNP

Copyright © 1977 by the University of Nebraska Press
Manufactured in the United States of America

Library of Congress Cataloging in Publication Data

Mickelsen, William C.
  Hugo Riemann's Theory of harmony.
  Bibliography: p. 239.
  Includes indexes.

1. Composition (Music)—History. 2. Harmony.
3. Riemann, Hugo, 1849–1919. Geschichte der
Musiktheorie im IX–XIX. Jahrhundert. I. Riemann,
Hugo, 1849–1919. Geschichte der Musiktheorie im
IX–XIX. Jahrhundert. Book 3. English. 1977.
ML430.M5   781.3   76–15366
ISBN 0–8032–0891–X

165594

Contents

List of Figures

List of Examples

Preface

THE superlatives found in various music dictionaries to describe **Hugo** Riemann are most impressive. He is mentioned alongside F. J. Fétis as being "the most universal and productive European scholar in the heroic age of musicology." [1] He has been called "the most prolific German writer on music in the nineteenth century next to Robert Eitner." He is classified as "the greatest European scholar of his generation and one of the last great universal musical personalities in which are united all the capabilities of the historian, pedagogue, composer, practicing musician, theorist, and seeker after fundamental truths." [2] The following quotation is the ultimate compliment:

> The mere bulk of Riemann's writings, covering every branch of musical science, constitutes a monument of indefatigable industry, and is proof of enormous concentration and capacity for work. When one takes into consideration that much of this work is the result of painstaking research and of original, often revolutionary thinking, one must share the great respect and admiration in which Riemann was held by his contemporaries. Although many of his ideas are now seen in a different light, his works treating of harmony were considered to constitute the foundation of modern musical theory. His researches in the field of music history have solved a number of vexed problems, and thrown light on others. And, finally, in formulating the new science of musicology, the labors of Riemann have been a most important factor. [3]

The study of Riemann's work in harmonic theory, to which this book is dedicated, is a prodigious undertaking, involving three different aspects of harmony: history, speculative theory, and practical theory: (1) His writings on the history of harmonic theory, especially *Die Harmonielehre,* Book III of *Geschichte der Musiktheorie im IX.–XIX. Jahrhundert,* serve as original material for later writers. (2) He succeeded in creating within the

realm of speculative theory a harmonic system wherein the meaning of harmonies and their relation to one another, and the evolution of the natural
laws of harmony are explained. (3) He wrote a number of practical textbooks on harmony and modulation. Closely connected to theory is his
research in acoustics, physiology, and psychology, which studies were
decisive in formulating his speculative theories.

Yet, meter is more important than harmony to Riemann and constitutes
the main focus of his interest, according to Denecke.[4] The problem of
meter is "a red thread" drawn throughout his works. Closely connected to
his preoccupations with meter are his studies of dynamic and agogic accent
and his theories of phrasing. His numerous publications and editions of
classical and romantic pianoforte music propounded a new interpretation
of musical punctuation which now, however, is not highly esteemed. His
theoretical output also includes textbooks in counterpoint and large collections of analysis of classical masterpieces.

As a teacher of composition he systematically treats the creation of form
from the motive to the symphony. His discourses include the study of
homophonic forms, contrapuntal techniques, the dramatic style, orchestra-
tion, melody, and modulation. He taught composition to Max Reger and
Hans Pfitzner. He also found the time to compose a number of piano
pieces, piano sonatas, songs, two string quartets, a string trio, a symphony,
a clarinet trio, several books of piano studies, and other works. Riemann
was also an accomplished pianist and piano teacher and found the time to
author several piano methods.

Still, Riemann is best known as a historian and musicologist. His
numerous publications treat almost every aspect of music from the ancient
through the late romantic period. A sample of the topics of individual
publications includes opera, the figured bass, history of musical instruments, analysis of Bach's works, organ construction, music since Wagner,
dance music, folk music, the dramatic song style, Gregorian chant, development of notation, *musica ficta,* and so on. He helped to establish musicology as a dignified and important discipline with the end result that it was
accepted in German universities as an academic discipline.[5] His many-
sided achievements and truly encyclopedic knowledge equipped him ad-
mirably for producing the *Riemann Musik Lexikon,* which attained eight
editions during his lifetime and has since reached its twelfth edition.

Karl Wilhelm Julius Hugo Riemann was born July 18, 1849, in
Grossmehlra, near Sondershausen. His father, a government agricultural
official, was a zealous amateur musician; however, although he taught
Hugo the elements of music, he opposed any early formal study of it. Also,
according to Riemann's own attestation, from his ninth year he devoted all

of his spare time to poetry.[6] Yet, he managed some theoretical training and piano study at nearby Sondershausen and his impulse toward music was later strengthened as a student at the Rossleben Klosterschule (1865–1868). After completing the Gymnasium curriculum he studied law, philosophy, and history at Berlin and Tübingen. He fulfilled his military obligation during the Franko-Prussian campaign of 1870–1871, and states that serious reflection toward music came during the siege of Paris. Upon his return to Germany he became a student at the Leipzig Conservatory. When his dissertation, "Ueber das musikalische Hören," was rejected he transferred to the University at Göttingen and received his Doctor of Philosophy degree in 1873. He then became a conductor and teacher in Bielefeld where he married in 1876. In 1878 he returned to Leipzig to qualify himself as a lecturer, hoping for an appointment at that esteemed institution. As the appointment did not come, he went in 1880 as a teacher of music to Bromberg. The years 1881–1890 were spent mainly as a teacher of piano and theory at the Hamburg Conservatory. From 1890–1895 he taught at the Wiesbaden Conservatory. In 1895 he returned to Leipzig as a lecturer and was appointed professor in 1901. In 1908 he became director of the newly established Collegium Musicum and in 1914 was made director of the newly established Forschungsinstitut für Musikwissenschaft. In Leipzig, in spite of opposition to some of his innovations, Riemann was one of the leading personalities of German and European musical activity. He attained many honors, one being the honorary doctorate from the University of Edinburgh in 1899. On his sixtieth birthday he was honored by a *Festschrift,* which contained papers from the world's most noted musical scholars. A second *Festschrift* was published in 1919, the year of his death.

As this book is dedicated to the study of Riemann's writings on harmonic theory, it is hoped that its presentation will fulfill two important needs in the literature of music theory: (1) a comprehensive presentation of Riemann's harmonic theories, especially in English, and (2) the translation of Riemann's history of harmonic theory, *Die Harmonielehre,* Book III of *Geschichte der Musiktheorie im IX.–XIX. Jahrhundert* (1898). Riemann's twenty or so books and articles on harmonic theory cover a period of forty-four years from 1872 to 1916. In addition to these publications the subject of harmonic theory constantly appears in his other works, particularly the historical books. For example, a chapter concerning the influence of harmony on Greek and Arabic theory appears in his *Studien zur Geschichte der Notenschrift,* and some ideas concerning Giuseppe Tartini's harmonic theories appear in *Katechismus der Musikgeschichte.* This profusion of material presents a tremendous task to the Riemann scholar.

Also, a full comprehension of Riemann's theories is difficult because they were in a constant state of evolution. I know of only four theoretical works which have been translated into English. The bibliographical list is small, consisting mainly of short articles in German publications, each concerning some aspect of Riemann's theories. Before this present publication, Elmer Seidel's article, "Die Harmonielehre Hugo Riemanns," *Beiträge zur Musiktheorie des 19. Jahrhunderts* (1966), and Renate Imig's book, *Systeme der Funktionsbezeichnung in den Harmonielehren seit Hugo Riemann* (1970) were the only extensive writings known to me. Practically the only source available in English is a rather derogatory section from a chapter in Matthew Shirlaw's *Theory of Harmony* (1955), which, by the way, is the only available history of harmonic theory in English before this present translation. In fact, it closely parallels Riemann's history and owes much to it. It is quite evident that a detailed compilation of Riemann's harmonic theories is needed.

In 1898 Riemann published his notable *Geschichte der Musiktheorie im IX.–XIX. Jahrhundert* in three books. As of this present date it is still the most complete history of music theory ever written, and in spite of its age and number of errors, based upon nineteenth-century preconceptions, the book is an important source for musicologists and theorists. A new history of music theory is badly needed. I suppose it has not come forth because of the enormity of such an undertaking. In view of this, one has to admire Riemann even more for taking on the awesome task of compiling such a history in the midst of so many other accomplishments. Books I and II were translated into English and published in 1962.[7] Book III, the history of harmonic theory, has been up to this time unavailable in English. It is hoped that this translation will be a helpful source for all those who prefer the convenience of a translation as well as for many who do not read German.

NOTES

1. *Riemann Musik-Lexikon,* 12th ed., s.v. "Riemann, Hugo."

2. *Die Musik in Geschichte und Gegenwart,* s.v. "Riemann, Hugo."

3. *Baker's Biographical Dictionary of Music and Musicians,* 5th ed., s.v. "Riemann, Hugo."

4. Heinz Ludwig Denecke, "Die Kompositionslehre Hugo Riemanns, historisch und systematisch dargestellt" (Inaugural diss., Kiel, 1937), p. 1.

5. *Die Musik in Geschichte und Gegenwart,* s.v. "Riemann, Hugo."

6. Hugo Riemann, *Encyclopaedic Dictionary of Music,* s.v. "Riemann, Hugo."

7. Riemann, *History of Music Theory,* trans. Raymond Haggh (Lincoln: University of Nebraska Press, 1962).

Acknowledgments

THE book has been published with the help of a grant from the Humanities Research Council of Canada, using funds provided by the Canada Council. A small grant was also received from the University of Victoria.

The writer wishes to acknowledge the assistance of Dr. Vernon Kliewer of the Indiana University School of Music for his helpful reading of this work and for his advice in the organization and presentation of the material. Mrs. Margot Hahn of the Utah University library staff assisted in the translation of many difficult German passages. Many of the Italian quotations found in *Die Harmonielehre* were translated by Robert Busse of Concordia Teachers College. Lloyd Tayson, a doctoral student in classical languages at Indiana University, translated the quotations from Latin sources. Professor Alexander Posniak of the Auburn University Language Department proofread the Italian translations and my translations of the French and made helpful corrections. I also wish to thank the many others who have helped in various ways to accomplish this study. Most of the numerous texts and sources necessary for the collecting of the material were available in the excellent music libraries at Indiana University and the University of Victoria. Other sources were procured by the interlibrary loan offices at those universities.

PART I

Hugo Riemann's Theory of Harmony

CHAPTER I

Riemann's Predecessors

*D*ualism AND *function* are the heart and soul of Riemann's mature harmonic system. Dualism, with its two aspects of major and minor; and function, with its three pillars of harmony, exist as the center of the system.

The term *dualism* means that major and minor tonalities, while being of perfectly equal value, are the antithesis of each other and are evolved from exact opposite sources. For example, when consonance is based on numbers the major triad can be derived from the geometric or harmonic series 1, 1/2, 1/3, 1/4, 1/5, 1/6 (C, c, g, c′, e′, g′). These fractions represent the divisions of a string. The minor triad, in opposite manner, can be derived from the arithmetic series 1, 2, 3, 4, 5, 6 (g″, g′, c′, g, e♭, c), which numerals represent the lengthenings of a string. The harmonic series might also represent a musical tone and its overtones. Riemann accepted the general theory that the original source of major harmony was the overtone series. He also believed in the physical existence of an undertone series as a source for minor harmony for a number of years. If the overtone series explains major harmony, then, he conjectured, minor harmony, being just as consonant as major and being the opposite of major, must result from undertones. As Riemann conceived it, every tone emits a series of undertones as well as

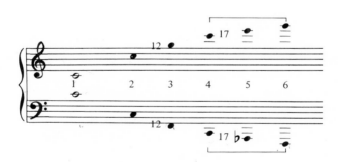

Example 1. The Fundamental and Its First Five Overtones and Undertones

3

overtones, as shown in example 1. Psychologically, one series becomes predominant and the other is erased. Thus, every tone belongs either to a major or a minor chord.

The term *Klang* (the English equivalent "sound") is used by Riemann to designate a fundamental note and its overtones or undertones of the twelfth and seventeenth, i.e., the natural triad, with all three tones reducible to the same octave in the form of a single triad. The term *Klang* or the English translation "clang" will thus be found in the above meaning throughout this writing. The term was not coined by Riemann. It was in common use by other German theorists and acousticians of the time (Hermann von Helmholtz, Arthur von Oettingen, Heinrich Schenker) in reference to the series of overtones which by nature forms the major triad. But these theorists and acousticians accepted only the overtone series, not the undertone series. It is well known that a vibrating string is capable of dividing into partials, thereby creating multiple higher sounds. But a string cannot multiply its length to create undertones. Presumably, Riemann realized this also. His justification of an undertone series was based on sympathetic vibration. In his *Dictionary of Music,* article "Clang," he states: "A sounding tone sets bodies capable of producing sound into sympathetic vibration . . . of whose ground tone it is an upper partial. In any case, bodies sounding by sympathetic vibration make, first of all, strong partial vibrations . . . but they also make total vibrations." This has, of course, been proved false, and later in life, Riemann himself rejected the idea of a physical basis for his undertone series. Yet, he rigidly adhered to dualism to the very end. I cannot accept the idea that major and minor are exact opposite key systems. Yet, the study of Riemann's brilliant dichotomous creation, if not exciting, is at least absorbing, and one can marvel at his ingenuity.

Function refers to the logical progression of harmonies within the major and minor key systems. There are only three fundamental chords, or clangs, sometimes called "the three pillars": tonic, dominant, and subdominant. The tonic chord originates from the given tone and its upper or lower partials of the twelfth (chord fifth) and the seventeenth (chord third). The second overtone (twelfth) provides the root of the dominant chord. The second undertone (twelfth below) provides the root for the subdominant chord.

The nucleus of Riemann's system consists of the major and minor modes with their fundamental chords of tonic and upper and lower dominants. All other chordal structures are alterations or mixtures of these three chords. In the theory of *Klang*-representation, first conceived by Helmholtz and expanded by Riemann, single tones are also understood as members of a primary triad. Riemann explains dissonant additions to these triads as notes borrowed from other fundamental triads. For example, in the chord of the dominant seventh, the seventh is really the root of the subdominant. The secondary triads of the key system are also explained as mixtures of notes from the primary clangs. This system, he claims, is not arbitrary. It is based upon natural and logical laws.

The basic features of Riemann's mature harmonic system can be summed up as follows:

1. The major and minor triads are derived from the overtone and undertone series respectively. Tones are always heard as representatives of either major or minor clangs. The major and minor key systems are the exact antithesis of each other and are equal in strength and value.

2. There are only three fundamental chords: the tonic and its upper and lower dominants. Therefore, harmonic function (and tonality) basically involves the movement away from the tonic to chords having dominant or subdominant significance and back to the tonic chord.

3. Chords other than the three primary harmonies are mixtures of notes from these chords and thus may be comprehended as representing two or even three of the primary chords. Yet, one primary chord is always more prominent. For example, the secondary triads of the key are such simultaneous representatives of two of the three primary chords in which one is comprehended as the main content (consonance), the other as a foreign addition (dissonance). Thus, all chordal formations can be explained as belonging to a key through the concept of chord-representation.

4. Modulation is the shifting of the significance of tonic to a new chord, and the interpretation of chords from their old to a new meaning.[1]

HARMONIC DUALISM

Riemann had forerunners. He never claims to have created truth, only to have discovered, or rediscovered, much of it. He believes that his system of harmony, existing as a natural truth, was slowly being discovered through the centuries by a few perceptive theorists, only to be lost again. Finally, truth can no longer be kept down. Thus, in his history he creates an illusion of a struggle between the forces of truth and error, the final result of which is the recognition of harmonic dualism and function as the ultimate truths within the harmonic system.[2] Riemann firmly believes that these concepts are natural, eternal, and of universal application. Even though composers of various cultures are not consciously aware of these natural laws, they are perceptibly or imperceptibly guided by them:

> One would think that the basic essence of monodic music, having existed for millenniums, would have been deciphered by the theorists of antiquity, but this was not the case. First, the entire development of polyphonic music from its crudest beginnings to its most sublime conceptions, and finally, a second analysis of harmony appearing in multiple melody was needed in order to completely disclose theoretically the essence of monody. *For even the simple one line melodies as they exist in the preserved monuments of antiquity rest upon a harmonic foundation.* [Italics mine.][3]

Gioseffo Zarlino

Riemann's assertions that Zarlino was the founder of harmonic dualism will be examined. Zarlino's *Le Istituzioni harmoniche* (1558) is the first published work to actually identify and name a harmonic structure.[4] Whereas earlier speculative theory involved only intervallic ratios, Zarlino exhibits the numerical relationships of some three-part combinations. He observes that all the consonances are found in the numerical proportions $1:2:3:4:5:6$, and gives this series of numbers the name *Senario*. The simultaneous sounding of all these tones produces for him the most beautiful of harmonies (*Harmonie perfetta*), and he advises the composer to make use of this triad of sounds whenever possible.[5] He discovers that the two forms of the triad result by dividing the fifth harmonically ($4:5:6$=major) and arithmetically ($6:5:4$=minor). He then states: "The minor harmony is less harmonious and perfect than the major; the reason being that in the minor harmony we find the consonances arranged 'contrary to the nature of the sonorous number.'" [6] He also advises the composer against using too many successive minor triads because the result would be too dreary. Zarlino also states that harmony results from diverse, rather than from similar elements. The union of two elements of the same species results in discords such as two fifths (C–g–d) or two major thirds (f–a–c♯). This is the extent of Zarlino's writings about harmony of more than two parts, but within these ideas is found the inception and emergence of harmonic theory.

In "Die Natur der Harmonik" (1882) Riemann gives his interpretation of Zarlino's contribution to the world:

> He gave to the world the conception of the consonant chord, in its double form of major and minor chord. . . . Zarlino . . . contrasted two modes of dividing a

string, which he called the "harmonic" and the "arithmetical." . . . By the "harmonical" division of the string he meant the determining of the pitch of the tones produced by the half, third, fourth, fifth and sixth of the string. By the "arithmetical" division, he meant the determining of the pitch of *multiples* of some small fraction of the string, $1:2:3:4:5:6$. . . . In other words: according to Zarlino, *the minor chord is mathematically the exact opposite of the major chord.* . . . Unfortunately, this splendid idea of Zarlino's came to naught; whether it remained unnoticed or whether it was not understood, no matter; it disappeared for a full two hundred years, and was then re-discovered by Tartini. . . . If the system which was to grow up had only been developed on the lines laid down by Zarlino, . . . then theory would have taken the direction in which the latest efforts of theorists are now being put forth; that of a consistent *dualism,* major being conceived of as formed *above* the fundamental tone, and minor *below* it.[7]

In *Die Harmonielehre* (see p. 108 this study) Riemann, through a misinterpretation, concludes that Zarlino means there are only two possible types of harmony, major and minor, in polyphonic composition, and that the only elements used in composition are the third and fifth and their inversions. Riemann's version of Zarlino states: "Not in the variety of consonances, but rather, in the two possible forms of harmony." According to Shirlaw, Zarlino is saying:

The variety of harmony does not consist *solely* in the variety of the consonances which two voices form with each other, but *also* in that variety of the harmony which is determined by the position which the Third or the Tenth occupies above the lowest note of the chord.[8]

The latter translation implies that the major and minor thirds are additional sources of variety, not the only source.

Riemann errs again in the same paragraph when he misinterprets the word *Replicati* as "inversions": "The third and fifth or their inversions (*Replicati*) constitute the only elements of compostion." Carl Dahlhaus points out that Zarlino's perfect harmony demands the third and fifth and their compounds the tenth and twelfth, not the third and its inversion the sixth, nor the fifth and its inversion the fourth.[9] That the term *Replicati* means octave compounds, not inversions, is substantiated in the text when Zarlino calls the minor sixth $(8:5)$ a consonance because the eighth is merely a replica (compound) of fourth and second.[10] Riemann's misinterpretation of Zarlino is given a sound condemnation by Shirlaw:

Dr. Riemann, in his eagerness to include Zarlino as one of the foremost representatives of the "newer school" of harmonic science, not only quite mistakes the real drift of his remarks, but fails to grasp the real nature of the important theoretical pronouncement which he makes. What Zarlino is chiefly concerned to demonstrate is that there is a certain position of the harmony which excels all others—the *Compositione*—or *Harmonie-perfetta*. He does not consider any consonance or harmony to arise from the principle of harmonic inversion. He is not to be regarded as the real progenitor of the Hauptmann-Oettingen, etc., school of modern theorists who recognize only one species of Third as "directly intelligible." He does not consider the Fifth of the minor Triad to be its fundamental note. He does not state that the Third and Fifth are the only elements of composition. Finally, he knows nothing of "ground harmonies," nor does he state that the only fundamental harmonies which exist are the major and minor chords.[11]

Riemann believed that Zarlino's supposed discovery of harmonic dualism was completely obscured by the practical aspects of the figured bass:

> Thus, the figured-bass system became the means of directing the development of the theory and practice of harmony into quite other channels than those marked out by Zarlino, the most learned and distinguished theorist of his time. The diametrically opposite character of the major and minor chord was totally forgotten. . . . The ideas of Zarlino as to the essential difference between major and minor chords, and the essential unity of any given chord, no matter what its inversion or distribution, were strangled in their birth.[12]

Jean-Philippe Rameau

Riemann then adds that more than a hundred years were to pass before theory was again turned in the true direction when Rameau discovered the overtone series as the basis for consonance.

Rameau's harmonic system, established with genius but full of inconsistencies, became the point of departure and set the course of harmonic theory for his successors. His original ideas on harmonic theory were conceived in his study of Zarlino and Descartes. From Zarlino he learned that all the consonances are found in the series of numbers 1–6. Zarlino had also stated that as unity is the source of numbers, the unison, representing the sounding body, is the source of consonance. From Descartes he learned that the primary consonances, as shown through sympathetic vibration, are the octave, the fifth, and the major third.[13]

With this background Rameau originated the fundamental bass theory. The entire string represented by the number one is the fundamental sound, the source, and generator of the multiples. The concept of harmonic inversion then resulted by identifying the octave with the fundamental sound. The octave is a replica, the same sound, not a different one; it is still the root, or fundamental, in whatever position it is found.[14] Here then are the three most important concepts presented in his first book, *Traité de l'harmonie*: (1) fundamental bass, or chord root; (2) harmonic generation—the other chord tones are generated from the fundamental bass; (3) harmonic inversion—when the fundamental bass is not in the lowest position.

One of Riemann's bitter disappointments with Rameau stems from the latter's rejection of a natural basis for the minor triad. Rameau was aware of this triad as a consonant entity, but finding its source in nature was a task with which he struggled throughout the remainder of his life. He came up with several different solutions. His first explanation of the minor triad is the theory of the divided fifth.[15] The fifth is the important interval, being generated directly from the root, and it makes no difference to the character of the fifth whether the minor third is the upper or lower of the two thirds. The minor triad is therefore explained as a variation of the major. Later, however, he contradicted his first principle of chord generation by the principle of adding thirds above one another. In this case the third and not the fifth is the generating principle.[16]

During the next eleven years prior to the publication of *Génération harmonique* (1737), Rameau did much research and study in the area of acoustics. He then returned to natural principles as a basis for the major triad and, in addition, thought that he had found a natural basis for the minor triad in the phenomenon of sympathetic vibration. He discovered that strings tuned to the twelfth and seventeenth below a given string will covibrate when the upper string is struck, thereby producing evidence of minor harmony. He now accepted Zarlino's explanation of the arithmetic series as the source of the minor mode, but with the added value of a supposed acoustical foundation.[17] In his fourth book, *Démonstration du principe de l'harmonie* (1750), having since been made aware that the lower strings do not vibrate in their entirety, but only in those segments coinciding with the unison of the original vibration, he conceded that undertones cannot serve as the basis for minor harmony. Riemann informs us of the situation in the following:

> He had discovered the true principle, but was talked out of it by the physicist D'Alembert, who told him that the lower strings did not vibrate sympathetically in their whole length, so as to give their fundamentals, but only in such fractions as correspond to the tone of the "generator."[18]

Because Rameau rejected the undertone series as a basis for minor harmony, Riemann cannot consider him a harmonic dualist. However, he feels that Rameau's great achievements in establishing an acoustical basis for major harmony helped point the way for the future dualists.

Giuseppe Tartini

In the "Die Natur der Harmonik" (1882) Riemann calls Tartini the first truly great thinker since Zarlino, for it was he who revived Zarlino's idea of the dual nature of harmony "after two hundred years of oblivion."[19] Tartini presents the polar opposites of major and minor in the following manner:

> Our musical practice is divided into two types of harmony: the one called the major third, derived from the harmonic division of the string into unequal parts, 1/2, 1/3, 1/4, 1/5, 1/6; the one called the minor third, derived from the arithmetic division of the string into equal parts, 1, 2, 3, 4, 5, 6. [See example 2.][20]

Example 2. Tartini's Derivation of the Major and Minor Triads

Tartini feels the necessity for having an acoustical basis for his harmonic system. He regards his discovery of combination tones as a confirmation of the overtone phenomena used by Rameau and maintains that they are manifestations of the same phenomenon. He specifies that if two sounds are played with sufficient strength and duration on a musical instrument, a third sound will be heard, as shown in example 3.

Example 3. Tartini Calculates the Third Sound an Octave Too High

However, Tartini errs in his calculations by placing the combination tone an octave too high. He states that if any adjoining two notes of the harmonic series be sounded, the third sound will always be that of half the string. Actually, the resulting third sound will be that of the whole string,

or equal to the lowest note of the harmonic series. In his second work (*De'
principi dell'armonia* [1767]) this error is corrected with the apology that
the particular timbre, namely, the simplicity of the combination tone,
deceived him into placing it an octave too high.[21]

But Riemann believes that Tartini's combination tones are caused by
coinciding undertones. In the two series extending downward below the
two notes of the interval there will eventually be an undertone common to
both series. The reinforcement of this particular tone will make it audible.
This tone will always be number one of the overtone series to which the
two notes of the interval belong. He misinterprets Tartini's explanation in
the following quotation:

He rated them [combination tones] equal to the overtones and explained both
manifestations as the same. He means by this that underneath the fundamental
lie the undertones (the exact opposite of the overtone series) which can be heard
when two tones sounding together cause them to be reinforced, i.e., in the case of
the two notes g' and e''. The first common undertone of g' and e'' is c.[22] [See
example 4].

Example 4. Combination Tones Caused by Reinforced Undertones

Example 5 shows how Tartini explains that minor harmony is based on
the same principle as the major. The intervals of the treble staff belong to

Example 5. Tartini's Explanation of the Physical Origin of Minor Harmony

the harmonic series of the lower tone (the combination tone). At the same time their resultant tones form a descending arithmetical series. This series is derived from strategically placed harmonic intervals, all built on C, after the order of those found in the overtone series: 8, 5, 4, ma.3, and so on. But the error, explained by Shirlaw, is as follows:

> They do not belong to one and the same harmonic system, but are derived from different systems. They are related to different fundamentals, and are strictly speaking in different keys. Thus the Fifth is related to c as its fundamental, or harmonic centre, the Fourth to F, the major Third to C, the minor Third to A♭.[23]

Moritz Hauptmann

According to Peter Rummenhöller, Hauptmann's approach to theory is different from all his predecessors. He goes back to the medieval concept, the all-embracing idea of universality, lost since Zarlino through progressive specialization. One manifestation of this "universality" is "music proceeding from one supreme universal binding principle."[24] The introduction to Hauptmann's treatise, *Die Natur der Harmonik und der Metrik* (1853), states that the entire work is after the order of Hegel in method and plan, i.e., Hegelian dialectics. The law anunciated by Hauptmann involves three stages in the process of thought: "a stage of simplicity or unity; a stage of division or separation; and a stage of reconcilement or restored unity.[25] The three stages are often referred to as unity, opposition, and union; or thesis, antithesis, and synthesis. In a brilliant manner he proceeds to organize a system of music wherein the aspects of harmony and meter are related to these three states. The elements of harmony which come out of the dialectical process are tone, triad, and key. All other phenomena, whether scalewise or dissonance, become intelligible only through the mediation of these three directly intelligible events. Only the triad will be discussed here. The conceptual principles of Hauptmann's system are found in the following concise statement:

> There are three directly intelligible intervals:
> > I. The octave
> > II. The fifth
> > III. The major third
>
> They are unchangeable.[26]

The octave expresses unity; the fifth, the idea of duality or opposition; the third, unity of duality, or union. He does not attempt to account for any of the other intervals, since he claims they are all products of these three. These three intervals, united become the triad, which is a two-sided concept; positive (major) and negative (minor). The major triad is shown as:

I	III	II
C	e	G

The numbers represent the three dialectic steps. The large letters show the interval of a fifth and the distance from a large letter to a small one represents the interval of a third. The positive concept of the major triad results from duality (G) being above unity (C). In the minor triad (F–a♭–C) the minor third is not a directly intelligible interval. The intelligible third is the upper major third. The minor concept therefore becomes negative when the duality is placed beneath unity:

II	—	I
F	a♭	C
	III	I

Thus, the root of the chord, F, is duality, while the fifth of the chord represents unity. Hauptmann also displays the minor triad in a different manner to give the root unity and the fifth duality:

I	—	II
F	a♭	C
	I	III

The note C now has the double meaning of duality and union.

Hauptmann ends the chapter of the minor chord with a statement that sounds much like Riemann:

> The minor triad thus being of passive nature, and having its starting-point above, and forming from it downwards, there is expressed in it, not upward driving force, but downward drawing weight, dependence in the literal, as well as in the figurative sense of the word. We therefore find in the minor chord the expression for *mourning,* the hanging boughs of the weeping willow as contrasted with the aspiring arbor vitae. [27]

Because of this explanation of the minor concept, Riemann acknowledges Hauptmann as the man who formulated the concept of harmonic dualism for the late nineteenth-century theorists:

> Hauptmann's memorable discovery that the minor chord ought to be regarded as a major chord upside down, developed negatively instead of positively, made a great sensation. Of course, when we now find, in studying the history of harmony teaching, that the same discovery had been made by Tartini a hundred

years before and by Zarlino three hundred years earlier, we cannot give Hauptmann the credit of its first discovery; historically it is not a new idea. But it would be very unjust to Hauptmann to deny him the merit of having discovered it for himself. So far as the present and future development of theory is concerned, Hauptmann is the originator of the idea. . . . The idea came to all of us from Hauptmann. There are his own faithful pupils, Köhler, Paul, and Rischbieter, who hold to the letter of his teaching. O. Tiersch, who seeks a compromise between Hauptmann and Helmholtz (see his "System und Methode der Harmonielehre," 1868); then the strictly consistent dualists, von Oettingen, Thürlings, myself, and with some reservations, Hostinsky, who have become more Hauptmannish than Hauptmann himself—all of us received the idea of dualism in harmony as a new conception from him.[28]

Because of his explanation of the minor concept, Hauptmann is usually ranked by harmonic dualists among their number. Rummenhöller disputes the claim that Hauptmann was a dualist: "The concept of dualism in its typical, needlessly inductive, theoretical interpretation is not to be associated with Hauptmann."[29] The dualists' idea of the music system arising from two opposing sources is completely different from Hauptmann's dialectic principle. Hauptmann says nothing about inverted minor harmony after the first few pages. Richard Münnich states that "Hauptmann . . . was for the consequent development of the dualistic idea as far removed as was Rameau a hundred years earlier. It was a mere episode in his musical thoughts."[30]

Arthur von Oettingen

According to Münnich, Oettingen's ideas on harmonic dualism were so original that if the dualist theory had consequently been recognized as correct it would have won for him an indisputable place of honor in the history of musical knowledge equal to that of Rameau and Helmholtz.[31] Oettingen's *Harmoniesystem in dualer Entwicklung* (1866) perhaps had more direct influence on Riemann's theories than any other book, for it was from Oettingen that he acquired a basis from which to develop his own ideas. Much of the terminology and nomenclature in Riemann's earlier works was taken directly from Oettingen's system.

The premise that major and minor are the exact opposites of each other is developed to its extremes by Oettingen in a most impractical manner. The notes of the major triad find their unity in a common lower fundamental. This is the same theory of harmonic generation first expounded by Rameau, wherein the fifth and third are the natural partials of the root tone. The notes of the minor triad, on the other hand, find their unity in a

common overtone (example 6).[32] The term *tonality* (tonic) refers to the
property of intervals and chords having the same fundamental, whereas

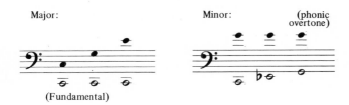

Example 6. The Source of Unity in the Major and Minor Triad

the term *phonality* (phonic) describes the property of intervals or chords
having a common overtone.

Riemann expresses misgivings over the fact that Oettingen uses overtones instead of undertones for deriving minor harmony.[33] But Oettingen
has a completely different definition of undertones. To him they are a
series of tones which have a common overtone. This occurs when these
tones are arranged in an arithmetical descending series. However, Riemann
expresses his approval over the way Oettingen proves the quality of major
and minor regarding their consonant and dissonant qualities. Oettingen
claims that since the minor is the exact opposite of the major their consonant and dissonant properties are identical. It is true, he claims, that the
minor triad is tonically dissonant while the major triad is tonically consonant; but from the reverse point of view the minor triad is phonically consonant while the major triad is phonically dissonant. The fundamental of a
major chord is exactly the same distance beneath the lowest tone as the
phonic overtone of a minor chord is over the highest tone.[34] Thus, the
symmetrical position of these two chords shows that the tonal systems are
exact mirrors of each other.

But Oettingen's analogy between major and minor is not wholly accurate. Wherein the root of major harmony can be considered a generator,
the common overtone of the minor chord is a determined note and, as such,
has nothing to do with the generating of minor harmony. Shirlaw explains
this very well:

> Oettingen cannot well maintain that there is any real analogy between the
> "tonic ground-tone" of the major and what he describes as the "phonic overtone"
> of the minor harmony. He cannot maintain that while c is the fundamental note
> of the major harmony c–e–g, g is the fundamental note of the minor harmony,

c–eb–g. This g of the minor harmony is a determined note, and is shown by Oettingen himself to be the Fifth of c. So that between c–g of the major harmony, and c–g of the minor harmony, there is absolutely no difference; c is fundamental and g is Fifth in each case. When, then, Oettingen shows us that in the minor harmony c–eb–g, g is Fifth of c, and Third of eb, his position does not appear to be materially different from that of Helmholtz, that is, he considers minor harmony to arise from two sources.[35]

The scale derived by Oettingen from the tonic system is the major scale, and the scale derived from the *phonic* system is its exact mirror, containing the same steps and half steps in the opposite direction (example 7).

Major

Phrygian

Example 7. The Major Scale and Its Opposite, the Phonic Minor

Oettingen points out that the two most important scales historically, the Dorian as the main scale of antiquity and the major scale as the main scale of modern times, are antagonistically opposite. Moreover, they are constructed equally and joined together with the same scale steps.[36]

Following his principles to the letter Oettingen constructs his chords and key system of major and minor as exact opposites of each other (example 8).[37] (1) The major tonic triad (c–e–g) mirrors the minor tonic triad

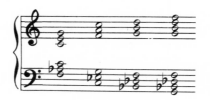

Example 8. The Major and Minor Key Systems as Exact Opposites

(c–ab–f). (2) The upper dominant (g–b–d) mirrors the underdominant, or the *Regnante,* as Oettingen calls the phonic dominant (f–db–bb). (3) The subdominant (f–a–c) mirrors the over-*Regnante* (g–eb–c), the counterpart of the subdominant. (4) The tonic dominant seventh chord (g–b–d–f) mirrors the phonic *Regnante* seventh chord (f–db–bb–g).

The concepts *Homonomic* and *Antinomic* are very important to Oettingen's theories. Homonomic refers to the relationship of two chords, intervals, or notes belonging to the same system, i.e., two major or two minor. Antinomic refers to the relationship of two chords or tones from different systems.[38] For example, altered chords are antinomic because they are a mixture of notes from both systems. Raising and lowering notes is only a borrowing from the opposite mode. There is no real altered chord; there are only mixed systems. Such an antinomic relationship is shown in the diminished seventh chord in example 9. Seventh chords, as Hauptmann

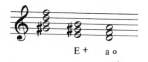

Example 9. Origin of the Diminished Seventh Chord

and Helmholtz explained earlier, consist of interlocking triads. The diminished seventh chord is a combination of antinomes a fifth apart, with missing roots (in minor triads the root is the highest tone (example 9). The resolution requires an antinomic resolution of a fifth. Riemann borrowed a number of symbols and terminologies from Oettingen, including the above, which are found in his earlier works (e.g., *Musikalische Syntaxis* [1877]).

HARMONIC FUNCTION

Riemann never claimed to have created the idea of three fundamental chords—tonic, dominant, and subdominant—in their logical succession. Natural truths are not created, only discovered. He lists a number of theorists who he feels preceived the true "meaning of harmony," most importantly, Rameau, Johann Friedrich Daube, and Heinrich C. Koch. Riemann was also familiar with *the rule of the octave,* which refers to harmonizing a bass scale using only the three above-mentioned chords and their derivatives and inversions.

The Rule of the Octave

The term *rule of the octave* became widespread after the publication of François Campion's book *Traité d'accompagnement et de composition, selon la règle des octaves* in 1716. (The Frenchman, François Campion, should not be confused with the English composer and theorist, Thomas Campion.) However, in *Die Harmonielehre,* Riemann implies that the rule of the octave has its roots in the thoroughbass rules of Bernardo Strozzi and Michael Praetorius.[39] In 1708 Francesco Gasparini was harmonizing bass scales in a manner much like the rule of the octave (see *Die Harmonielehre,* this study, page 232, note 32. F. J. Fétis, in his *Biographie universelle* (1837–1844), article "Delair," mentions that the rule of the octave was known in Italy long before François Campion published his work. The rule of the octave is also found in the works of Johann David Heinichen and Johann Mattheson, as well as in those of Rameau. The two former men, however, were concerned only with its practical aspects. Rameau's writings on the subject are distinguished by his efforts in the realm of speculative theory—his attempts to prove that melody, and hence the scale, is derived from harmony.

Jean-Philippe Rameau

Riemann mentions Rameau's establishment of the "three pillars of harmony," the tonic with its upper and lower dominants (dominant and subdominant).[40] He credits Rameau with conceiving and naming the subdominant and giving it (with added sixth) equal significance along with the dominant (with added seventh). In the *Traité,* Rameau stresses the importance of the V–I relationship; he understands the importance of the tonic as the center of gravity and point of repose. Yet, in the *Nouveau système de musique théorique* he considers that the tonic has two dominants, an upper and a lower, in the triple progression $1:3:9$ (C–G–D). The central term, G, represents tonic, and the most perfect progression is that of a fifth away from and back to tonic. Shirlaw's critcism of this progression is in having the number three represent tonic. Since the number one always represents the generator, three cannot be tonic because it is a sound determined by the number one. Therefore, C has to be tonic, G the dominant, and D the dominant of the dominant. The subdominant cannot be determined by numbers representing geometrical progressions.[41]

In the *Génération harmonique* Rameau explains the natural relationship of the subdominant to tonic through the principle of sympathetic vibration. He has learned that a string tuned to the twelfth below covibrates with the sounding string. Although he knows that the longer string divides into three segments, he thinks that it also vibrates in its entirety. This is incorrect, as has been discussed in reference to the minor triad. However, he presents a key system in which the three primary harmonies represent the fundamental chords of the key.[42] He was the first theorist to write about the three chords in their primary perspective.

Rameau's efforts in harmonizing the major and minor scales with the tonic and two dominants is of great significance to Riemann. In the *Traité*, Rameau harmonizes the scale according to the rule of the octave (example 10), using the subdominant with added sixth.[43]

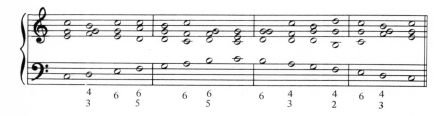

Example 10. Rameau's Harmonization of the Scale According to the Rule of the Octave

Rameau writes that melody is derived from harmony.[44] Melody in its pure form, the scale, is derived from the three basic sounds: the tonic, dominant, and subdominant and their upper partials. These chords, representing the triple progression $1:3:9$ (C–G–D), give all the notes of the major scale. By a fundamental bass progression of a minor third the tonic (E) of the minor mode is reached.[45] This tonic then becomes the middle term of another triple progression, A–E–B, which yields the notes of the melodic minor scale. Riemann states that Rameau is the first theorist to express the idea that melody is derived from harmony.

Of great interest to Riemann is Rameau's handling of dissonance and seventh chords. In the *Traité*, Rameau states that a triad on each step of the scale can become a seventh by the addition of a third on top. The most important of these is the dominant seventh because of its natural resolution to the tonic.[46] The subdominant chord, however, may carry a sixth above the bass. The purpose of the added sixth is to add a note of dissonance in order to impel the chord onward. In the *Génération harmonique* he explains these two dominant dissonants in much the same way Riemann does his characteristic dissonances 150 years later. The new note added to the dominant is the root of the subdominant. The new note added to the subdominant is the fifth of the dominant chord. Rameau distinguishes between the subdominant with added sixth and the supertonic-seventh chord in first inversion (grand sixth) according to their resolution.[47] If the resolution is to the dominant, the chord is considered a supertonic six-five chord. If it resolves to tonic, then it is a subdominant chord with added sixth.[48]

Riemann laments the fact that Rameau's presentation of the three fundamental harmonies did not become standard. Instead, influential writers such as Rousseau and Johann Phillip Kirnberger gave a name to every note of the scale on which to construct triads and seventh chords. Riemann's bias stems from the fact that his own system calls for three acoustically derived chords and none other.

Johann Friedrich Daube

Riemann's remarks concerning Johann Friedrich Daube's *Generalbass in drey Accorden* (1756) reveal an interesting but almost forgotten theorist. Daube's primary goal was to organize a system for thoroughbass based on as few rules and chords as possible. His book is entirely practical, as were nearly all thoroughbass texts, with no speculation whatever as to the origin of chords and key systems. He merely states that the three primary chords have their origin in the natural progresssion of the key.[49] These chords are the tonic, the chord of the fourth scale degree with added sixth, and the chord of the fifth scale degree with its seventh. "These chords contain all others which may be found in the figured bass."[50] At the time of the writing of the book the principle of inversion was still a completely new theory. He therefore goes into much detail to show that many chords are not really new structures, but only inversions of the three primary chords. Although he does not use the term *rule of the octave,* he nevertheless constructs ascending and descending scales from the notes of the three primary chords.[51]

Daube's handling of the subdominant (he does not use the term) with added sixth is especially interesting (example 11). He classifies the fourth

Example 11. Daube's Chord on the Fourth Degree and Its Inversions

scale degree as the *Grundton* (root), and when other chord members are in the bass the chord is inverted. The third inversion then is the seven-five-three chord of the second scale degree. The seventh chord on the second degree is not a fundamental chord at all, but an inversion of the chord on the fourth degree.

Strangely, Daube makes no direct mention of the secondary triads of the key. There is the direct statement that the seventh chord on the second scale degree is the third inversion of the subdominant with added sixth.[52] The former chord must therefore be considered as a subdominant chord lacking its fifth. The leading-tone triad would be an incomplete dominant seventh, since he calls the seventh chord on the leading tone a first inversion dominant with suspension, i.e., the seventh is suspended over from the third of the previous subdominant chord.[53] The chords on the third and sixth scale degrees are not specifically discussed. All other chord formations are of chromatic and enharmonic origin. An example of such are the secondary dominant seventh chords which are explained as fifth degree chords of another key.

Heinrich Christoph Koch

Koch is mentioned by Riemann as being the first to classify the triads within the key as essential or nonessential.[54] The essential triads in the major mode are the three major triads, and in the minor mode they are the three minor triads (including the major dominant) because the scale in both cases is derived from them. The nonessential chords are those of the other scale steps in each key. In his *Musikalisches Lexikon* (1802), article "Akkord," Koch distinguishes between consonant chords and dissonant chords. The consonant chords are those in each mode which consist of a root, major or minor third, and perfect fifth and their inversions. From these arise all consonant combinations of tones, aside from which there are no such consonances. The diminished and augmented triads are classsified as dissonant along with other dissonant formations, such as the seventh chords.

Koch gives the six-four chord a double meaning.[55] It can be considered a consonant inverted triad or a dissonant suspension, according to how it is used. As a suspension it is a type of consonant dissonance, which Riemann calls the first presentation of a feigning consonance. Because of Koch's presentation of the three primary chords and his concept of consonance, Riemann regards him very highly.

In addition to the theorists already mentioned, there are a number of eighteenth- and nineteenth-century theorists who harmonize the notes of the scale using only the three primary chords, including Tartini, Hauptmann, and Helmholtz. Their objective is to show that melody is derived from harmony.

It might be appropriate at this point to include a remark of Jacques Handschin regarding the predominance of the three harmonies in classic and romantic music: "The claim, that each chord should be either tonic, dominant, or subdominant is by no means purely theoretical. It corresponds to a tendency which appears to be valid in classic and romantic music."[56]

It therefore appears that Riemann is very seriously attempting to find the source of harmonic logic within musical practice. It is important to him that theory should truly be able to discover the natural laws of music and use these laws as a basis for musical analysis and for gaining an understanding of the logic of melodic and harmonic organization. As has been shown, Riemann had many sources from which to draw inspiration for his theories of harmonic dualism and function. From his viewpoint the men discussed in this chapter, with the addition of Gottfried Weber (chord symbols), F. J. Fétis (tonality), and Hermann Helmholtz (physiology), are the most important theorists because through them he can trace the emergence of "the true meaning of harmony" and harmonic dualism.

Yet, bias is revealed in Riemann's choice of theorists. Other important eighteenth- and nineteenth-century theorists who give little service to Riemann are almost dismissed with contempt. Of Georg Andreas Sorge he states:

It would be difficult to name the person who initiated the disastrous idea of erecting triads, and for the future, seventh chords, etc., on every degree of the scale. I would almost like to believe that Sorge be held responsible.[57]

Kirnberger's works, which were so influential to the course of the development of theory after Rameau, are also condemned:

Because of Kirnberger's adroit and penetrating presentation, the rules of composition as Fux had formulated them became the universal norm for the following period, and free thinkers such as Daube and Koch . . . remained unnoticed.[58]

Even Rameau is assailed because he rejected the undertone series and used successive thirds for his principle of chordal construction. Riemann calls him a mediocre mathematician and physicist and a poor logician. Daube is held in greater esteem: "Evidently, Daube is more consistent than Rameau in accomplishing an entirely new theory of the meaning of harmony, actually succeeding in his efforts" (see this study, p. 195).

NOTES

1. Hugo Riemann, *Die Harmonielehre*, this study, pp. 218–219.
2. *Ibid.*, pp. 197–201.
3. *Ibid.*, p. 185.
4. Gioseffo Zarlino, *The Art of Counterpoint*, trans. Guy A. Marco and Claude V. Palisca (New Haven and London: Yale University Press, 1968), pp. 68–71.
5. Oliver Strunk, *Source Readings in Music History* (New York: W. W. Norton & Co., 1950), pp. 242–243.
6. Gioseffo Zarlino, *Le Istituzioni harmoniche*, no page given, quoted in Matthew Shirlaw, *Theory of Harmony*, p. 54.
7. Riemann, "The Nature of Harmony," trans. John C. Fillmore in his *New Lessons in Harmony* (Philadelphia: T. Presser, 1887), pp. 7–8.
8. Shirlaw, *Theory of Harmony*, p. 50.
9. Carl Dahlhaus, "War Zarlino Dualist?" *Die Musikforschung* 10(1957): 288.
10. See this study, p. 109.
11. Shirlaw, *Theory of Harmony*, pp. 52–53.
12. Riemann, "The Nature of Harmony," pp. 10–11.
13. René Descartes, *Compendium of Music*, trans. Walter Robert (Rome: American Institute of Musicology, 1961), p. 21.
14. Jean-Philippe Rameau, *Traité de l'harmonie*, pp. 3–15.
15. *Ibid.*, p. 12.
16. *Ibid.*, pp. 30–31.
17. Joan Ferris, "The Evolution of Rameau's Harmonic Theories," *Journal of Music Theory* 3 (April, 1959): 235–256.
18. Riemann, "The Nature of Harmony," p. 12.
19. *Ibid.*, p. 17.
20. Guiseppe Tartini, *Trattato di musica secondo la vera scienza dell'armonia* (Padua: G. Manfre, 1754), pp. 65–66.
21. Hugo Riemann, *Katechismus der Akustik* (Leipzig: 1891), p. 82.
22. Riemann, *Katechismus der Musikgeschichte* 2d ed. (Leipzig: Max Hesse, 1906), p. 153.
23. Shirlaw, *Theory of Harmony*, p. 295. See also Alejandro E. Planchart, "A Study of the Theories of Guiseppi Tartini," *Journal of Music Theory* 4, no. 1 (April 1960): 34–40.
24. Peter Rummenhöller, "Moritz Hauptmann, der Begründer einer transzendental-dialektischen Musiktheorie," in *Beiträge zur Musiktheorie des 19. Jahrhunderts* ed. Martin Vogel (Regensburg: Gustav Bosse, 1966), p. 11.
25. Moritz Hauptmann, *The Nature of Harmony and Meter*, trans. W. E. Heathcote (London: Swan Sonnenschen & Co., 1888), p. xviii.
26. *Ibid.*, p. 5.
27. *Ibid.*, p. 17.
28. Riemann, "The Nature of Harmony," pp. 23–24.
29. Rummenhöller, "Moritz Hauptmann," p. 27.
30. Richard Münnich, "Von der Entwicklung der Riemannschen Harmonielehre" in *Riemann-Festschrift*, p. 61.
31. *Ibid.*, p. 62.
32. Shirlaw, *Theory of Harmony*, p. 386.

33. See this study, pp. 214–215.

34. *Ibid.*

35. Shirlaw, *Theory of Harmony*, pp. 386–387.

36. Martin Vogel, "Arthur v. Oettingen und der harmonische Dualismus," in *Beiträge zur Musiktheorie des 19. Jahrhunderts,* p. 128.

37. Münnich, "Von der Entwicklung der Riemannschen Harmonielehre," pp. 61–63.

38. Peter Rummenhöller, *Musiktheoretisches Denken im 19. Jahrhundert* (Regensburg: Gustav Bosse, 1967), p. 87.

39. See this study, p. 156.

40. See this study, p. 191.

41. Shirlaw, *Theory of Harmony,* p. 138.

42. *Ibid.,* pp. 219–220.

43. *Ibid.,* p. 119.

44. Jean-Philippe Rameau, *Nouveau système de musique théorique,* p. 34. Also, see this study, p. 191.

45. See this study, p. 192. Also, see Joan Ferris, "The Evolution of Rameau's Harmonic Theories," *Journal of Music Theory* 3, no. 1 (1959): 245–246.

46. Rameau, *Traité de l'harmonie,* pp. 31–39.

47. See this study, p. 230, note 20.

48. Jean-Philippe Rameau, *Génération harmonique,* pp. 107–119.

49. See this study, pp. 194–195.

50. J. F. Daube, *Generalbass in drey Accorden* (Leipzig: Johann Benjamin Andra, 1756), p. 19.

51. *Ibid.,* p. 20.

52. *Ibid.,* p. 17.

53. *Ibid.,* p. 33.

54. Heinrich Christoph Koch, *Handbuch bey dem Studium der Harmonie* (Leipzig: J. F. Hartknoch, 1811), pp. 60–61. Also, see this study, pp. 202–203.

55. Koch, *Handbuch,* p. 76.

56. Jacques Handschin, *Der Toncharakter, eine Einführung in die Tonpsychologie* (Zürich: Atlantis, 1948), p. 268.

57. See this study, p. 198.

58. See this study, p. 201.

CHAPTER II

The Early Period (1890-1909)

*H*ARMONIC theory is for Riemann twofold: speculative theory and practical instruction in four-part writing. The following definition appears in the Riemann *Dictionary of Music,* article "Theory":

> The theory of music is either an investigation of the technical manipulations of composition established by practice, reduced to fixed rules, and presented as instruction, or method (general-bass, systems of harmony, counterpoint, and composition), or it is an inquiry into the natural laws of musical hearing, the elementary effects of the various factors of musical art, and of the final perception of completed musical works of art (speculative T. of music, musical esthetics). Practical and speculative T. are, it is true, closely correlated, yet very distinct domains of intellectual activity. Of both there is a rich literature, although, naturally, rational speculative T. has been and is, much slower in development than purely empirical technology.

Riemann always takes this distinction between the two forms of theory very seriously. Nevertheless, the distinction is not always easy to maintain. In books devoted to one form of theory Riemann constantly contributes from the other and often the two forms overlap each other. The twenty or so books and articles devoted essentially to harmonic theory cover a period of forty-four years (1872–1916). The chart in figure 1 lists the essential writings in chronological order.[1] Its division into speculative and practical theory must be general for the above given reason. This chapter will provide a chronological outline of Riemann's theories as they are developed within the various publications of the early period.

THE DISSERTATION: MUSICAL LOGIC

The basis for Riemann's theory of harmony was established in his doctoral dissertation ("Ueber das musikalische Hören" [1873]) twenty years after Hauptmann's *Natur der Harmonik und der Metrik,* ten years after

Figure 1.
Riemann's Published Writings
on Speculative and Practical Harmonic Theory

YEAR OF PUBLI- CATION	SPECULATIVE HARMONIC THEORY	PRACTICAL HARMONY
1872	"Musikalische Logik," *Neue Zeitschrift für Musik*	
1874	"Ueber das musikalische Hören" Dissertation at Göttingen	
1874	Dissertation published as *Musikalische Logik*	
1875	"Die objective Existenz der Untertöne in der Schallwelle," *Allgemeine Deutsche Musikzeitung* 5	
1877	*Musikalische Syntaxis*	
1878	Major and Minor Concepts in Early Music, Chapter 3 of *Studien zur Geschichte der Notenschrift*	
1880		*Skizze einer neuen Methode der Harmonielehre*
1881	"Zarlino als harmonischer Dualist," *Monatshefte für Musikgeschichte*	
1882	"Die Natur der Harmonik" No. 40 in Waldersee's *Sammlung musikalischer Vorträge*	
1887		*Skizze* revised and expanded as *Handbuch der Harmonielehre*
1887		*Systematische Modulationslehre als Grundlage der musikalischen Formenlehre*
1890		*Katechismus der Harmonie- und Modulationslehre*
1891	*Katechismus der Akustik*	
1893		*Vereinfachte Harmonielehre, oder die Lehre von den Tonalen Funktionen der Akkorde*
1898	*Geschichte der Musiktheorie im IX.–XIX. Jahrhundert*	*Handbuch der Harmonielehre,* 3rd ed., revised
1901	"Zur Theorie der Konsonanz und Dissonanz," *Präludien und Studien* 3	

YEAR OF PUBLI-CATION	SPECULATIVE HARMONIC THEORY	PRACTICAL HARMONY
1902		*Grosse Kompositionslehre* Vol. 1, *Der Homophone Satz*
1905	"Das Problem des harmonischen Dualismus," *Neue Zeitschrift für Musik*	
1906		*Elementarschulbuch der Harmonielehre*
1914–1915	"Ideen zu einer 'Lehre von den Tonvorstellungen,'" *Jahrbuch der Musikbibliothek Peters* 21/22	
1916	"Neue Beiträge zu einer Lehre von den Tonvorstellungen," *Jahrbuch der Musikbibliothek Peters* 23	

Helmholtz's *Lehre von den Tonempfindungen,* and seven years after Oettingen's *Harmoniesystem in dualer Entwicklung.* Although Riemann received the idea of harmonic dualism from Hauptmann, it was from Oettingen that he found a model from which to build his own system. From Helmholtz he gained a penetrating insight into physiological aspects, as well as an acoustical penetration into the entire problem of harmony, and Helmholtz's investigations and conclusions with their strengths and weaknesses were the basis for Riemann's scientific position.[2]

In the year 1872, when Riemann was still a twenty-two-year-old student at the Leipzig Conservatory, an article entitled "Musikalische Logik" appeared in the journal *Neue Zeitschrift für Musik* under the pseudonym Hugibert Ries.[3] This first publication by Riemann, consisting of excerpts from the dissertation of the following year, points directly to Hauptmann as the first major influence in shaping his concept of theory. Riemann later acknowledges Hauptmann as the originator of the idea of harmonic dualism.[4] The article "Musikalische Logik," however, is not concerned with dualism. Rather, it uses Hauptmann's dialectic principles of thesis, antithesis, and synthesis to show the logic of harmonic and metric movement. This is highly significant, for it shows that from the very beginning Riemann's two most important principles, (1) harmonic dualism and (2) the logical harmonic succession of tonic, dominant, and subdominant, are being formulated, both under the influence of Hauptmann.[5]

In the second paragraph of the article, "Musikalische Logik," Riemann states his goal—to attempt a continuation of Hauptmann's dialectic theory beginning where he left off, with the application of harmony and meter. He goes on to say that Hauptmann's work, as it stands, is neither complete nor pleasing because he could not decide, or it did not occur to him, to attempt to place his concept of octave unity, fifth duality, and third union in the temporal succession without which a musical work is unthinkable. Although Hauptmann is able to define the abstract concepts of tonal systems, he is incapable of bringing three chords together in a reasonable and practical succession. He has placed the three primary chords together within a key, but has not grasped the meaning of these chords in musical composition. Riemann, then, will remedy this deficiency by showing the logical meaning, or harmonic function, of the various scale degrees within the key. He will show how the freest and most complicated chords may be developed out of the simple principles of thesis, antithesis, and synthesis.

Although Riemann is dependent upon Hauptmann, his objectives differ greatly. This, according to Elmer Seidel, is very significant:

> While Hauptmann proceeds with the three dialectic steps and attempts to prove that it is the formative principle of all musical phenomena (*Die Natur der Harmonik und der Metrik*, p. 10), Riemann begins with a concrete musical event, the cadence. Dialecticism is for him only a means of realizing the various chordal meanings [functions]. His criticism of Hauptmann is significant for his position. . . . Above all, Riemann perceives that Hauptmann's theoretical views have nothing to do with the direct involvement of musical practice.[6]

Of fundamental importance to the development of the tonal function of harmony is Riemann's analysis of the I–IV–I–V–I cadence in major. Historically, it is the beginning point of his harmonic theory. Riemann transfers Hauptmann's dualistic concept of octave, fifth, and third to the temporal succession of chords. First, he describes the two cadences, I–V–I and I–IV–I. The first sounds full and satisfying while the second sounds weak and cold.

> Why? because in the plagal cadence the keynote temporally becomes the chord fifth and again immediately becomes root, although there is no constraint. On the other hand, in the I–V–I it [the tonic root] is completely suppressed so as to be forcibly demanded by the third of the upper dominant, the leading tone.[7]

The cadence C–F–C–G–C contains both cadences combined for a satisfying close. The second appearance of the tonic is different from the third appearance because the second appearance is almost always in second inversion, in which position it has little authority. The tonic root, C, becomes the chord fifth in four, then the fourth above the bass in the six-four chord, where it seems to be in disunion with itself. In this second appearance of the tonic Riemann sees Hauptmann's *Quintenbegriff,* or antithesis, the opposite of the concept of unity that the tonic chord gives in its first appearance. In the following dominant chord the tonic note is completely suppressed in order to be summoned forth again. The synthesis then occurs in the resolution of the dominant to the tonic with roots in fundamental position. "This form of the cadence is the prototype of all musical form."[8] The tonic represents thesis, the subdominant with the tonic six-four chord, antithesis, and the dominant with the final tonic in root position, synthesis.

In the cadence I–IV–V–I the tonic six-four is missing after the subdominant in which case the independent appearance of the subdominant is designated as the antithesis. The tonic root is found as the fifth in the subdominant in antithesis to its former position as root in tonic, in which case the six-four chord brings forth nothing new, only the same thing in a more easily understood form.

"The tonic is thesis, the subdominant, antithesis, the dominant, synthesis."[9] In this sentence one can see very clearly the formulation of the principle of harmonic logic so important to his mature system: "The relationship that all harmonies maintain to the tonic finds its most conceivable and significant expression in the primary pillars of logical harmonic progression: the tonic and its two dominants."[10]

Riemann then explains the meaning of the secondary chords of the key: "Their logical meaning depends upon the degrees of relationship with one or the other of the primary chords."[11] The thetic chords in major are I and possibly VI and III. The VI chord contains the major third interval of the tonic and often substitutes for the tonic. The III chord is an unhappy chord which, having tones of both the tonic and dominant, can be either thetic or synthetic according to its use. The antithetic chords are IV, II, and possibly VI. The II chord is decidedly antithetic because it has no tones in common with I, and often substitutes for IV. Because the VI chord contains the upper third of the IV chord, it is often antithetic. The synthetic chords are V, VII, and possibly III. Here is found the embryo of the later concept of parallel clangs and leading-tone-change chords which are an important aspect of Riemann's mature harmonic system. These are the secondary chords of the key whose components are composed of a mixture of two of the primary chords.

In the introduction to the dissertation ("Ueber das musikalische Hören"), Riemann pays honor to four theorists whom he calls the "new harmonists." He then states his goals:

I shall, in the following, attempt to unite the results of the investigations of Rameau, Hauptmann, Helmholtz, and Oettingen. However, I need a small hypothesis which is nothing more than the consequence of evidence furnished by Helmholtz concerning the construction of the inner ear and the analysis of clangs.

My explanation of the minor chord and the minor system is based on it [the hypothesis], while my explanation of consonance and dissonance, at least for the major system and even without the minor, proves the conformity between acoustical theory and musical practice. It also allows for the final resulting assertion of musical logic as self-evident throughout. It can also be seen as a continuation of Rameau's theory of the fundamental bass.[12]

His "small hypothesis" is a subjective explanation of undertones on physiological grounds, influenced by Helmholtz's hypothesis of tone sensations in the fibers of the inner ear. Helmholtz had put forth the hypothesis that the fibers in the inner ear vibrate sympathetically with the musical tone and its overtones.[13] As a supplementary hypothesis Riemann constructs his minor system also on physiological principles and adds his own supposition: "The fibers of the vascular membrane corresponding to the undertones of a given tone vibrate in partials, and we have the implicit presentation of undertones."[14]

Hence, not only do fibers vibrate which correspond to the given tone, but also, longer fibers vibrate in segments at those upper partials which correspond to the given tone. Riemann adds, it is further conceivable that the vibration of elastic bodies in partials (with nodes) corresponding to the given tone will cause displacement, and hence, vibration of the entire length of the bodies. Thus, one fiber covibrating at the octave, a second at the twelfth, and so forth, and each one vibrating in its entirety will bring forth the entire undertone series. Since the tones in the undertone series quadratically decrease in strength toward the depths, they unavoidably fuse with the higher fundamental in such a way that their separate identity becomes impossible. And so, although the actual undertones are not perceptible in sound waves, their demonstration as a reality in our sensations is, nevertheless, of the greatest significance.

I disagree with Seidel's opinion concerning the meaning of the above quotation from Riemann. Riemann says: "Ich behaupte daher: die den Untertönen eines angegebenen tones entsprechenden Fasern der Membrana basilaris schwingen partiell mit und wir haben daher die Vorstellungen der Untertöne implicite." After quoting this passage Seidel adds:

Above all, only the concept [Vorstellungen], for it did not escape him at that time that undertones exist only in our sensation and not in sound waves entering the ear. He first fell prey to the illusion of the existence of undertones within the tone itself several years later (1877) and then only for a short time.[15]

The word *Vorstellung* has several meanings. It may mean (1) "the idea or concept of," (2) "the representation of," (3) "the demonstration of," or (4) "the presentation of." Seidel seems to be of the opinion that Riemann is saying the "implicit idea," or representation of undertones. I believe that Riemann means something stronger—the demonstration, or presentation of undertones. Why? Because Riemann's belief in real undertones continued for more than "a short time." In 1875 the article, "Die objective Existenz der Untertöne in der Schallwelle," appeared.[16] As late as 1891 in the *Katechismus der Akustik,* he gave an acoustical explanation of undertones, and the allusions to the continuing belief in major and minor clangs and a natural harmonic foundation are found in the *Geschichte der Musiktheorie* of 1898. Also, considering the fact that publications take time for preparation, this belief must have begun before 1875. And so, the "illusion" of undertones was maintained for over a period of twenty-five years.

In Chapter II of the dissertation Riemann discusses his concept of consonance and dissonance arising from the two sources. The undertone vibration ratios are naturally the exact reciprocal of the overtone ratios, thereby producing the double series:

$$\begin{array}{ccccccccccccc}
 & & & & & & & & c & c' & g' & c'' & e'' \\
1/8 & 1/7 & 1/6 & 1/5 & 1/4 & 1/3 & 1/2 & 1 & 2 & 3 & 4 & 5 & 6 & 7 & 8 \\
 & & & AA^\flat & CC & F & C & c & & & & &
\end{array}$$

Riemann has now succeeded in establishing a basis for consonance from the overtone and undertone series. From the primary numbers of the series (1, 2, 3, 5, 7, 11, etc.), those not recognized in music are removed (7, 11, 13, etc.) and the remainder are placed together as the primary clang. From this comes the definition: "Consonance is the simultaneity of tones belonging to the same clang."[17] In other words, consonance is the sounding together of notes with the ratios $1:2:3:5$ and $1:1/2:1/3:1/5$ (the major and minor triads and their derived intervals, and notes representing the triads). Dissonance, then, includes (1) all notes that do not correspond to the primary overtones or undertones of a given pitch, and (2) within a tonality, all intervals and chords having notes which do not come from the same series.

Riemann's concept of dissonance stems directly from Oettingen, who wrote that dissonance arises from the simultaneity of components of two or more clangs. The terms *homonomic* (two chords of the same system, e.g., two major or two minor) and *antinomic* (two chords from different systems) explain the derivation of seventh chords. The diminished seventh chord has already been shown as a combination of antinomes a fifth apart (pages 16–17).

In Riemann's system the formula becomes: Dissonance appears as (1) a mixture of tonic and subdominant, (2) a mixture of the tonic and dominant, and (3) a mixture of dominant and subdominant.[18] In addition, all chords which are mixtures of over-clangs and under-clangs are dissonant. From this last sentence arises the concept of the feigning consonance [Scheinkonzonanz].

A feigning consonance is a chord having the appearance of a consonance but with a dissonant origin. The triad on the second degree in the major scale is a good example. It is essentially a subdominant triad with missing fifth and added sixth (f–a–(c)–d). The d is a foreign element derived from the dominant triad. The chord therefore sounds consonant, but musical logic confirms it as a dissonance.[19] He then states that consonance is not established by proving which combinations sound well, but it is established when we can distinguish between the relationships of overtones and undertones. This distinction between consonance and dissonance is the first confirmation of our instinct for logic in music.[20]

The term musikalische Logik appears frequently. Seidel says it is found throughout Riemann's works "wie ein roter Faden" (as a red thread).[21] The term is the title of Riemann's first publication (1872) as well as the final chapter in the Geschichte der Musiktheorie. It has to do with proven acoustical occurrences and unproved as well. The unproven is that which has no acoustical basis, but yet stands as valid for the comprehending spirit. The logic of dissonance and chordal succession needs more than an acoustical basis. It also needs a psychological foundation. For example, a note can be understood as a prime, third, or fifth, of either a major or minor triad. It can be interpreted six different ways according to its logical meaning in the composition. Psychology is, then, an important concept alluded to in the dissertation. Münnich states that Riemann erred in maintaining his system was to be established upon the foundation of physiology; the foundation was psychology. All that he had established through acoustics depended entirely upon self-observation and pure logical processes, without having the slightest connection with physiology.[22]

The concept of tonality is also a process of musical logic. The same psychological process of relating two tones through the clang concept is used to unite all chords by means of a central spiritual band. This is the process of maintaining in the memory one tone as the tonic.[23] Seidel states that this is the same definition invented by Fétis, who asserts that the idea of a relationship forms itself into an order which can be termed *tonality*.[24]

Riemann derives the notes of the major scale from the three primary chords as Rameau had done.[25] The tonic and its upper and lower dominants collectively contain all the notes of the major scale, i.e., the complete material for the logical development of melody. Correspondingly, the minor scale is derived from the notes of its three primary chords. The scale is the descending e minor scale, the one used by Oettingen as the scale opposite to the major scale.[26]

The Objective Existence of Undertones

In 1875 Riemann published an article entitled "Die objektive Existenz der Untertöne in der Schallwelle" [The objective existence of undertones in soundwaves]. The writer does not have access to this article, but Riemann discusses its contents in both the *Musikalische Syntaxis* (1877) and in "Die Natur der Harmonik" (1882). In the first book he states:

> I attempted another explanation [of undertones] in the pamphlet "Die objektive Existenz der Untertöne in der Schallwelle" (Cassel: Luckhardt) by pointing out that in order to generate tones of a determined pitch nothing else is necessary but a specific number of impulses. If, say, a given tone makes x vibrations per second, so must also the tones of $1/2$ x, $1/3$ x, $1/4$ x, etc., be sympathetically stimulated, because by those impulses of 2 to 2, 3 to 3, 4 to 4, etc. of the tone of x vibrations, the impulses to produce the tones $1/2$ x, $1/3$ x, $1/4$ x, etc., must be [sympathetically] imparted. In this way also, the entire undertone row results, of course, in evenly diminishing strength toward the depths. A single reinforcement of any one of the undertones would be impossible and a uniform reception is self-evident. These notions can be proved. Minor consonance can definitely be obtained from the series of undertones in the same way as major consonance is obtained from the overtone series. If the overtones from C are:

c		g		c′		e′		g′		*b♭′		c″		e″		etc.
2		3		4		5		6		7		8				

in comparison, the undertones from c‴ are:

etc. A♭		B♭		c		d*		f		a♭		c′		f′		c″
1/10		1/9		1/8		1/7		1/6		1/5		1/4		1/3		1/2

> Only the primary overtones (corresponding to the prime numbers) amalgamate to a unity with c . . . while the remaining are regarded as secondary, as overtones of the first order of overtones. In like manner the undertones amalgamate with c.[27]

In essence, Riemann seems to be saying that since the minor consonance is related to the undertone series in the manner in which major consonance is related to the overtone series, this is proof of the existence of undertones. This may be a logical assumption, but it can hardly be considered as proof.

Tartini, mentioned in the Riemann dissertation but not listed among the great harmonic theorists, is now presented as an earlier exponent of dualism. Riemann states, "I myself had brought to light the fact that there had been earlier advocates of this idea; as regards Tartini, in my pamphlet, "Die objective [sic] Existenz,' etc., published in 1875." [28] Of course, as seen earlier, Tartini's derivation of the minor triad is based on overtones, not undertones, as Riemann mistakenly implies.

Before the publication of *Musikalische Syntaxis* in 1877, Riemann completed the writing of two practical textbooks for teaching harmony based on dualism. The first, "Neue Schule der Harmonik," established the minor principle on undertones and involved the naming of the minor triad after its highest note rather than after its lowest. However, no publisher would accept it because of its huge size and compositional complications. A second practical handbook, "Musikalische Grammatik," was written to replace the traditional figured-bass system with new symbols. The book was to be a detailed presentation for practical instruction in harmony, with many lessons and examples. This manuscript also was never published.[29]

In the *Musikalische Syntaxis* Riemann makes a surprising announcement. In the preface he states that he had sent word to Helmholtz about his discovery that undampened strings corresponding to the series of the given tone will vibrate in their entirety, making the undertones audible. He claims that when the note g′ is struck on the piano and quickly released while c is held down (but not struck), the c is heard faintly though clearly but disappears quickly. This c has the same esthetic qualities as the combination tone and is easily confused with its upper octave (as was Tartini's experience with combination tones). He believed that the note E♭ and other lower notes of the series can also be heard.[30] In the appendix he mentions Oettingen's admission of being unable to hear undertones on his piano. Although most of the world's great authorities had said "we do not hear them," Riemann felt the reason that he heard them was that he had been attempting for years to hear the phenomenon that explained minor harmony. He also discusses his experiments with tuned glass resonators. The resonators emit sounds in sympathetic vibration to other sounds corresponding to their own particular pitch. This pitch is also actuated by sounds at the higher octave, the twelfth, and double octave, demonstrating the definite proof of an objective undertone series. Need-less to say, Riemann was not a physicist. He explains his results but not the causes. He gives no explanations as to how these objective tones he thought he heard are actually produced.

The chord symbols in *Musikalische Syntaxis* are especially devised to fit a dualistic system.[31] The symbol + to the right of a letter and the symbol ° to the left designate the major and minor chords respectively, with the difference that the minor triad is spelled downward (e.g., c+ = c–e–g, °c = f–a♭–c). The seventh chords are designated, e.g., c+^{7} = c–e–g–b♭, or $^\circ_7$c = d–f–a♭–c. The note e with c+ above it designates the note as third of the c major triad. The same note e with °b above it means the root of the e minor triad, or with ° means the fifth of the a minor triad. The Roman numerals I, III, V, or VII beneath + or ° indicate which chord tone is in the bass of a major or minor chord, for example, the note e with $\frac{+}{\text{III}}$ = e–g–c. A seventh chord with omitted root is shown, e.g., C + 7 = e–g–b♭. Ninth chords are shown as combinations of two chords: c + g = c–e–g–b–d (both major) and f°c = b♭–d♭–f–a♭–c (both minor). These symbols (incomplete here), showing the combined influence of Rameau, Weber, and Oettingen, are Riemann's replacement for the figured bass.

MUSICAL SYNTAX

Seidel mentions that the dialectic concept, so important in Riemann's dissertation, has gradually become nothing but a mere formal designation in *Musikalische Syntaxis*.[32] The tonic as the center of the harmonic structure is still termed thesis, but the antithesis and synthesis have lost their former significance. In fact, the term thesis is the central point of the book. The first four of the five chapters are entitled (1) One-sided Thesis through Two Chords, (2) One-sided Thesis through Three Chords, (3) Two-sided Thesis, and (4) The Linking Together of Theses. *Thesis* means unity, and *side* refers to major or minor. Thus, the central goal of the book is to systematize, classify, and name all important chordal progressions found in the major and minor key systems.

In Chapter I, relationships of one chord to another are made in the major key system and then its minor opposite. He begins the chapter with an explanation of how tones and chords are conceived as belonging to either the major or minor key system. He states that musical hearing is a comparative sensation. It is psychological. The simplest concept is that of a tone, but there is no such thing as a simple tone. That which we call a tone is only the middle point of the upper and lower series of overtones designated collectively as clang. Clangs can be conceived as representing either major or minor according to relationships formed with one another. Such clangs are then understood in regards to, and become identified with, either the overtone or undertone series. A single note may have six different interpretations, i.e., one, three, or five of a major or minor clang. A clang can also have six different interpretations according to its function. Tone-representation and chord-representation are the designations for this important mental concept. Chord-representation, the meaning of chords within the key system, however, depends upon the reference to a central tone or clang (tonality). For example, a chord functioning as tonic is conceived as absolute consonance; the same chord in a different meaning has not this some connotation.[33]

After the above acoustical and psychological explanation for the basis of his system, Riemann proceeds to designate chordal relationships. These relationships are none other than Hauptmann's directly intelligible intervals of the octave, fifth, and third, as well as Rameau's explanation of chordal progressions.[34] Thus, the progression of a second, or ninth, is a combination of two fifths (*Doppelquintschritte*), and the leading-tone step is a combination of fifth and third (*Leittonschritte*). Much of the terminology comes directly from Oettingen. *Homonom* refers to two clangs related through the same series (major or minor). *Antinom* refers to two chords from different series. An example of a homonomic two-clang thesis would be C major–F major–C major (c+ − f+ − c+). An antinomic two-clang thesis would be C major–f minor–C major (c+ − °c − c+). In the minor triad the letter always designates the highest note of the triad (c minor = °g, f minor = °c). The term *Homolog* refers to an interval rising above a major chord or descending below a minor chord. The series c+ − e+ − c+ or °e − °c − °e would thus be designated a homologic-homonomic-third step.

In this first type of two-sided thesis the representation appears to correspond to the acoustical ratios, insofar as the main clang relates to a clang of one of its partials. But when the direction to the next chord is opposite of the first chord concept it is an antilogic exchange. The progression from tonic to subdominant, moving downward from a major clang to another major clang, or a move from a minor up to e minor and back to a minor (°e–°b–°e) is an antilogic-homonomic exchange.

Riemann continues defining progressions that occur from one-sided thesis and ends the chapter with a summary of all such progressions. The terminology in the following examples, awkward as they are, are typical:

1. c+ − g+ − c+ = +Tonic and+overdominant (homologic-homonomic fifth clang).

9. c+ − a♭+ − c+ = +Tonic and antilogic-homonomic-third clang.

17. c+ − °e − c+ = +Tonic and third-change chord (homologic-antinomic third clang).[35]

In Chapter II Riemann continues with progressions of one-sided thesis, using three clangs instead of two. He also derives the dominant seventh chord from the natural seventh of the overtone series (g–b–d′–f′), and its opposite, the underseventh beneath the minor subdominant from the natural seventh of the undertone series (b–d–f–a).[36] Yet, he cannot justify pure tuning. Pure tuning does not allow for enharmonic identification, which he claims is a positive fact in our musical hearing and is of greatest significance in our twelve half-tone system for making all kinds of chordal connections.[37]

In Chapter III, "Two-sided Thesis," he states: "It is a fact that successions of chords further related from one another stimulate the expectation of a mediating chord which is closer related to both chords."[38] The position of two dominants, one above and one below the tonic, is an example. In the cadence the tonic is usually placed between them (I–IV–I$_4^6$–V–I) as a mediator. The specific idea of the two-sided thesis is that two distantly related chords may follow each other without becoming unintelligible because the tonic is maintained in the memory, thus dividing the progression into two parts. And so, clangs not directly related in terms of the same upper or lower partials of the fifth and third, or compounds of them, need to be directly related to a third clang in order to form an intelligible progression. This is, of course, the concept of clang-relationship formulated by Helmholtz.[39] Riemann therefore succeeds in laying out systematically a large number of harmonic progressions with their terminologies.

In Chapter IV, *Thesenverkettung* ("linking of theses"), the progressions are joined together and expanded into greater harmonic constructions. Riemann points out, however, that the mere succession of many such theses cannot result in a clearly ordered, unified whole.[40] The principle of antithesis with increasing strength must prevail, and the synthesis as the settlement of the conflict concludes the perfectly logical process. A thetic occurrence is a simple cadential progression similar to a singly represented tone or chord, first conceived as isolated and independent, afterward to become individualized in this or that sense. Just as the tone c can be conceived as being relatable in the major or minor sense to a large number of tones but at first relating to none, and just as the c major or c minor chord can be conceived as being relatable to a large number of chords but at first relating to none, so also can the thesis, represented by a chord, be understood as the unifying point in the relationships of a limited number of chords without further relationships. A particular chord emphasized through the thesis can later become the tonal center for all chords in a period or even for an entire composition. Yet, another chord can replace it as the tonal center in which case the first chord appears as antithetic, and then synthetic when it again becomes tonic.

In Chapter V, "Syntax," the expansion process continues.[41] The thesis, as tonality, unites the large sections of compositions. The expansion continues into multimovement works where widely spaced harmony steps of one movement are joined to those of the next movement. The thesis here is, of course, the central tonality. As Seidel points out, thirty years before Schenker formulated his step theory Riemann succeeds in achieving a step theory through his harmony steps which he identifies as theses.[42] In this fifth and final chapter, Riemann attempts to apply his rules and terminologies to the harmonic and metric analysis of a number of compositions.

Musikalische Syntaxis shows the high point of Oettingen's influence, which markedly declines thereafter. The awkward terminology and much of the organization, according to Riemann's own admission, is taken directly from Oettingen. However, he is not entirely satisfied with Oettingen's system because it is based entirely on overtones and does not account for minor harmony on the basis of real undertones. The system, therefore, is only an indication of minor, not proof. He therefore rejects Oettingen's phonality and along with it the *Regnante* as the mirrored dominant. Other things in the system bother him, such as the major chord in cadences becoming an inverted phonic minor in six-four position (e'–c'–a–e), which Oettingen had very earnestly considered.[43] This mirroring of the major also throws the bass with all of its harmonic directive implications into the highest voice, and the fetters of a "phonic general discant notation" (in contrast to a general bass notation) is a danger that Riemann must avoid. From Riemann's above deviations from Oettingen we see the basic difference between his concept of presenting an empirical system, compatible with the current musical practice, and Oettingen's attempt at a completely theoretical presentation of the minor concept, regardless of harmonic practice. Yet, there are inconsistencies in Riemann's system. The minor harmony is generated downward, making the note e' in the a minor chord the generator. But the e' is important only theoretically, since he still regards the note a as the fundamental. It is certainly illogical to claim that the minor harmony is generated downward, and then to call the lowest and last derived note of the chord the fundamental.

The Major and Minor Concept
Applied to Prebaroque Music

Musikalische Syntaxis is followed one year later by Riemann's history of notation, *Studien zur Geschichte der Notenschrift* (1878). Apparently, Riemann is still much involved with dualism, for in this book he digresses from the subject of notation for thirty pages to present his concept of the historical development of harmonic dualism. This historical excursion throws much light on certain aspects of Riemann's views of the history of harmonic theory only touched on in the *Geschichte der Musiktheorie* and is therefore too important to be omitted. He considers major and minor as natural truths and the polar opposites of each other and believes that a continuous struggle has existed between them throughout musical history for the dominant position. Accordingly, in ancient Greek monody the minor viewpoint prevails, and the theoretical system which developed was unconsciously created from that point of view.

The Greek Dorian Mode

Riemann believes that the ancient Greek Dorian mode was the pure minor scale, the same descending scale used by Oettingen and himself to form the polar opposite of the major scale (see figure 2).[44] He adds that since

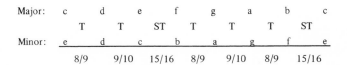

Major:	c		d		e		f		g		a		b		c
		T		T		ST		T		T		T		ST	
Minor:	e		d		c		b		a		g		f		e
		8/9		9/10		15/16		8/9		9/10		8/9		15/16	

Figure 2. The Major and Minor Scales as Polar Opposites

the ancients viewed the *mese* as the real tonic, the Dorian octave species was essentially such that an a minor chord represented the central point: e f g a b c d e with an e minor and a d minor chord situated on each side as dominants:[45]

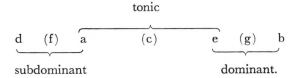

tonic

d (f) a   (c)   e (g) b

subdominant   dominant.

Riemann realizes that the Greeks themselves were completely unaware of such a harmonic basis and that it was not a part of their theoretical formulations. Nevertheless, he feels that the Greeks probably heard the Dorian scale (with the note a *mese* as the real tonic) just as it is understood by the harmonic dualists (i.e., descending). Their letter notation revealing a descending scale is evidence of this concept. The three genera (diatonic, chromatic, and enharmonic) were comprehended in the Dorian mode as descending, and the octave species were also understood in the same manner.

The above position of Riemann is untenable for several reasons. The Greek Dorian scale did not have a chordal derivation based on just intonation as shown in figure 2. It was a Pythagorean scale derived from a spiral of fifths resulting in a very different tuning. The minor scale Riemann presents in figure 2 as the exact opposite of the major mode does not even exhibit just tuning, since the 9/8 and the 10/9 whole tones between e'–d and d'–c are in reverse positions. All Greek tetrachords and scales (before Ptolemy) are written from high to low, but why should Riemann assume that this has anything to do with the minor scale? The fact that today we normally think of all scales as ascending does not make them all major. The step and half-step arrangement is the basis for judgment. Of course, the whole idea is unfortunate. It is an unnecessary complication to force a harmonic foundation on the monodic music of antiquity as Riemann has done.

The Arabian Messel Theory

According to Riemann (see this study, page 110), the minor concept was even more pronounced in the *messel* (measure) theory of the Arabs and Persians.[46] The basis of this system is a stretched string divided into twelve equal parts, as shown in figure 3. The symbol β represents the right side of the string from which the measurements begin. If the string length from I–β, which is 1/12 of the entire length, equals g''', then the tones of the series are as shown from right to left, corresponding to the arithmetic

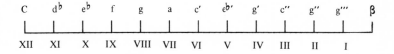

Figure 3. Arithmetic Divisions of a String

series (the string length and its multiples). The term, *messel*, means a unit of measure. This unit is the length of the string from the right side to the higher note of the interval; e.g., VI–β is half of XII–β. The string length from XII is therefore twice that of VI (VI–β). The *messel* is in this case VI, and the interval is XII–VI, which is designated 2M (the octave). In another case, VIII–β equals the *messel*. XII–VIII is the interval (3/2 or 1 1/2). The designation is M + 1/2 (perfect fifth). The first degree consonances are therefore (2M = octave, M + 1/2 = perfect fifth, M + 1/3 = perfect fourth, M + 1/4 = minor third, M + 1/5 = minor third. Because the *messel* system derives intervals arithmetically from the string lengths, Riemann interprets it as a minor concept. He adds that it is astonishing to find a system which has the undertone series as a basis. But the arithmetic series is not synonymous with undertones, and the fact that the Arabs evolved their just scale through the arithmetic series hardly justifies calling it a system based on minor. The just system can also be derived from the harmonic division of the string. Both divisions result in a series of notes from which many scales can be derived, including the major and minor. The following quotation reveals more recent research on the matter:

The messel has nothing to do with an early recognition of the third or the sixth as consonances as was formerly believed (R. G. Kiesewetter, *Die Musik der Araber* [1842] and many others after him.). The third (5/4) is simply one in the long series of consonant *mathal* intervals, while the sixth (5/3) does not occur in this series and hence was not a consonance. [47]

Medieval and Renaissance Music

In Part I of the *Katechismus der Musikgeschichte* (1888) Riemann's historical point of view is again influenced by his theoretical concepts, and he continues to outline the struggle between major and minor for the dominant position. He believes that the minor outlook prevailed in the early church modes. The final tones of the modes do not begin on C, but rather on D (D E F G a b c d), which shows the influence of Greek theory in its strict diatonically reduced form and minor concept.[48] The minor point of view is also found in notation. A system of letter notation starting with the letter A for the present tone of C seems to have been used for some instruments such as the monochord.[49] It is significant to Riemann that the early medieval writers (Notker Balbulus, Hucbald) converted the new notation to the minor principle instead of leaving it in major. He thinks that if this had not occurred our C major scale would now begin on the letter A rather than on C. This, he says, was the last victory of the minor over the major. Of course, since the concept of major and minor did not evolve until much later, the real reason had to do with the medieval writers' comprehension of the modal system in current usage. They set the letters to begin with the lowest note of the lowest mode, the Hypodorian.

Riemann then goes on to explain further victories by the major principle. The Franconian notation arranged the notes from low to high, a symptom of major. Also, in solmization the hexachord was taken from a section of the major mode. The major mode came more and more into the foreground when the authentic and plagal modes were fused into the same mode. Then the bass voice usurped the authentic mode from the tenor, and along with it the basic harmony tones, especially at closes. During the figured-bass period, all harmony was figured from the bass note upward. And so, the concept of major prevailed until the latter part of the nineteenth century, when theorists began to perceive the equality of the two modes. He goes on to say that long before the establishment of the major and minor systems of the late baroque, the unconscious awareness of them began to be perceived, effecting a reduction of the number of modes through *musica ficta*. The necessity of major and minor became more and more evident, especially in the popular songs that were springing up around the year 1500 (the German *lied,* the French *chanson,* and the Italian *frottola* and *villanella*) which did not seem to be accommodated by the old church modes. Riemann expresses the situation as he sees it in the following:

> The harmonic instinct had been discovered, which theory was only to understand later (to be clearly expressed for the first time during our century). A completely satisfying closing effect, actually, a clear, definite harmonic framework, is possible only within a harmony which consists of the main chord (our so-called tonic) with its over-dominant and under-dominant.[50]

He therefore claims that a completely satisfying close was not possible in any of the modes without *musica ficta,* for none of the modes produced the tonic chord surrounded by its two dominants. As he shows in figure 4,

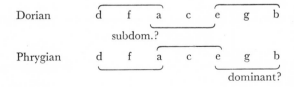

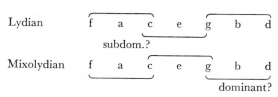

Figure 4. Dominant and Subdominant Functioning as Tonic of the Various Modes

the chord which should be the tonic of the given mode really functions as an upper or lower dominant. A dominant chord in each case has become the central harmony.[51]

The necessary result was a compromise between respecting the purity of the scale and the demands of the ear by a reasonable cadence, in such a manner that the harmony of the closing tone could have its own dominant harmony provided through the introduction of raised or lowered tones. He then shows how *musica ficta* gave the modes a completely new sense (figure 5).[52]

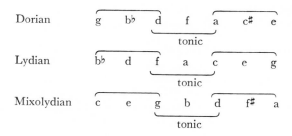

Figure 5. The Tonic Assumes the Central Position with Aid of *Musica Ficta*

Riemann states that the Phrygian mode was another matter. The half step, f–e, was retained, and the final chord was changed into major (e–g♯–b), thereby creating an entirely different system:

Phrygian   d   f   a   c   e   g♯   b
                                    dominant

Riemann's view is summed up by Willi Apel in *Accidenten und Tonalität in den Musikdenkmälern des 15. und 16. Jahrhunderts:*

Following earlier investigations of the nineteenth century, the problem of accidentals maintains its decisive expression through impetus from two sides: through the Riemann idea of "presumed tonality," and through the "voice-leading rules" formulated by J. Wolf. Riemann (*Verlorengegangene Selbstverständlichkeiten in der Musik des 15. und 16. Jahrhunderts,* 1907) . . . concludes that the distinctions between the eight or twelve church modes had already been removed from practice in earlier times. The number was reduced to three, namely, the *cantus mollaris,* the *cantus naturalis,* and the *cantus duralis,* which have become known as the minor, major, and Phrygian. The *cantus* can be determined by examining the separate accidentals within the composition, after which, accidentals are added in all other places to the extent that the presumed tonality is fully revealed.[53]

But adding accidentals to Renaissance music until it looks like classical music is not acceptable to Apel. Apel's discussion of the leading tone will suffice to show that Riemann's conclusions have not solved the problem of interpreting Renaissance music:

The leading tone, the raised seventh, can be seen as the decisive characteristic of the major-minor principle in contrast to the church modal music. The stronger the presence of the leading tone, the more similar are the various modal scales to each other, until the variety is reduced to those two types which rule the classic tonal consciousness. From the point of view of contemporary musicology, the objective, as is indicated in the use of accidentals in the numerous new editions, is to shift these developments which have categorically set in since 1600 back a considerable time, even back to the beginning of musical tradition. While we attempt to show that this point of view is false, we should not be understood to mean that the leading tone was foreign to the older comprehension of tonality. There has been no music in Europe, apart from Gregorian choral music, which has not used the leading tone. The new music is characterized by the complete application, the unconditional mastery of the leading tone. This is the simplification of harmonic and melodic elements, in contrast to the church modal music, which was indispensable for the construction of great forms beginning in the Baroque and completed in the classic period. Therein lies the peculiarity of the language of the Renaissance; two possibilities are left open, the altered or the diatonic seventh, according to need or taste.[54]

THE NATURE OF HARMONY

In 1881 Riemann published an article entitled "Zarlino als harmonischer Dualist."[55] This article is not available to the writer, but Riemann's views on Zarlino are again stated in "Die Natur der Harmonik" of the following year.[56] The latter treatise, first presented in a lecture at the Hamburg Conservatory of Music, February 4, 1882, contains an easily read history of harmonic dualism as well as a general summary of Riemann's speculative accomplishments up to that time. The history traces the development of harmony through the Greeks, Arabs, medieval theorists, Zarlino, the thoroughbass period, Rameau, Tartini, Oettingen, Helmholtz, and Haupt-mann. "Die Natur der Harmonik" is, in this respect, the forerunner to the *Geschichte der Musiktheorie*. As a summary of Riemann's speculative theories after ten years of writing, it contains some remarkable observations.

Psychology has become the predominant issue. Early in the treatise he discusses the three sources of theory:

> Scientific investigation in the domain of music concerns itself, primarily, with ascertaining the laws which govern *sounding bodies,* and is thus a department of *physics;* i.e., the science of acoustics. Then, pursuing tones still further, and in-quiring into the effects they produce on the human ear, and the mode in which those effects are produced, it becomes a special department of *physiology.* Final-ly, concerning itself with tone-perceptions, with the *mental effects* of these acoustic and physiological phenomena, and with the mental connections and rela-tions of the sensations produced by sound, it enters the domain of *psychology.* Out of the results of scientific investigation in all three fields of physics, physiology and psychology, we get the elements of an exact theory of the nature of harmony.[57]

The idea of psychology is not new to Riemann; it is part of the concept of tonal logic seen from the very beginning. But the emphasis is new, and chord-representation replaces acoustics as the predominant issue:

> With Helmholtz, all complex tones are overtone combinations, i.e., major chords. The minor chord c–e♭–g, he conceived as a compound of two major chords, those of c and e♭. . . . But von Oettingen has widened the range of this conception of Helmholtz to an unexampled degree, by treating the minor chord as a real chord which may be represented in the mind when one of its tones is present. In this view, the principle of chord substitution (or representation in the above sense) is no longer a principle of acoustics or Physiology but of Psychology. If we really find by experience that we are able to conceive a tone as representing a minor chord just as easily as a major chord, neither chord being audibly present, then that is a scientific fact on which we may build quite as well as we can on acoustic phenomena. When we have once acknowledged this, it seems of very little account whether the minor chord can be based on acoustic facts or not. . . . This latest advance in scientific knowledge has transformed the science of Harmony from a doctrine of the mathematical relations of musical in-tervals to a doctrine of mental tone-representations and their connections. Acoustics and the physiology of hearing are remanded to their proper place at auxiliary sciences.[58]

Nevertheless, the continuing belief in the objective existence of undertones is confirmed. He strongly regrets Rameau's rejection of minor harmony based on covibration:

He did try to find a series of *undertones* corresponding to the *overtones,* to account for the minor chord. He discovered that those strings of *which a given tone is an overtone* (i.e., according to Rameau, the *under* twelfth and seventeenth), will vibrate strongly whenever that string is struck, while others remain silent. He could not distinguish these tones in the mass, but he assumed that they must be there, since the strings were in vibration. So he thought he had discovered in the phenomenon of *sympathetic vibrations* the principle of the *minor chord;* for the *under* twelfth and seventeenth of a note make, with the original note (Rameau's "generator"), a *minor* chord; just as the *over* twelfth and seventeenth make a *major* chord, thus:

He *had* discovered the true principle, but was, unfortunately, talked out of it by the physicist, D'Alembert, who told him that the lower strings did not vibrate sympathetically in their whole length, so as to give their fundamentals, but only in such fractions as corresponded to the tone of the "generator." We know now that these lower strings *do* vibrate in their whole lengths; although their fundamental tones are much weaker than the partial tones which reinforce and correspond to the tone which generates them.

Thus, Rameau had to give up his attempt at a scientific basis for his minor chord, and was forced to build up his system of harmony one-sidedly, on the major principle exclusively.[59]

The following quotation is also very informative concerning Riemann's views on undertones in 1882.

I have already pointed out that the phenomenon of *sympathetic vibrations* gives us the series of undertones. The phenomenon of *jarring* tones belongs to the same category. If a tuning-fork in vibration be set lightly (not firmly) on a sounding board, or if a loosely-fastened metallic plate be set violently vibrating, we hear, *not the fundamental tone* of the plate or fork, but its under octave, under twelfth, even the under double octave, under seventeenth, or other low undertones. But it is indeed probable that every tone *always* generates not only a series of *overtones,* but a series of *undertones* also, decreasing in power in the direct ratio to their depth, and more difficult to detect and separate from the mass of tones in our consciousness than are the overtones. I have diligently collected all possible information on this point, so far as the facts have been observed, and I find nothing inconsistent with this hypothesis.[60]

Riemann concludes the article with a very important discussion of consonance and dissonance with regard to chordal and tonal relationships. These ideas will be discussed in detail in the following chapter under "Modulation."

THE PRACTICAL WORKS OF THE EIGHTIES

The period between 1880 and 1890 is particularly distinguished by a number of works in practical theory. The first, *Skizze einer neuen Methode der Harmonielehre* (1880) was intended to bring theory and practice into unity, "to utilize in practice the latest scientific advances in the knowledge of the natural basis of harmonic theory."[61] It is the conclusive result of the two earlier unpublished books and of *Musikalische Syntaxis,* which had achieved little popularity due to its complicated terminology. Yet, it is intended for the teacher rather than for the student. The second edition (1887), by contrast, is an introduction to the rudiments of four-part writing. The more theoretical explanations are given at the beginning of each chapter. Both editions are divided into two parts: Part I, primary and secondary chords of the key, and Part II, dissonance. The theory of parallel clangs and other feigning consonant chords are not yet conclusively developed. The subject of modulation, covered in one short section, is handled extensively in another work entitled *Systematische Modulationslehre* (1887). Here Riemann, as in the *Musikalische Syntaxis,* attempts to connect the elements of harmony and form. Two other books, *Neuen Schule der Melodic* (exercises in counterpoint, 1883) and *Handbuch der Kompositionslehre* (1889) round off the practical instruction of the eighties. The terminology and chord symbols are much like those found in the *Musikalische Syntaxis.* One significant change is found in the way inversions are indicated. The Arabic numerals 3 and 5 (in place of Roman numerals) beneath the note show which member of the chord it is. For example, c_3 = e–g–c', and c_5 = g–c'–e'.

The works of Riemann's early period are not well known. Their importance is historical, for in them Riemann's continuously expanding conceptual theories can be traced. They provide the ground work for the mature works of the following period. These latter works are those known to the world at large, for in them are found his final, definitive theory of the tonal functions of chords.

NOTES

1. Elmer Seidel, "Die Harmonielehre Hugo Riemanns," in *Beiträge zur Musiktheorie des 19. Jahrhunderts*, pp. 41–42. The writer acknowledges his debt to Elmer Seidel for the form of figure 1.

2. Richard Münnich, "Von Entwicklungen von der Riemannischen Harmonielehre," p. 60.

3. Hugibert Ries [Hugo Riemann], "Musikalische Logik," *Neue Zeitschrift für Musik* 28 (1872); reprinted in Hugo Riemann's *Präludien und Studien* (Leipzig, 1901)3 : 1–22.

4. Riemann, "The Nature of Harmony," p. 24.

5. Mortiz Hauptmann, *Die Natur der Harmonik und der Metrik* 2d ed. (Berlin: Breitkopf und Härtel, 1873).

6. Seidel, "Die Harmonielehre Hugo Riemanns," p. 46.

7. Riemann, *Präludien und Studien*, 3:2.

8. *Ibid.*, p. 3.

9. *Ibid.*

10. Hugo Riemann, *Handbuch der Harmonielehre*, 9th ed. (Leipzig: Breitkopf und Härtel, 1921), p. 215.

11. Riemann, *Präludien und Studien*, 3:4.

12. Riemann, "Ueber das musikalische Hören" (Ph.D. diss., Leipzig, 1874), pp. 4–6.

13. Hermann von Helmholtz, *On the Sensations of Tone*, 6th ed. p. 129.

14. Riemann, *Ueber das musikalische Hören*, p. 12.

15. Seidel, "Die Harmonielehre Hugo Riemanns," p. 44.

16. Riemann, "Die objective Existenz der Untertöne in der Schallwelle," in *Allgemeine Deutsche Musikzeitung* 5 (1875).

17. Riemann, *Ueber das musikalische Hören*, p. 17.

18. *Ibid.*, pp. 55–57.

19. *Ibid.*, pp. 21, 59.

20. *Ibid.*, p. 21.

21. Seidel, "Die Harmonielehre Hugo Riemanns," p. 47.

22. Münnich, "Von der Entwicklung der Riemannschen Harmonielehre," p. 68.

23. Riemann, *Ueber das musikalische Hören*, p. 17.

24. François Joseph Fétis, *Traité complet de la théorie et de la practique de l'harmonie*, 2d ed. (Paris: Braudwe, 1853), p. ii.

25. Riemann, *"Ueber das musikalische Hören,"* pp. 42–44.

26. *Ibid.*, pp. 45–56.

27. Hugo Riemann, *Musikalische Syntaxis*, pp. 6–7.

28. Riemann, "The Nature of Harmony," p. 24.

29. Riemann, *Musikalische Syntaxis*, p. xiv.

30. *Ibid.*, p. 6.

31. *Ibid.*, p. 8.

32. Seidel, "Die Harmonielehre Hugo Riemanns," p. 50.

33. Riemann, *Musikalische Syntaxis*, pp. 1–14.

34. See this study, pp. 12 and 196.

35. Riemann, *Musikalische Syntaxis*, pp. 21–22.

36. *Ibid.*, p. 33.

37. *Ibid.*, pp. 33–34.

38. *Ibid.*, p. 37.

39. Helmholtz, *On the Sensations of Tone,* pp. 256–257.

40. Riemann, *Musikalische Syntaxis,* p. 50.

41. *Ibid.,* p. 84–90.

42. Seidel, "Die Harmonielehre Hugo Riemanns," p. 52.

43. Münnich, "Von der Entwicklung der Riemannschen Harmonielehre," p. 63.

44. Riemann, *Studien zur Geschichte der Notenschrift* (Leipzig: Breitkopf und Härtel, 1878), pp. 72–77.

45. Riemann, *Katechismus der Musikgeschichte,* p. 156. Also, see Otto Gombosi, *Tonarten und Stimmungen der Antiken Musik* (Copenhagen: Ejnar Munksgaard, 1939), pp. 6–19.

46. Riemann, *Studien zur Geschichte der Notenschrift,* pp. 77–85.

47. Willi Apel, *Harvard Dictionary of Music,* 2d ed., rev., s.v. "Messel."

48. Riemann, *Studien zur Geschichte der Notenschrift,* pp. 86–95.

49. Apel, *Harvard Dictionary of Music,* 2d ed. rev., s.v. "Letter Notation."

50. Riemann, *Katechismus der Musikgeschichte,* p. 156.

51. *Ibid.,* p. 157.

52. *Ibid.,* p. 158.

53. Willi Apel, *Accidenten und Tonalität in den Musikdenkmälern des 15. und 16. Jahrhunderts,* 2d ed. (Baden-Baden: Valentin Körner, 1972), pp. 6–7.

54. *Ibid.,* p. 14.

55. Hugo Riemann, "Zarlino als harmonischen Dualist," in *Monatshefte für Musikgeschichte* (1881), no page given.

56. Riemann, "Die Natur der Harmonik," *Sammlung musikalischer Vorträge,* 4th ser. 40 (1882): 157–190.

57. Riemann, "The Nature of Harmony," pp. 3–4.

58. *Ibid.,* pp. 27–28.

59. *Ibid.,* pp. 12–13.

60. *Ibid.,* p. 20.

61. Riemann, *Handbuch der Harmonielehre,* pp. v–vi (Preface to *Skizze einer neuen Methode der Harmonielehre* [Leipzig, 1880]).

CHAPTER III

The Mature Speculative Harmonic Theory
(1890–1909)

THE mature period is highlighted by the appearance of the *Geschichte der Musiktheorie im IX.–XIX. Jahrhundert* (1898). This great work contains three books. The first book, entitled *Organum. Dé chant. Faux-bourdon.*, covers the period from the ninth through the thirteenth centuries. The second book, *Die Mensuraltheorie und der geregelte Kontrapunkt*, contains the history of counterpoint from the beginning of the fourteenth century to the middle of the sixteenth century. The third book *Die Harmonielehre*, is the study of harmonic theory from the middle of the sixteenth century to the end of the nineteenth century. In the introduction Riemann states that his original intent was to limit his history to the earlier centuries, up to Johannes Tinctoris (1475). Most of the material of Books I and II were collected in the years 1878–1879. However, these materials were laid aside while he sought better methods for teaching harmony and counterpoint. He states that during this period his theories of harmonic dualism matured, resulting in part from his studies of the writings of Zarlino and Tartini. He then decided to expand his earlier intentions and present a history of theory up to his own time. Nevertheless, he did not cover the later theorists with the same completeness as the earlier ones for fear that the large size of the book would make it unsaleable. The material in Book III is therefore sketchy and biased toward harmonic dualism. This bias should be well understood by its readers in order for them to maintain a balanced perspective of harmonic theory.

In *Die Harmonielehre* Riemann summarizes in four short statements the essence of his mature harmonic theories. As the purpose of this chapter is to make a study of his theories of this period, these statements provide four categories on which to base such a study.

51

Dualism: Major and Minor Consonance

We always hear tones as representatives of clangs, i.e., consonant chords, of which there are only two kinds, namely, major (over-clangs) and minor (under-clangs).[1]

It is interesting to note that not one of Riemann's so called predecessors (Zarlino, Rameau, Tartini, Hauptmann, Oettingen) used undertones as a basis for minor harmony. Rameau, in his *Génération harmonique* described sympathetic vibration at the twelfth and seventeenth below, but as was shown in Chapter I, he later discovered his error and rectified it. It was not until 1891 (*Katechismus der Akustik*) that Riemann was able to give a plausible explanation for undertones. This time, in contrast to his earlier pronouncements, he demonstrates why they cannot be heard. He first presents the conditions under which higher tones will generate lower pitches:[2]

1. A tuning fork in motion set loosely on a sounding board will produce the under octave and twelfth, and even the lower double octave. These tones, known as "jarring tones," are proof to him of the possibility that every tone generates a series of undertones as well as overtones.

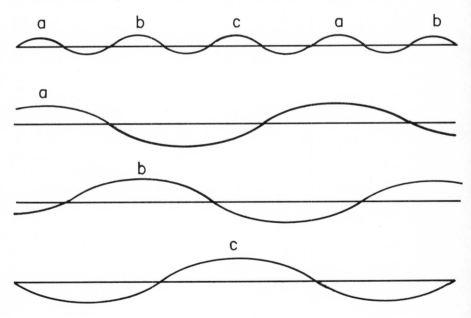

Figure 6. Conditions for Generating the Undertone C

2. According to Helmholtz, resonators (tuned jugs) have only irregular and very high overtones. These resonators will yield their own tone when a pitch equal to one of the overtones is sounded.

3. Two sounds which belong in the same overtone series of a particular ground tone will make this ground tone audible (combination tones).

Riemann gives the futile but entertaining explanation that undertones are not heard because of the occurrence of interference. Pitch is determined through the time interval of successive vibrations. For instance, g will make three times as many vibrations in the same period of time as C, the twelfth below. It therefore happens that the conditions for generating C occur not one time, but three times, at each point of the maxima (figure 6). The fact that the tone C is not heard when g sounds is explained through the law of interference. The rule is that two cycles (in this case three) of the same period and amplitude, set simultaneously, cancel each other out. It may be more easily perceived by studying the under octave (figure 7). In this case, *a* and *b* cancel each other out. And so, each tone generates its

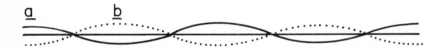

Figure 7. Interference in Undertones

own series of undertones every two, every three, four, and so forth, vibrations of the main tone. They remain inaudible because they appear several times, annuling themselves. In view of the argument that might arise over the fact that combination tones could not possibly occur if all undertones were cancelled out, he adds that, since the tone is undisputably heard, it may be that two tones set in motion together set off irregular vibrations so that total interference does not take place, allowing the combination tone to be heard.

It is doubtful if Riemann ever fully accepted Helmholtz's explanation of difference tones. He preferred to believe that Tartini's combination tones were coinciding undertones. He also placed little value on Helmholtz's summation tones. He was more interested in Oettingen's observation of a so-called much stronger upper combination tone resulting from the multiple, rather than through the sum (not $3 + 5 = 8$, or $g + e' = c''$, but $3 \times 5 = 15$, or b''). The multiple is the first common overtone of the separate tones of the interval or chord, just as the combination tone is the first common undertone. Therefore, according to Riemann's calculation, the multiple tone, rather than the summation tone is the real upper combination tone. In example 12 Helmholtz's scientific results are compared to Oettingen's

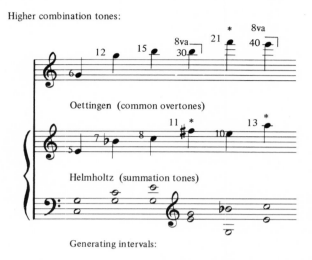

Example 12. A Comparison of Helmholtz's Summation Tones to Oettingen's Common Overtones

multiple or phonic overtone.[3] Riemann adds that it can be proved by listening that multiple tones are more audible than summation tones. However, he admits the existence of difference tones and summation tones, giving a completely different explanation for them. They are merely individual resultant tones from a large group of secondary combination tones, namely combination tones of the overtones. He means by this that the overtones also have undertones and that two overtones can produce or make audible undertones that are common to both (example 13).[4] The first interval in example 13, g–e', is struck, each note producing its series of overtones. The intervals formed by these overtones (treble clef) generate a coinciding undertone. Thus, a large group of combination tones of overtones is produced. But the first and strongest (NB) is Helmholtz's difference tone. This has to be the most fantastic hypothesis of combination tones ever put forth.

One of the first explanations for combination tones (by Th. Young, 1773–1823) was that they were quick beats. But the theory of beat tones was refuted by Helmholtz, who advanced the theory that combination

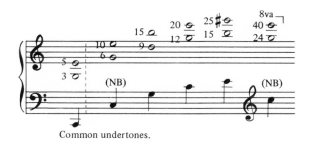

Common undertones.

Example 13. Riemann's Explanation of the Source of Difference Tones

tones can be generated objectively in the air and subjectively in the middle ear. According to Stanley Smith Stevens and Hallowell Davis, combination tones are produced in the cochlea of the inner ear:

> Simultaneous stimulation of the ear by two pure tones produces an electric potential, out of which not only the several harmonics of these two tones but also the sum- and difference-tones representing combinations of these harmonics can be analyzed (Newman, Stevens, and Davis). . . . The procedure here was identical with that used to investigate the aural harmonics: the electrical output of the cochlea of an animal was analyzed by means of a wave-analyzer. This method shows clearly that two pure-tones, led simultaneously to the ear, produce in the cochlea all the combination-tones that can be easily detected by the method of "best beats" and a great many more besides.[5]

In the *Geschichte der Musiktheorie* (1898) mention of the undertone phenomena is avoided. Yet, Riemann states that there are only two kinds of chords, *Überklänge* and *Unterklänge*.[6] Also, throughout the book he continually alludes to a belief that music of all periods is based on natural, physical laws. This is in spite of the fact that chord-representation is emphasized.

In the article "Das Problem des harmonischen Dualismus," of 1905, Riemann drops physiology and acoustics as a basis for harmony and completely rejects his former belief in undertones:

> For a long time, as I frankly confess, I was deceived by the pseudo logic of an undertone series constructed as the opposite of an overtone series. Evidence of this false reasoning may be found in any number of my earlier works on harmony and theory.[7]

After discarding the overtones as well, Riemann asks, "What should

hinder an acceptance of consonant relationships for two structures conceived upward and standing side by side, the one termed major and the
other termed minor?" He answers the question by pointing out that such
a procedure would require complicated mathematical figures for either one
or the other of the chords (figure 8).

This comparison between two forms of chords demonstrates that the minor
consonance is correctly derived from the relative size of sound waves (length of
string, size of pipe, etc.); and that the major consonance is derived from relative
rapidity of vibrations.[8]

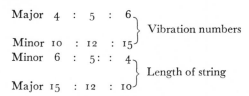

Figure 8. Both Chords Conceived Upwards Produce Complicated Ratios

The principle of major consonance, then, is that of increasing intensity
and the principle of minor consonance is that of an increasing length, as
shown by the following series of numbers:

	Minor					Major		
5	4	3	2	1	2	3	4	5

"The usual series of fractions devised by Zarlino for expressing harmonic
and arithmetical divisions may now by discarded." Thus, Riemann's new
explanation for the source of harmony is found in the arithmetic series
proceeding outward in two opposite directions. The source is still
acoustical, but there are no overtones or undertones.

The source of consonance had long been a subject of speculation. Antiquity and the Middle Ages judged consonance by the simplicity of the
numerical ratios. Even as late as the early eighteenth century the
mathematician Leonhardt Euler believed that the mind unconsciously
counted the ratio of the vibrations. The less one had to count, i.e., the
simpler the ratio, the greater the consonance.[9] The acoustical approach to
the problem was first promoted by Rameau, who found a natural basis for
the harmony of the major triad in the upper partials. Since then a number
of physical approaches to consonance have originated. Tartini explained
combination tones as the determining factor for consonance. Later
Wilhelm Preyer and F. Krüger propounded the theory that the degree of

consonance between intervals depends upon the number of difference tones: the fewer the number, the more consonant the interval. For instance, the octave has no differentials; the fifth, one; the fourth, two; and so on. Paul Hindemith has carried this on, showing a definitie relationship between the consonance of intervals and combination tones.[10] Helmholtz measured consonance and dissonance by the rapidity of beats. He also gave a second measurement: consonance is due to notes having common overtones (clang-relationship).[11] Hauptmann, refuting numbers and physics, gave a metaphysical interpretation of dissonance as arising from ambiguity, the understanding of which is found in the chord of resolution.[12]

For Riemann the clang is the source of consonance. Every note is either a root, third, or fifth of an over-clang or under-clang, and it has a natural consonant relationship to the other two members of that clang. Consonance is, therefore, distinctly separate from dissonance. Helmholtz's theory of beats, as well as Krüger's difference tone theory, gives a graduated scale of consonance into dissonance with no clear-cut division. This, Riemann could not accept, for consonance is already clearly defined for him in the triad. Of course, Helmholtz's *Klangverwandschaft* (relationship of sounds), because it establishes a definite line between consonance and dissonance, was acceptable.

Riemann's concepts were rather well defined by the time Carl Stumpf's first work, *Tonpsychologie,* was published in 1883, and it is doubtful that the latter's experiments with amalgamation of tones had much influence on him. Stumpf measured consonance by the degree to which musically unschooled listeners heard intervals as one unified sound instead of two different tones. Although Riemann admitted the fact of fusion, he probably disagreed with the results. In the first place there was no clear line of distinction between consonance and dissonance; instead there was a graduated scale away from the most consonant interval toward less consonant intervals.[13] Secondly, there was the implication that chords were made by placing consonant intervals together. But Riemann already had his over-clangs and under-clangs from nature with clearly defined consonant entities. A third objection was that Stumpf regarded intervals as isolated psychological perceptions. The implication from Riemann's writings is that consonance and dissonance cannot exist in isolation, for they are musical entities; and tones, intervals, and clangs do not exist as isolated phenomena. In most of his theoretical works no mention whatever is made of intervals as separate entities. In the *Katechismus der Harmonie und Modulationslehre* he does include an early chapter on consonant and dissonant intervals, but he hastens to add that they are only consonant when they belong to the major or minor triad.[14] His definition of consonance is so bound up with the clang concept that he can only accept amalgamation, or fusion, as it fits into his system as follows: (1) fusion of the octave, (2) fusion of thirds and fifths, (3) fusion of components of the major and minor triads, and (4) fusion of the components of more than one primary triad into musically intelligible discords (e.g., dominant seventh and subdominant added sixth chords).[15] Riemann does feel, however, that Stumpf made a great contribution by taking the problem of consonance out of acoustics and placing it in psychology where it belonged.[16] The aspect of psychology will be discussed in detail later.

Riemann, like Rameau, does not regard the tones of the octave to be different tones, only different appearances of the same tone. The clang concept is therefore not involved, for the octave is but an extension of the same tone. The other intervals also maintain their intervallic meaning through octave extensions. For example, the relation does not vary between a fifth and three octaves and a fifth.[17] Attempts to give a rational explanation for the octave phenomenon reach back to the beginning of musical science. The earliest theorists explained it on the basis of the simplest mathematical ratio (2 : 1). But this is untenable for octaves wide apart. Riemann mentions that Euler placed the fifth octave ($1:32$, $C - c^4$) in the scale of consonance correctly behind the sharpest dissonance ($1:15$, $c - b^2$) because its ratio is more complex. Helmholtz, the first to make a scientific investigation of the octave, based its similarity on the lack of dissonance between the overtones.[18] Yet, the music psychologist Géza Révész refutes this with the argument that when the overtones are eliminated the similarity still exists.[19] Stumpf attributed the similarity of octaves to the high degree of fusion, or blending. But Révész also points out that blending can only occur when both notes are sounded simultaneously, whereas equivalency takes place in successive octaves as well as in simultaneous octaves.

To the above theories Riemann adds the thought that perhaps there is a psychological basis for octave equivalency. Although Stumpf (*Tonpsychologie* [1883, 1890]) remains famous for his psychological experiments with amalgamation of tones, Riemann was writing on the subject some years earlier. In *Musikalische Syntaxis,* he writes, "It appears that even in a single clang with overtones the octave fuses in a very special manner with the ground tone."[20] In the *Katechismus der Akustik,* he states that when C and c are sounded simultaneously the commensurability is heard, not because one tone vibrates twice as fast as the other, or because both tones excite the same nerve endings, but because the commensurability is psychologically heard by the ear as a perfect fusion of tones. Riemann continues with the idea that, psychologically, fusion of the octave may have a melodic basis.[21] In the scale from the smallest interval ascending there are a number of intervals of which the third and fifth are most intelligible, and last of all there is the octave, the most intelligible of all. The major third (5 : 4) is not as intelligible as the seventeenth (5:1), and the fifth (3:2) is not as intelligible as the twelfth (3:1). These large intervals, however, are denied to the voice, while the voice can reach a number of tones at both octaves. Riemann continues that while mathematicians, physicists, and physiologists remain perplexed, further study is required from the psychological aspect.

In 1912 Révész brought forth his two-component theory, which attempts to explain octave equivalency through a synthesis of its two characteristics, pitch and quality. Pitch is expressed as the continuity of direction, quality, the periodicity of direction. In his graphic representation (figure 9), pitch is indicated by a continuous line curving upward. The quality, or periodicity, is expressed by the vertical dotted lines. The chart reveals two factors: first, the phenomenon of ascension characterized as pitch, and secondly, a cyclical repetition, characterized as quality:

> One characteristic is that which changes with the vibration number, apprehensible phenomenologically through the rising or falling. This fundamental characteristic we call the musical pitch. The second characteristic recurs from octave to octave—in other words, with the doubling of the vibration number—and this we call the musical quality of the tone sensation. Consequently that in which the octave notes differ one from another is the pitch. That in which they are similar is the quality of the tone sensation.[22]

My criticism of the two-component theory is that Révész never explains what he means by quality. He merely assumes the fact that octaves are equivalent because they have the same quality. The closest he comes to defining quality is that it "recurs from octave to octave—in other words with the doubling of the vibration number—and this we call the musical quality of the tone sensation." This is hardly different from the old idea that octave similarity is caused by the doubling of the vibration number, or ratio. Révész states that Riemann at first took a rather negative attitude toward his views, but he later retracted his criticism and came out in support of the Révész theory.[23] Révész states that Stumpf also discarded his former views in favor of Révész.[24]

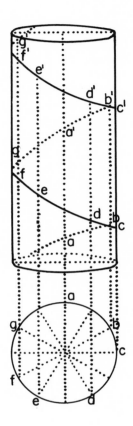

Figure 9. Graphic Representation of Révész's Two-Component Theory

THE THREE PILLARS OF HARMONY

Chordal successions (also melodies, since they represent the principle of chordal succession in its simplest form) are heard much like one hears the relationship of chords to a central clang (Rameau's *centre harmonique,* the tonic) against which the other chords, being harmonically related, are understandable. The two primary chords in question . . . were first theoretically established by Rameau. They are the dominant (the closest related by an ascending fifth) and the subdominant (the closest related descending progression of a fifth).[25]

It was shown in Chapter I that three-chord harmonizations of melodies and scales have a long history before Riemann. In his first publication

("Musikalische Logik") his goal was to establish harmonic progression in reference to the three dialectic steps. Even the secondary chords and seventh chords are categorized into the three functions according to their logical use. After that, however, we read of primary chords and secondary chords. The idea of only three functions is taken up again only after twenty-one years in *Vereinfachte Harmonielehre* (1893). Here, and in the third edition of *Handbuch der Harmonielehre* (1898) Riemann's theory of harmony becomes complete.

Riemann gives Rameau credit for establishing the tonic-dominant relationship. Rameau states that the bass progression from the fifth to the first [scale step] is the most perfect because "in the perfect cadence the fifth seems to return to its source." [26]

This dominant-tonic relationship is based on the root and its third upper partial. Riemann merely had to apply the same logic to the third under partial to obtain the tonic-subdominant relationship. He makes the extraordinary statement that the three tonal functions are actual acoustical results of the dualistic system:

The relationship that all harmonies maintain to the tonic finds its most conceivable and significant expression in the primary pillars of logical harmonic progression: the tonic and its two dominants. The limitation of primary functions to the number three is not an arbitrary act; it is a logical law of necessity as readily understood by those who have grasped the natural truth of the principle of harmonic dualism. There is only one tonal relationship in the positive (ascending) and one in the negative (descending) sense. The former yields not only the concept of the major chord, but also its dominant, the latter not only that of the minor chord, but also that of its subdominant. All dominant relationships are, therefore, major, and all subdominant, minor. This is already apparent in the attempts to give the minor mode a major dominant and the major mode a minor subdominant, while the opposite (major subdominant in minor and minor dominant in major) is out of the question.[27]

The tonal relationships of a tonic and upper and lower dominants was first established by Rameau in 1726 when he discovered the subdominant chord and classified it as a lower dominant.[28] Then, in 1737 he presented a key system based on the harmonic and arithmetic series. The tonic with its two dominants stand in the center of the system, with the harmonic system moving upward and the arithmetic system downward.[29]

But Rameau never claimed that there were only three tonal functions. He meant the three to be the center of the entire system of chords arranged in progressions of fifths above and below, with the tonic and its two dominants standing symmetrically in the center.

Handschin, Riemann's relentless critic, discusses Riemann's functional theory in relation to classic and romantic music:

The claim, that each chord can be considered either tonic, dominant, or sub-dominant, is by no means purely theoretical. It definitely corresponds to a valid tendency in classic and romantic music. Nevertheless, this generality should not be exaggerated. First, . . . harmonic function has a naïve, effortless character in classic music and a pleasant, striving character in romantic and nineteenth-century music. . . . The above-mentioned functionalism [Riemann], which places everything into a mold, institutes to an extent a mechanical chord succession in the Cartesian sense, which also obliterates the individuality of the chords.[30]

Seidel counters by stating that the function theory is not a pure logical construction imposed upon major and minor tonal music, but that it corresponds throughout to the inner essence of the music.[31] Seidel also answers Hellmut Federhofer's objection that Riemann's function theory suggests to the listener nothing more than a series of one-after-the-other functionally rotated chords.[32] Riemann's statements regarding the comprehension of large harmonic connnections did not remain on paper. Federhofer does not mention Riemann's analysis of Beethoven's Sonata, opus 53, rondo (measures 1–9) as a great cadence in F major. Here, already in 1877, Riemann has foreshadowed Schenker's *Stufen*. Seidel adds that Riemann as well as Schenker realized the organic connection between horizontal and vertical dimensions.

Carl Dahlhaus, another critic of Riemann's function theory, states that Riemann leaves it undecided as to whether tonic, dominant, and sub-dominant are designations for chordal degrees or chordal functions.[33] For example, he adds, the subdominat parallel (Sp) is a modification of the subdominant chord (S), yet, it has the same function. Therefore, function and chord are independent occurrences. But Riemann has made the meaning of his three pillars decidedly clear. Function and clang are identical. The tonic functions as the central position. The two dominants function as chords standing a fifth above and below tonic. Whenever the chordal shape is modified (e.d., S to Sp), the function is also modified to the same extent. The modified tones are foreign elements from other clangs, recognized as dissonant additions. Dahlhaus also adds that the functional concept is superfluous and that the chords can be interpreted as a rigorous step theory of three chords with modifications by dissonant additions.[34] This charge can also be refuted. The creative theorist is free to formalize his own principles. The function concept has been a great contribution to theoretical speculation, not only for Riemann's disciples, but to proponents of various step theories.

Dahlhaus also discusses the incompatibility of harmonic function and dualism in Riemann's system:

If the subdominant in major is antilog and antithetic, in minor it is on the contrary, homolog and synthetic. The term *subdominant* therefore has not the same meaning, but contrary meaning. The function S and the *Logos,* and the expressions *homolog* and *antilog* contradict each other.[35]

Continuing on, he states that the divergence would be avoided if Riemann had given up the dualism caused by interpreting the "natural" minor cadence as I–V–IV–I = T–D–S–T. If he had left it the same as the major cadence, then subdominant would still be antithetic, and dominant would be synthetic, and function and *Logos* would be identical. Riemann's defense against the same argument by Ary Delinfante in 1904 might also apply to Dahlhaus:

> To be logical, he, and possibly others, would have me call as dominant in A minor the D minor chord, and as sub-dominant the E minor chord, that is, °D and °S, respectively. Then they would be strictly the opposite of D+ and S+ in major. But in that he overlooks the fact that since 1873 I have used these same symbols in their present meaning. I did not choose the names. They have been in general use since the time of Rameau. I had quite the same right to use them as I had to employ the terms major, minor, parallel, fundamental, etc. . . . That no confusion arises relative to the dominants is demonstrated by the fact that the prime of the minor tonic and the prime of the major dominant are the same note. [36]

The Feigning Consonant Chord: Dissonance

> It is possible to comprehend two kinds of clang-representation at the same time. However, one clang is always more prominent, and the presence of the other appears as a disturbance of the primary clang, as dissonance (not haphazardly, but also, according to the relationship of the second to the primary clang, which is evaluated differently). Such a duality of clang-representation can also be understood in cases where there is a tonal relationship, the one uniform interpretation allowable in the sense of another (third) clang. For example, the secondary triads of the key are such simultaneous representatives of two of the three primary harmonies in which one is always comprehended as the main content (consonance); the other is the foreign addition. For example, a–c–e in c major is either a dissonant form of the tonic (with sixth instead of the fifth) or a form of the subdominant (with the leading tone as a substitute for the prime). Besides the three primary harmonies, all other possible and intelligible chord formations originate through such dissonant formations without abandoning the key (viz., without changing the key center, the tonic).[37]

Evidently, Riemann's earlier concept of dissonance, borrowed from Oettingen, that dissonance arises from the simultaneity of two chords, has undergone further development. The two or more chords always represented in a dissonance are no longer equal; one chord is conceived as the prominent function and the others modify it. The *characteristic dissonances,* both major and minor dominant sevenths and the major and minor subdominants with added sixth, are examples.[38]

Thus, all chords having other tones than those understood as the prime, third, and fifth are considered dissonant.[39] Dissonance is defined as a disturbance of the unity of the meaning of the clang through foreign elements. This definition also explains why many chords having the appearance of consonance (feigning consonant major and minor triads) show a dissonant derivation, for it is not sufficient for a chord to show the tones of a prime, third, and fifth. A chord is only really consonant when its components are understood as prime, third, and fifth of the same clang. From this aspect a musical consonance is neither a physiological nor an acoustical concept, but a psychological one; not the result of sound waves or tone sensations, but of tone-representation. The chord of the added sixth with omitted fifth, f–a(c)–d, is an example. The note d, an added foreign element to the major triad, gives the chord the appearance of being minor as soon as the fifth (c) is omitted. But with the appearance of the added sixth the chord, with or without the fifth, does not change its meaning. As another example, the major triad with fifth in the bass (six-four position) is understood as dissonance, since the bass (the real root, the dominant) has two upper tones belonging to a different clang (the tonic). From this psychological aspect of feigning consonances Riemann developed the theory of parallel clangs and leading-tone-change clangs. The secondary triads in the key are such simultaneous representatives of two of the three primary harmonies in which one is always understood as the main representative, the other as dissonance. From this point of view the minor chord a–c–e is either a dissonant form of tonic (parallel clang) with added sixth and omitted fifth, or a form of the subdominant with tonic replaced by its leading tone (leading-tone-change chord).

The term *parallel* is the German equivalent of the English *relative* in pertaining to the relationship of major and minor keys. The parallel key is that of the distance of a minor third having the same key signature. Riemann adopts the term to show the relationship of chords, e.g., the parallel clang of the subdominant clang F is d–f–a. The latter is not a true clang since it is not derived from the undertone series. Its derivation as already mentioned is from the clang with added sixth (its characteristic dissonance) and omitted fifth, f–a–(c)–d. The note d is a foreign element from another clang, G. Shirlaw misrepresents Riemann's explanation of parallel clangs in the minor mode in the following statement:

This explanation of the secondary triads on the second, third, and sixth degrees of the scale would appear to apply to the major key system only; there are obviously serious difficulties in the way of its application to the minor key-system. For example, the triad of the second degree of the minor scale is a diminished triad, while that on the third degree is augmented.[40]

In the minor mode the parallel keys are not found on the second, third, and sixth degrees, but rather on a minor third above each primary chord; thus in a minor the tonic parallel is on the third (c–e–g), the subdominant parallel on the sixth (f–a–c), and the dominant parallel on the seventh (g–b–d). Just as the parallel major mode is a minor third above, so are the parallel clangs a minor third above the clang they represent (example 14).

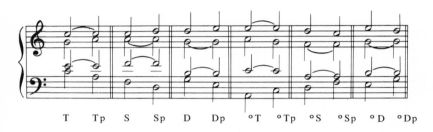

T   Tp   S   Sp   D   Dp   °T   °Tp   °S   °Sp   °D   °Dp

Example 14. Riemann's Parallel Klangs

Shirlaw also misinterprets Riemann's concept of the leading-tone-change chord: "But we find another explanation of these 'clangs' as 'leading-tone-change clangs' (*Leittonwechselklänge*)."[41] However, the leading-tone-change is not another explanation. In Riemann's concept of the feigning consonance such chords can, according to how they function, be considered either parallel clangs or leading-tone-change clangs. For example, the chord e–g–b in C major may be the dominant parallel (Dp) if it represents the dominant, or a leading-tone substitute of the tonic if it follows directly after the tonic in such a way as to substitute for it. In example 15, the second chord in each measure is a leading-tone-change clang.

Shirlaw again proves that he does not understand Riemann's theory of feigning consonance:

It is impossible to understand why he should describe the triad d–f–a as a "parallel clang," seeing that it is derived from, and represents, in incomplete form, the Subdominant discord f–a–c/d. There is another reason why this triad cannot be considered a "clang": it consists of not only a dissonant Fifth, d–a (27–40), but of a dissonant Third d–f (27–32).[42]

Example 15. Riemann's Leading-Tone-Change Chords

But the whole point of the feigning consonant chord is that it is not a clang at all; it is merely a quasi chord standing in place of a clang. The notes f–a are components of the major subdominant; the so-called dissonant d is from the major dominant. The result is, as Shirlaw points out, a dissonant fifth and third. Riemann would be the first to acknowledge this. In another of Shirlaw's attacks he states the following:

> Dr. Riemann, in several of his works has made it one of his principal tasks as a theorist to demonstrate the utter impossibility, even absurdity, of any such explanation of the minor harmony, which must be regarded as the antithesis of the major and as being generated downwards, not upwards.[43]

In defense of Riemann it must be again mentioned that the feigning consonances in the major mode do not belong to minor harmony, even though they appear as minor chords. Feigning consonances are chords whose components are composed of a mixture of two of the three primary harmonies of that same mode. This is what he means in *Die Harmonielehre* when he discusses the possibility of hearing a minor chord in the sense of a major.[44] There may be disagreement over the real value of his system, but whatever we think of it his presentation of feigning consonances is entirely consistent within the bounds of consonance and dissonance which he has set up.

The dissonant structures covered so far are all conceived vertically. There is another category called *figurative dissonance*. These dissonances arise as the melodic consequences of passing tones, suspensions, unprepared dissonances, and so on. Included herein are augmented triads ninth chords, altered chords, and sequences. He accepts Fétis's definition of the sequence as a nonfunctional series of chords of melodic derivation. Inasmuch as the scale itself is derived from the notes of the primary harmonies, tones in a single melodic line are comprehended as either consonant or dissonant according to whether they are felt as prime, third, or fifth of a clang, or as a foreign tone. In example 16 it is not a problem of dissonant intervals or chords but of a dissonant note, which does not belong to the C clang.

Example 16. Melodic Tones Comprehended as Chord Members

MODULATION

Modulation is nothing more than a new interpretation of the chords from the meaning they have in the key being left, to that which they hold in the new key. Therefore, it is, above all, a change of the significance of tonic to a new chord.[45]

Modulation in the above sense will be discussed in the next chapter, on practical theory. Psychologically, however, modulation for Riemann does not signify a change of tonic, but only a more distant removal from it. In speaking of the psychological aspects of tonality Riemann claims that only the tonic chord itself contains absolute consonance. Thus, in the concept of tonal logic wherein all chords are reduced to the function of tonic and its two dominants, chordal successsion is a continual movement out from tonic and a return to the tonic center. The unrest felt in movement away from the tonic is a sense of dissonance, while the return is a return to consonance. Consonance and tonal repose, then, are synonymous to Riemann. He cites Tartini as insisting that all tones of a key are dissonances except those belonging to the tonic triad,[46] for it is the only chord that does not require a progression. Referring to the two dominants, Riemann states: "The effect of these chords is dissonant-like; or better, the perception of them contains something which disturbs their consonance; and this is simply their relation to the chord of C Major [tonic chord]."[47] Consequently, all variations of the two dominant harmonies are related to the tonic in the sense of dissonance. This is the key to the reason why the dominant and subdominant chords can have their characteristic dissonances of the seventh and added sixth respectively, without changing the character of the chords. Because they are not completely consonant, their meaning is made clearer.[48]

Rameau's view of consonance in respect to tonality differs to some degree. In the *Traité de l'harmonie* he states that the perfect triad should be placed only on the tonic because every note bearing the perfect harmony must be considered tonic. Therefore, we would be hearing as many different keys as there are perfect triads.[49] Here, Rameau, like Riemann, sees consonance as tonality, with the difference that Rameau was guided only by acoustics, whereas Riemann used mental perceptions for clarifying the tonic center. (Rameau later modified his position.) Tonality is therefore regarded as a mental perception. For example, if the g chord is thought of as being fifth to c, then the central point lies outside of the chord of g. This gives to the chord an element of unrest, making it necessary to move to the c chord. Rameau thought it necessary to give the g chord a dissonant note in order for it to acquire the feeling of unrest, but for Riemann the mental instability of the pure triad itself constitutes dissonance. This is his "modern concept of tonality as distinguished from the old idea of key."[50] (Münnich wondered why Riemann did not also classify the dominant and subdominant as feigning consonances, considering they represent tonal dissonance to the tonic chord.)[51]

In continuing, Riemann adds that the modern concept of key is not confined to the notes of the scale. All twelve tones are ultimately connected to the tonic chord.[52] Thus, he clearly predicts Hindemith's Series I (see p. 97). The closest related chords after the two dominants are the major thirds above and below because the major third is the first overtone after the fifth.

The consonant concept of tonal relationships is also extended to keys. Seeing that their positions are not permanent, all modulations are positions of dissonance. Riemann attributes to Hauptmann the concept of the third relationship of keys, but Rameau deserves the honor. Rameau states that modulation from one key to the next can only be done naturally by a consonant interval. In other words, modulation can be made to the third, fourth, fifth, or sixth above or below, i.e., the consonant intervals of the major triad (see p. 196).

Hauptmann's key relationships are expounded in a similar way, on the basis of the intervals in the tonic triad. For modulations to the dominant and subdominant the fifth can become root, or the root can become fifth. In modulations of a third the process involved is "Making the Root or Fifth of the Tonic the Third, or its Third, the Root or Fifth of the new Tonic."[53] What happens is that elements of the tonic chord appear in more remote keys. This involves relationships of both major and minor thirds above and below. Apparently, third-relationship of keys was not clearly defined before Hauptmann; both Riemann and Shirlaw make statements to the effect that theorists were unable to account for these modulations in Beethoven's music. Rameau was a hundred years ahead of his time in this respect.[54]

Riemann's concepts of closely related keys are like Hauptmann's. The idea of third-related keys is equally valid along with fifth-related keys. Riemann implies in "The Nature of Harmony"[55] that third-related keys, both major and minor, are more closely related than major second relationships. But in *Harmony Simplified* he states that the minor third progression can only be understood in regard to a third clang. For example, the progression from C major to A major would require an intermediary chord such as E major, resulting in the progression up a major third and down a fifth: C–E–A.[56] The inference, of course, is that the minor third is not directly intelligible like the major third.

Riemann's concept of consonance has rather far-reaching implications. The entire system inherent in musical composition has its involution in the major and minor clangs. The single note is understood only as a member of the clang. The same is true for the interval. All chords from the single triad to complex dissonant structures are in their final analysis only modifications of the clang. All progressions within the key system are dissonant steps from the central position of the tonic consonance. Finally, modulations to the most remote keys are journeys through dissonance, which must need return to the home key and chord to find final repose in consonance. These views of Riemann are seen in the following quotation:

> As the principle tone of a chord is related to its accessory tones (the third and the fifth, and more distantly related tones), and as the tonic chord in a key is related to the accessory chords (chords of the fifths, thirds, etc.), so the principle key of a piece is related to the accessory keys which occur in it (the key of the fifth above and below, the third above and below, etc.). . . . Thus the fundamental laws of chord succession, as well as of the succession of keys (Modulation) may be deduced directly from the extension of these simplest musical conceptions, consonance and dissonance.[57]

Basing a musical system on psychology brings up a great problem of inconsistency. Riemann insists that only major and minor triads can be consonant, and these only in their correct context. If psychology alone is sufficient, the question may be asked, why cannot other chords or intervals be considered consonant. Riemann replies, somewhat unsatisfactorily, in the following manner.[58] The seventh, eleventh, and thirteenth partials are very audible in some chords, and their existence in the series of overtones and undertones, as well as their ability to amalgamate, cannot be denied. He adds that Helmholtz does not assume too much when he says that the g–b♭′ (3:7) generally sounds more pleasing than e′–g″ (5:12). Nevertheless, Riemann believes that our music system and our ears which have been trained in this system do not recognize relationships of the seventh or of the higher partials which are not octave extensions of the first five partials. For this reason the partials, seven, eleven, thirteenth, and seventeenth, and their divisions cannot be comprehended as clang components. The ninth partial is a different problem for it is in tune with the scale. As a single sound the ninth partial is as intelligible as the third, but the ear denies its direct relationship to the tonic and inserts the third partial in between as an intermediary. In other words, the ear distinguishes between direct relationships and secondary relationships. The reason the ear cannot comprehend chords with components beyond the fifth partial is that the other notes would be out of tune with our scale, except the ninth, which is a relationship of the second degree. As to why the ninth partial has a secondary relationship Riemann points back to Helmholtz's theory of *Klangverwandtschaft,* wherein two notes are defined as consonant if their harmonies have common overtones. The two notes forming the interval of the major ninth (C–d) also have a common overtone (c″), but it is the seventh partial of the upper note (d) and is, therefore, not in tune with the overtone of the lower note (C). The fallacy of Riemann's reasoning is that we no longer use pure tuning at all. In our even-tempered system all notes except the octave are out of tune with the upper partials. The ear adjusts rather well to such changes. Even during the nineteenth century fundamental chords of the seventh were constructed on every scale degree by other theorists, and there is no reason to doubt that they were heard as such.

So while giving a psychological reason for consonance Riemann goes right back to acoustics as the real basis for his system. Even chordal progressions proceeding by fifths and thirds relate to the natural scale of partials. This is also true of modulation. Riemann's entire thesis (and Schenker's) that the clang is the only source of consonance is based directly on Rameau's theory of harmonic generation. Rameau attempted to show that the entire music system can be reduced to the single generating tone. From this tone is generated the chord, chordal progressions, and further extensions. Riemann's extensions of this acoustical basis into the realm of psychology are, nevertheless, important contributions. Weakness comes in his attempt to limit the possibilities of intelligibility. He says that we hear a tone as being the root, third, or fifth of a triad, but nothing else. Yet, psychologically, we know today that the ear can also hear a tone as being a seventh of a chord. Chords with their sevenths on every scale degree can be heard as fundamental chords, which is the case in the standard ninetenth-century music system. Concerning the tonic chord Riemann declares:

> All that can be experienced musically is heard either in the concept of a major chord or of a minor chord. A major chord, or a minor chord, is always the central chord (Rameau's "Centre harmonique') in every melody, or succession of harmonies. There positively is no third chord, nor can there ever be.[59]

Before Riemann's death in 1919 all these and many more dissonances were serving intelligently as tonics in the music of Stravinsky, Schönberg, Bartók, and Ives. The psychological perception of the materials and organization of music, along with stylistic aspects, have changed constantly throughout musical history. Psychologically, Riemann could have justified the modal system instead of condemning the modes for not conforming to major and minor. He could have heard the Phrygian cadence as terminal as well as progressive. Could it not have occurred to him that the Renaissance ear heard it as such, psychologically? Helmholtz would agree that the music of any era can be justified by its own inherent rules of tonal logic and will sound esthetically satisfying if the listener is psychologically adjusted to the stylistic features of that era.[60]

NOTES

1. See this study, p. 218.
2. Riemann, *Katechismus der Akustik,* pp. 78–80.
3. *Ibid.,* p. 83.
4. *Ibid.*
5. Stanley Smith Stevens and Hallowell Davis, *Hearing, Its Psychology and Physiology* (New York: Wiley and Sons, 1938), p. 197.
6. See this study, p. 218.
7. Hugo Riemann, "Consonance and Dissonance, A Discussion of the Principles of Harmonic Dualism," trans. S. Harrison Lovewell (typewritten, 1925), p. 10. Further, G. Révész, in his *Introduction to the Psychology of Music* trans. G. I. C. de Courcy (Oklahoma City: University of Oklahoma Press, 1953), p. 14, makes the following comment: "Riemann himself was not convinced that the undertones were an objective reality. He believed them to be merely subjective. It was only recently that B. van der Pol was able to verify experimentally (and make audible) the physical existence of these hitherto only theoretical suppositional undertones through the synchronizing properties (frequency demultiplication) of relaxation oscillations." Van der Pol's experiments ("Frequency Demultiplication," *Nature* 120 [September 10, 1927]: 363–364) are of little significance to music theory. With an electrical current he was able to produce tones with decreasing frequencies in the ratios of 1000/1, 1000/2, 1000/3, and so on, by increasing the capacity of a variable condensor. His series of tones corresponds to the ratios of the undertone series, but instead of all the tones being

generated by the first they are all produced singly and by a deliberate change of electrical current. Hindemith also discusses these electrically produced tones in *The Craft of Musical Composition* trans. Arthur Mendel (London: Associated Music Publishers, 1942), 1:78. Révész also makes a similar statement regarding the actual physical existence of combination tones: "The objective presence of combination tones has recently been established by means of resonators of varying pitch (Waetzman in 1906, and Ramann in 1915)" (p. 18). But as far as I am aware, such latent existing undertones and combination tones are not mentioned anywhere in our more recent texts of acoustics, a proof of either their lack of importance or that such findings are not based on sufficient proof to be considered scientific facts.

8. Riemann, "Consonance and Dissonance," p. 17.
9. G. Révész, *Introduction to the Psychology of Music*, p. 80.
10. Paul Hindemith, *Craft of Musical Composition*, 1:57–89.
11. Hermann Helmholtz, *On the Sensations of Tone*, p. 168.
12. Moritz Hauptmann, *The Nature of Harmony and Meter*, p. 54.
13. Riemann, "Consonance and Dissonance," p. 14.
14. Riemann, *Katechismus der Harmonie- und Modulationslehre* (Leipzig: Max Hesse, 1906), p. 12.
15. Riemann, *Katechismus der Akustik*, p. 94.
16. Part II of Jacques Handschin's *Der Toncharakter, eine Einführung in die Tonpsychologie* is a comprehensive and detailed source for the study of the consonance problem.
17. Riemann, *Katechismus der Akustik*, pp. 96–98.
18. Helmholtz, *On the Sensations of Tone*, pp. 187–188.
19. Révész, *Introduction to the Psychology of Music*, pp. 59–61.
20. Riemann, *Musikalische Syntaxis*, p. 10.
21. Riemann, *Katechismus der Akustik*, p. 96.
22. Révész, *Introduction to the Psychology of Music*. p. 58.
23. Hugo Riemann, "Révész Tonqualität," *Zeitschrift der intern. Musikgesellschaft* (no date), p. 8.
24. A historical survey of the octave problem is found in Jacques Handschin, *Der Toncharakter*, pp. 238–250.
25. See this study, p. 218.
26. Rameau, *Traité de l'harmonie*, p. 129.
27. Riemann, *Handbuch der Harmonielehre*, p. 215.
28. Rameau, *Nouveau système de musique théorique*, p. 38.
29. Rameau, *Génération harmonique*, pp. 38–49.
30. Handschin, *Der Toncharakter*, p. 268.
31. Seidel, "Die Harmonielehre Hugo Riemanns" pp. 88–89.
32. Hellmut Federhofer, "Die Funktionstheorie Hugo Riemanns und die Schichtenlehre Heinrich Schenkers," in *Bericht über den Internationalen Musikwissenschaftlichen Kongress, Wien, Mozartjahr 1956*, ed. Erich Schenk (Graz: H. Böhlaus Nachfolger, 1956), pp. 183–190.
33. Carl Dahlhaus, "Ueber den Begriff der tonalen Funktion," in *Beiträge zur Musiktheorie des 19. Jahrhunderts*, p. 93.
34. *Ibid.*, p. 94.
35. *Ibid.*, p. 95.
36. Riemann, "Consonance and Dissonance," pp. 27–28.
37. See this study, pp. 218–219.

38. Riemann, *Harmony Simplified,* trans. H. Bewerung, pp. 55–69.
39. Riemann, *Handbuch der Harmonielehre,* pp. 138–213.
40. Matthew Shirlaw, *Theory of Harmony,* p. 399.
41. *Ibid.,* p. 400.
42. *Ibid.*
43. *Ibid.,* p. 401.
44. See this study, p. 215.
45. See this study, p. 219.
46. Guiseppe Tartini, *Trattato di musica,* p. 112.
47. Riemann, "The Nature of Harmony," p. 30.
48. Riemann, *Harmony Simplified,* p. 55.
49. Rameau, *Traité de l'harmonie,* pp. 248, 266.
50. Riemann, "The Nature of Harmony," p. 30.
51. Richard Münnich, "Von Entwicklung der Riemannschen Harmonielehre," p. 75.
52. Riemann, "The Nature of Harmony," p. 30.
53. Hauptmann, *The Nature of Harmony and Meter,* p. 152.
54. Shirlaw, *Theory of Harmony,* p. 115.
55. Riemann, "The Nature of Harmony," p. 26.
56. Riemann, *Harmony Simplified,* p. 169.
57. Riemann, "The Nature of Harmony," pp. 30–31.
58. Riemann, *Katechismus der Akustik,* pp. 96–97.
59. Riemann, "Consonance and Dissonance," p. 16.
60. Helmholtz, *On the Sensations of Tone,* p. 236.

CHAPTER IV

The Mature Practical Harmony (1890–1909)

R IEMANN'S practical theories became fully developed in the two books *Vereinfachte Harmonielehre* (1893) and the third edition of *Handbuch der Harmonielehre* (1898). Numerous editions and translations establish these two as the best known of Riemann's theoretical works. They will, therefore, serve as the basis for our discussion of Riemann's practical theories. I am using the ninth edition of the *Handbuch* (unchanged from the sixth and last edition of Riemann's lifetime) and the English translation of *Vereinfachte Harmonielehre, Harmony Simplified.* The content of the two books is essentially the same, except that the chapter on modulation is far more extensive in *Harmony Simplified* than in the *Handbuch.* The *Handbuch* justifies its meagerness by saying that the real schooling in modulation lies in the analysis of the works of the masters. Student exercises are of necessity too short to show all types of modulations. Necessary instructions for the study of the ways and means of modulation can be found in the works of the masters of composition, not in the study of harmony.[1] The lessons in composition which began with studies in harmony are extended and are concluded in the three volume work, *Grosse Kompositionslehre* (1902–1913). The first volume, *Der Homophone Satz,* is a study of form and the techniques of analysis, beginning with the motive and working up to the modulation and development techniques of the sonata form. The *Elementarschulbuch der Harmonielehre* (1906) is the last of the works treating practical theory.

THE NEW FUNCTION AND CHORD SYMBOLS

Riemann's chord and function symbols reach their final form in *Verein-fachte Harmonielehre.* The two different classifications, the *Funktionsbezeichnung* (function symbols) and the *Klangschlüssel* (chord symbols) serve specific purposes.

75

The Function Symbols

The function symbols as a type of designation separable from any particular key constitute a generalization applicable to all keys. They are designed with the idea of clarifying the function of every chord within the key, even chromatic chords not revealing their diatonic origin.[2] Of course, the function theory replaces the step theory (*Stufenlehre*) with its Roman numeral designations of chords on every scale degree.

The basic function symbols relate directly to the three primary harmonies in the key and distinguish between major and minor: major, T+ D+ S+; minor, °T °D °S. The parallel chords are designated by adding p to the above letters: Tp, Dp, Sp, and °Tp, °Dp, °Sp. The leading-tone-change chords also use the letters T, D, and S with the symbols < and > added to distinguish between major and minor. The above symbols are all shown in the previous chapter in examples 14 and 15.

Riemann designates the secondary dominant (*Zwischendominante*), a chord functioning as dominant to a chord other than tonic, by placing D in parenthesis. For example, c–e–g–b♭ is secondary dominant to the following subdominant, f–a–c: (D)S. The chord in parenthesis always refers to the following chord unless other symbols are given. The arrow ⟵―――― indicates that the chord is dominant to the previous chord. If the normal chord of resolution is missing, the symbol for the missing chord is placed in brackets, as in example 17.

The dominant of the dominant and subdominant of the subdominant are shown as in example 18.

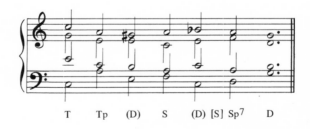

T   Tp   (D)   S   (D) [S] Sp⁷   D

Example 17. Secondary Dominant of a Preceding Chord and of a Missing Chord

Example 18. Dominant of the Dominant and Subdominant of the Subdominant

Modulations are indicated by giving a common chord its meaning in the original key and also in the new key, as in example 19. A repeated function is indicated by the use of two dots.

Example 19. Modulation by Means of a Common Chord

The Chord Symbols

The chord symbols may be compared to a figured bass. They are used in direct reference to a given line of music to be realized in four parts. These symbols are as follows: [3]

> \+ = major chord   (c+ = C major)
> ° = minor chord   (°e = a minor)

(The minor triad is spelled downward from the highest note.) Chord letters without the symbols + or ° are always understood as major.

Arabic numerals always refer to the interval above the major chord root, and Roman numerals always refer to intervals below a minor chord prime. These are designated *plain steps*, i.e., the natural prime, third, fifth, and even the natural seventh. The numerals in figure 10 and other numerals up to ten designate specific intervals of the prime, major second, major third, perfect fourth, perfect fifth, major sixth, minor seventh, perfect octave, major ninth, and major tenth, which are termed the *plain intervals*.

The plain intervals can be expanded or contracted by raising ($<$) or lowering ($>$) the notes by one half step as follows:

$$2 < \quad \text{in c} \quad \text{becomes d}^\sharp.$$
$$2 > \quad \text{in c} \quad \text{becomes d}^\flat.$$
$$\text{III} > \quad \text{in } ^\circ\text{e becomes c}^\flat.$$
$$\text{V} < \quad \text{in a}^\flat \text{ becomes d.}$$

The consonant intervals are, of course, 1, 3, 5 (I, III, V) and the dissonant intervals are 2, 4, 6, 7 (II, IV, VI, VII). (See figure 10.)

	c+	g♭+	f♯+
The meaning of the numerals in the keys of:			
1 = major prime (root of major chord)	c	g♭	f♯
2 = major second above	d	a♭	g♯
3 = major third above	e	b♭	a♯
The meaning of the numerals in the keys of:	°e	°a♯	°b♭
I = minor prime (highest note of the minor triad)	e	a♯	b♭
II = major second below	d	g♯	a♭
III = major third below	c	f♯	g♭

Figure 10. The Meaning of Arabic and Roman Numerals

If the figure is given above a tone which is chord root, the letter may be omitted, as is shown in example 20. If the note is not root, then the root letter is given with the appropriate figure.

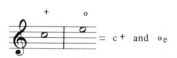

$= \text{c} + \text{ and } _{\circ}\text{e}$

Example 20. The Letter is Omitted when the Given Tone is Root

Inversions are indicated by placing numerals under the bass note. The numerals show which tone is in the bass, for example: $\frac{\text{c}}{5}$ = g–c–e or $\frac{\text{c}}{\text{III}}$ = c–e–a. (Note that the figure ° is omitted from the °e chord, above. Whenever the Roman numeral is present showing the minor direction, the chord as being minor is self-evident without the figure.)

Positioning the number above a determined pitch indicates which tone is to be written in the highest voice (soprano), for example, $\frac{3}{c}$ or $\frac{V}{e}$.

A solidus through a letter or numeral indicates the omission of that note from the chord:

The symbols shown are to be used with a given line of music to be worked out in four parts. Example 21 shows a given problem and the solution.[4]

Soprano

Example 21. The Soprano Line with Chord Symbols and a Four-Part Realization

CHORD CONNECTIONS

The book *Harmony Simplified* is divided into four chapters with an introduction. The introduction establishes the source of major consonance from string divisions and minor consonance from string multiples. There are only two kinds of clangs, major and minor, and three kinds of tonal functions. Chapter I deals specifically with the connecting of the three primary chords in each of the two modes, Chapter II deals with parallel clangs and leading-tone-change clangs, Chapter III with dissonance, and Chapter IV with modulation. Thus, in logical sequence, he presents a practical theory in the same order as the four categories used in organizing the previous chapter of this present work.

In Chapter I, Riemann presents a new terminology to define the various connections between the three primary chords. The terms refer to the interval relationships between chords, the direction of movement, and the change of mode whenever it occurs. The term *plain* refers to progressions upward in major and downward in minor. The term *contra* refers to an interval opposite the natural direction of the mode, downward in major and upward in minor. The two words replace the terms *Homolog* and *Antilog* introduced in *Musikalische Syntaxis*. The following progressions are used in Chapter I.

The *plain-fifth step (schlichten Quintschritt)* is the connecting of the tonic with the *plain-fifth clang* (T–D and °T–°S). "The one, therefore, soars upwards, the other dives downwards, the former case entailing, for the return to the tonic, a sinking downward; the other, a rising aloft."[5]

The *contra-fifth step (Gegenquintschritt)* is the connecting of the tonic with the *contra-fifth clang* (T–S and °T–°D). The major tonic down to the subdominant, or the minor tonic up to the minor dominant is explained "as a forcible pressing back beyond the starting-point of harmonic relations" (pp. 28–29).

The *whole-tone step (Ganztonschritt)* is the connecting of the two dominants (S–D and °D–°S). "The contra-fifth clang is the stretched bow which slings the arrow beyond its mark (the tonic)" (p. 29). He adds that for this reason the contra-fifth clang is generally not followed by its tonic, but moves beyond it to the clang the same distance to the other side of tonic. This results in the progressions T–S–D–T and °T–°D–°S–°T.

The *turn of harmony (Seitenwechsel)* produces a mixture of major and minor relations (p. 44). These are chords of the same prime, but of opposite modes (T–°S = c–e–g — f–a♭–c, and °T — +D = c–e♭–g — g–b–d). One chord is the contra-clang of the other. The term *turn of harmony* replaces the older term *Antinom*.

The *contra-fifth change (Gegenquintwechsel)* is a progression from the minor subdominant (fifth below the minor tonic) to the major dominant (fifth above the major tonic, °S–D+).

The *fifth-change (Quintwechsel)* identifies a change from a major to a minor chord (°S – +S = f–a♭–c — f–a–c, and °D–D+ = e–g–b — e–g♯–b).

On page 17 of *Harmony Simplified* Riemann strictly prohibits the movement of consecutive octaves and fifths, even in contrary motion. According to Seidel, this is one of two voice-leading rules of Riemann which are different from those of his predecessors and contemporaries. The other is the removal of restrictions against hidden octaves and fifths.[6]

In Chapter II Riemann begins with a discussion of how the feigning consonances arise from *characteristic dissonances*. "Since the dominants are never perfectly consonant, in so far as they are always conceived and judged from the tonic," they often appear with additional tones which make their meaning still clearer (p. 55). The characteristic dissonances are the seventh added to the dominant and the sixth added to the sub-dominant. The added tone is in each case a note borrowed from the other dominant of the same mode, as follows:

In C major: D7   = g–b–d/f/   (root of the subdominant)
               S6   = f–a–c–/d/   (fifth of the dominant)

In a minor: °S^{VI} = /b/–d–f–a   (prime of the dominant minor)
             °D^{VII} = /d/–e–g–b   (fundamental, or lowest note
                                      of the subdominant)

The additional note is either a sixth or seventh above the root in major, or a sixth or seventh below the prime in minor.

The diminished triad b–d–f is either the dominant seventh chord in major with omitted root: g̶–b–d–f (Ɗ7) or the subdominant seventh chord in minor with omitted prime: b–d–f–a̶ (S̶^{VII}).

Two *parallel clangs* result from the omission of the fifth in the added sixth chords (S6 and D^{VI}). By omitting the fifth a chord apparently of the opposite mode arises: f–a̶–d (S $^{6}_{3}$) in major, or d–f̶–g–b (DV̶I) in minor. "Thus, we become acquainted with a new category, and, indeed, a very important one, of dissonances under the cloak of consonances (*feigning consonances*)" (p. 71). The remaining parallel clangs do not originate from the chords of characteristic dissonances, but they also consist of notes from two clangs. In the major modes the parallel clangs are chords a third below the primary chord, while in the minor mode they are a third above the primary chords. With the addition of the parallel clangs and the diminished triad further progressions are defined.

The *third change (Terzwechsel)* is a progression from a primary chord to its parallel clang. *Third* means major third, and *change* means that the prime of the second chord is on the opposite side of the chord, for example, T – Tp = /c/–e–g – a–c–/e/.

The *leading-tone change (Leittonwechsel)* is a half-step progression between major and minor chords, keeping in mind that the minor prime is the upper note (T–Dp, S–Tp: °T–°Sp, °D–°Tp).

The *minor-third change (Kleinterzwechsel)* is the equivalent of the deceptive cadence, the dominant to the tonic-parallel (T–Sp, D–Tp; °T–°Dp, °S–Tp.) (p. 84).

The *whole-tone change (Ganztonwechsel)* connects the subdominant parallel to the dominant in major and the dominant parallel to the sub-dominant in minor (Sp–D and °Dp–°S).

The *tritone change* (Dp–S; °Sp–°D) contains the danger of parallel fifths, which can be avoided by contrary motion between the bass and the three upper parts (p. 76).

The symbols for the *leading-tone-change clangs (Leittonwechselklänge),* or leading-tone substitutes, are in major, ⁺𝕯 ⁺𝕾 in minor ⁺𝕱 𝕯 𝕾. The tonic substitute ($T_7^< = $ e–g–b or $T^{VII>} = $ f–a–c) "forms a natural connecting link between tonic and contra-fifth clang" (p. 80). Further progressions result from the addition of the leading-tone-change clangs:

The (plain) *third step,* the connecting of two major or two minor triads a major third apart, such as a minor to f minor (𝕾 – °S) ;

The (plain) *minor-third step,* such as d minor to f minor (Sp – °S) ;

The (plain) *leading-tone step,* such as e minor to f minor (𝕱 – °S).

Riemann then goes on to explain other diatonic formations which result from the modal scales (pp. 88–103). The Mixolydian seventh (lowered seventh) of the major scale and the Dorian sixth (raised sixth) of the minor scale give the major key a minor dominant and the minor key a major subdominant. However, he adds that the Dorian sixth in minor must be followed by the major dominant in order to avoid the modal treatment. The Lydian fourth (raised fourth) and the Phrygian second (lowered second) are represented by the leading-tone substitutes 𝕯 in C major (f♯–g–b–d) and 𝕾 in a minor (d–f–a–b♭). The latter chord is, of course, the Neapolitan sixth.

In Chapter III, dissonance is classified (p. 107). Characteristic dissonances have already been defined as sevenths and sixths added to the plain-fifth and contra-clangs. *Figurative* dissonances are those resulting from passing and auxiliary notes. Numerous chords arise as a result of passing sevenths and ninths. Chromatically altered chords also belong to this class, for example the tonic with raised fifth (c–e–g♯ = $T^{5<}$). Suspensions and unprepared dissonances also produce variations of the primary chords. Figurative dissonances are not placed on a level with the characteristic dissonances.

Sequences, Riemann states, lead theorists astray because they contain illogical progressions. It was Fétis who opened their eyes: "Sequences are, . . . not really harmonic, but melodic formations—i.e., their ruling principle is not the logical progression of harmonies, but the proceeding by degrees through the scale" (p. 122).

On page 127 of *Harmony Simplified* Riemann begins a discussion of the chord known to many as the secondary dominant *(Zwischen-dominante).* The translator calls it a *transition,* "the indication of harmonies as dominants of the following harmony" (p. 128). This relation is expressed by placing the chord in parenthesis. "Chord signs in brackets [parenthesis] are not to be understood as relating to the principle key, but as circumscribing the chord immediately following the bracket, as tonic." For example, in the four-chord progression T (S D7) S the two chords in parenthesis are considered as being in the key of the last chord, and the appropriate accidentals are added to fit the key of the subdominant. For the dominant of the dominant, Riemann uses the sign ♭.

In Chapter IV, modulation is defined as "the change of meaning of tonal functions" (p. 141). Any two-chord progression in the original key that can be interpreted in the sense of a different progression in a new key can bring about a modulation. The progression from tonic to subdominant in C major, c+ − f+, is the same as the plain-fifth close in F major (D–T). "It is evident, therefore, that we only require to add 6 to the T to prompt its change of meaning to S, or the VII to make °S of the °T, or 7♮ to stamp the T as D; similarly, the sudden entry of 4< in the figuration of the major tonic will give the latter under-dominant significance, the merely passing 7♮ will prepare its change of meaning to dominant, and the minor tonic, with a IV>, becomes minor upper-dominant, with a VII♮, under-dominant" (p. 142).

A further means of modulation is by the whole tone step. "Every whole-tone step, because it corresponds to the transition from one dominant to that of the other side (S–D, D–S; °D–°S, °S–°D), has power to modulate to the clang skipped" (p. 146). In C major the possible progressions to other major keys are:

$$
\begin{aligned}
\text{T–}\natural\flat &= \text{c+ − d+ in G major} \\
\text{T–}\S &= \text{c+ − b}\flat\text{+ in F major} \\
\S\text{–°Sp} &= \text{b}\flat\text{+ − a}\flat\text{+ in E}\flat\text{ major} \\
\text{°Tp–}\S &= \text{e}\flat\text{+ − d}\flat\text{+ in A}\flat\text{ major.}
\end{aligned}
$$

There are also such steps from minor keys to major keys, from major to minor keys, and from minor keys to other minor keys, in all a surprising number of modulating possibilities. Examples are given for each of the eighteen possibilities.

Riemann then demonstrates the numerous possibilities of modulating through the diminished triads and the diminished seventh chords (p. 152), after this by means of "bolder harmonic progressions" (p. 162), and finally by "far-reaching harmony steps" (p. 170). An example of the latter is the *chromatic semitone change* as seen in the progression from C major to A major (figure 11) (p. 172).

$$T \; / \; S \; - \; \mathcal{B}$$
$$= \; ^{\circ}Sp \; - \; ^{+}Sp \quad D \; / \; ^{+}T$$

The chords are:

$$c+ \; / \; f+ \; - \; ^{\circ}f\sharp$$
$$= \; f+ \; - \; ^{\circ}f\sharp \quad e+ \; / \; a+$$

Figure 11. Modulation through the Chromatic-Semitone Change

It is obvious at this point that Riemann's *Harmony Simplified* is actually a very complicated harmony textbook. On the other hand, it cannot be denied that the organization of the book, the explanations, and the problems have all been laid out by a master pedagogue.

NOTES

1. Riemann, *Handbuch der Harmonielehre,* p. 223.

2. Renate Imig, *Systeme der Funktionsbezeichnung in den Harmonielehren seit Hugo Riemann* (Düsseldorf: Gesellschaft zur Förderung der systematischen Musik-wissenschaft, 1970), pp. 7–16.

3. Riemann, *Handbuch der Harmonielehre,* pp. 11–20.

4. *Ibid.,* p. 152.

5. Riemann, *Harmony Simplified* (London: Augener and Co., 1896), pp. 16–17; all subsequent text references to *Harmony Simplified* in this chapter are to this edition.

6. Seidel, "Die Harmonielehre Hugo Riemanns," p. 73.

CHAPTER V

The Late Period (1909–1919)

*I*N HIS last two theoretical treatises, "Ideen zu einer 'Lehre von den Tonvorstellungen'" and "Neue Beiträge zu einer 'Lehre von den Tonvorstellungen,'" *Jahrbuch der Musikbibliothek Peters* (1914/15 and 1916), Riemann's thoughts focus entirely on the mental perception of music. In the first article he expresses his disappointment that Stumpf has not succeeded in establishing a real psychological foundation for music, and he proposes to point out for the first time a new postulate—"the important role that tonal conception and the conception of tonal movement have had in music." [1] The concern is no longer simply for the "confirmation of logical functions in actual sounding music, but even more, the newly arising relationships in the phantasy of the composer and in the mind of the listener." [2]

Throughout Riemann's productive years he repeatedly proclaimed that "music listening is not merely a passive sensation of the sound waves in the ear, but is a highly developed confirmation of logical functions of the human intellect." [3] In the dissertation he discusses the logic of basic harmonic progressions. Progressions are logical because they can be associated with antithesis and synthesis. Later, in the treatise, *Musikalische Syntaxis*, he states that harmonic progressions are logical because they can be directly associated with acoustical phenomena. Also, here and in later works progressions are logical because their chordal relationships are understandable within the tonality. Then, in "Die Natur der Harmonik," the psychological term *chord-representation* becomes an important principle. A single tone may be conceived in the mind as having six different relations, or a major chord itself may be thought of in six different keys. It may be a consonantlike tonic, or dissonantlike related chord. The idea of the relationship of keys is also a mental concept. A modulation away from the central key is thought of in terms of a state of dissonance. In order to present these concepts in a clear and orderly manner Riemann created both function symbols in harmony and phrasing symbols in rhythm and meter.

In his latest theoretical writings he moves further into the realm of mental perception. The article "Ideen zu einer 'Lehre von den Ton-vorstellungen'" [Ideas for a theory of tonal concepts] deals specifically with the inner hearing and interpretation that takes place in the imagination, rather than in the actual hearing of a performance. It was only after many years of intensive activity with Beethoven's late works that Riemann was able to formulate his ideas on tonal concepts. He states:

> The alpha and omega of music are not to be found in actual musical performance, but are to be found in the newly arising tonal relationships in the musical phantasy of the composer before they are notated, and again in the musical phantasy of the listener. The notation of a musical composition and even the actual performance are only expedients for transplanting the musical experiences from the mind of the composer into that of the listener.[4]

He also adds that Beethoven's sketchbooks are proof that a composition may have a latent existence in the mind of the composer for years before it reaches its final shape in notation. A formerly composed work might also have the same existence in the memory of a performer enabling him to reproduce the work without a score. The same experience takes place when we read a score after hearing a performance of a work, or even when one follows the score at a concert and reads one line ahead. He adds that when the performing artist has his eyes on several measures ahead of the sounding tones, that artist is displaying one of man's greatest gifts.

Thus, Riemann's theory of *Tonvorstellung* includes the ability of the mind to hear (or imagine) music not actually being performed. It also includes the ability of the mind to interpret the logic or illogic of musical activities on the basis of past experiences. As one's familiarity with music from older epochs and foreign lands grows so does one's concept of its imminent logic.[5] Riemann is also able to connect his theory of tonal concepts directly to his former psychological teachings. He states that "the principle of the greatest economy in tonal concepts rejects complicated formations."[6] This is the reason why the mind conceives as consonant the chords derived from tones corresponding to the numbers one through six, chordal relationships of thirds and fifths, or the position of the triads within the key. From this point of view, tonal organization results from the quest for simplicity. As specific examples, he states that "each tone can be conceived as having six clang-representation possibilities"[7] and that "the simplest concept is doubtlessly the step from one clang constituent to another."[8] Even in complicated progressions the mind seeks simplicity. For example, intervals not directly conceived need "helping concepts." The singing of the tritone f'–b can be more easily rendered by associating it with c': f'–b–c'. In this regard, he gives a number of helpful hints to the sight singer.[9]

Economy is also a factor in Riemann's comparison of just tuning and equal temperament.[10] Certainly, pure tuning is a joy to hear, but it is attained at the price of freedom in harmonic movement and modulation. Thus, he asks, "What is our mental concept? Do we think in pure or tempered intervals?" He answers by saying that the ear hears pure intervals. However, the production of such tones is hardly possible, and voices only approximate the clearly outlined demands of the ear through artistic deviations. Thus, temperament is an official falsehood. Nevertheless, this "artistic deviation" blurs the mental concept so that the difference of a comma between two notes of the same pitch becomes unrecognizable. The enharmonic identification of tones is therefore not only possible, but indispensable.

Handschin discusses these aspects of Riemann's *Tonvorstellung*:

> It seems clear that Riemann's later theory of *Tonvorstellung* is genuine Kantism. . . . On the one hand one hears even in tempered tuning what is intended (actually, the correspondence between the inner and outer is not the question). On the other hand Riemann states that we hear each tone either as root, third, or fifth of a triad ("chord-representation"). This is an exaggerated, but not completely arbitrary assumption, which essentially within a limited sphere has as its basis a prevailing historically musical interpretation. However, with the catchy term *Tonvorstellung* the problem of the relationship between tonal concepts and tonal reality is pushed aside, just as is the problem whether or not it is a coincidence that others have the same tonal concept as I have.[11]

Seidel, in defense of Riemann, states that he did not push the problem aside.[12] As early as his dissertation Riemann had distinguished between involuntary tonal concepts brought forth by listening to music and voluntary concepts such as those conceived purely in the mind of the composer in the process of creation. Then later Riemann states that the preliminary question in establishing a theory of tonal concepts must be: "What do we generally conceive mentally? What are the recognizable qualities that a mentally conceived tone, if conceived correctly, has in common with an actually sounding tone?"[13] The other problem, as to "whether it is a coincidence that others have the same tonal concept as I," was not discussed by Riemann. Seidel asks whether it was possible for him to do so.

Riemann's thoughts on the concept *seelisches Erleben* (mental experience) are noteworthy. A series of single tones form into a concept of tonal movement. These in turn form into chains of musical events. Mental concepts can then be formed of wordless stories, or emotional happenings.[14]

In the second article, "Neue Beiträge zu einer Lehre von den Tonvorstellungen," Riemann seeks to expand these concepts to include all the elements having a share in musical organization:

The entire theory of practical composition and form is concerned only with those elements conceived and combined by the composer. Musical understanding must, therefore, be trained to grasp all rhythmic, metrical, melodic, and harmonic concepts in familiar music, as well as in strange or exotic music. Each misinterpretation of the composer's intent destroys to an extent the eminent logic and distorts more or less the artistic product.[15]

Riemann states his feelings that out of the art of composition a theory of *Tonvorstellung* may be created:

In spite of everything we have come along far enough that we can say: a considerable part of the material used for general instruction serves directly the aim of making familiar to the beginning musician those concepts with which music *Vorstellungen* function.[16]

Riemann has not the slightest doubt that his own theoretical works are building stones, contributions to the creation of such a theory.[17]

NOTES

1. Hugo Riemann, "Ideen zu einer 'Lehre von den Tonvorstellungen,' " *Jahrbuch der Musikbibliothek Peters,* 21/22 (1914/15):3.

2. *Ibid.,* pp. 1–2.

3. *Ibid.,* p. 1.

4. *Ibid.,* p. 2.

5. Riemann, "Neue Beiträge zu einer Lehre von den Tonvorstellungen," *Jahrbuch der Musikbibliothek Peters* 23 (1916): 3.

6. Riemann, "Ideen zu einer 'Lehre,' " p. 7.

7. *Ibid.,* p. 6.

8. *Ibid.,* p. 24.

9. *Ibid.,* p. 25.

10. *Ibid.,* pp. 18–19.

11. Jacques Handschin, *Der Toncharakter,* p. 126.

12. Seidel, "Die Harmonielehre Hugo Riemanns," pp. 84–85.

13. Riemann, "Ideen zu einer 'Lehre,' " pp. 4–5.

14. *Ibid.,* pp. 10–11.

15. Riemann, "Neue Beiträge zu einer Lehre von den Tonvorstellungen," p. 10.

16. *Ibid.,* p. 1.

17. Riemann, "Ideen zu einer 'Lehre,' " p. 3.

CHAPTER VI

Riemann's Successors

RIEMANN'S system of harmony was neither generally accepted nor understood in its entirety. According to Renate Imig, Riemann's complicated manner of presentation more than anything else prevented it from being generally received.[1] Also, Ernst Kirsch was of the opinion that Riemann's manner of expression was difficult to understand.[2] Similarly, Herman Grabner states that many who realized the necessity for a reform seriously considered teaching Riemann's function theory, but after a few unsucessful attempts returned to the old familiar step theory.[3] Even in his own lifetime Riemann felt the sting of opposition. Embittered enemies of his new theories prevented him from teaching theory at the Leipzig University.[4] In self-defense Riemann declares: "My harmony text-books doubtless [*sic*] contain passages that on account of polemical discussion are of no great value and because they are perplexing are even detrimental to the young student." Nevertheless, he adds: "I state . . . that the naming of the minor chord after its highest tone does not in the least irritate elementary students and even very young children."[5] After much study of Riemann, I also admit the difficulty of the system. The analysis of minor harmony downwards is a tedious and mind-boggling task. No less complicated is the problem of connecting the various change steps, which involve spelling major chords upward and minor chords downward. The challenges in the chapter on modulation from *Harmony Simplified* are tremendous, not so much because of the modulations themselves, but because of the figures, terminologies, and procedures involved. Nevertheless, although the original Riemann system did not survive beyond Riemann's own lifetime, there are numerous simplified versions of it, most of them omitting the dual aspect and presenting a simplified version of the function theory and symbols for pedagogical purposes. Several dual systems of harmony have come forth, one an extension of Riemann (Erpf) and another a modification (Karg-Elert). According to Imig the chord symbols have been disseminated far and wide.

89

DUAL SYSTEMS AFTER RIEMANN

Sigfrid Karg-Elert (1877–1933), a brilliant pianist and composer, was for years a teacher of piano, theory, and composition at the Leipzig Conservatory. In his theoretical treatise, *Polaristische Klang- und Tonalitätslehre* (1931), he goes much further than Riemann in his mathematical-speculative creation of two polar opposites. According to Karg-Elert, the real existence of undertones is not important. His harmony system is based on the numbers one, three, five and seven, the seventh being a natural consonance. The polar opposite of the ascending C major scale and its triads is the descending e minor scale with its upside-down triads.[6] The chord symbols also mirror each other, for example, the symbols for the major primary triads are T, $\overline{\text{D}}$, and C *(Contradominante)* and for the minor primary triads are ⊥, ⊔, and ⊃. Like Riemann's, his system includes the three primary functions with the addition of the feigning consonances. Dissonance results from combinations of tones out of different clangs, which he calls clang complexes. The natural seventh leads to an essential expansion of fifth and third-related chord progressions and tonalities to include natural relationships of seconds and sevenths.[7] Paul Schenk states that the Karg-Elert system is of little value to musical practice because its pure minor mode, its inverted aspect, and its abstract mathematical-acoustical foundation ignore both the psychological aspects of music and musical practice. Also, in the age of Stravinsky and Ernst Krenek a system based on major and minor is outdated.

Karg-Elert's students include Fritz Reuter, Paul Schenk, and Siegfried Bimberg. Fritz Reuter wrote his *Praktische Harmonik des 20. Jahrhunderts* (1952) as an introduction to Karg-Elert's harmonic *"Buch der Bücher."* [8] Paul Schenk acknowledges Karg-Elert as his teacher, but his own book, *Modulationslehre* (1954), out of didactic considerations, departs from the polarization of the minor tonality and arrives at a compromise between Riemann and Karg-Elert.[9]

Hermann Erpf (1891–1957), a student of Riemann, pedagogue, composer, and theorist, was Riemann's only successor, according to Denecke,[10] who accepted the Riemann system in its entirety as a basis for further development. This further development was, above all, the explanation of the meaning of harmony in the new music. The most important concept in his *Studien zur Harmonie- und Klangtechnik der neueren Musik* (1927) is the *Mehrklang,* a chord constructed from constituents of two or more clangs. There is no dissonance, just chord combinations. The first group of *Mehrklänge* are combinations of the primary chords. The

Doppeldominant chords are combinations of the dominant and sub-dominant as seen in example 22. Signs at the upper right of the letter refer to the dominant and signs at the lower right refer to the subdominant.[11]

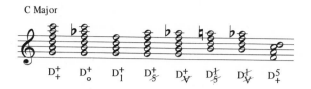

Example 22. *Doppeldominantklänge* (Double Dominant Chords)

The *Dominanttonikaklang* is a formation constructed from notes of either or both dominant chords and the tonic chord. The symbol is the T and D placed together: ^T_D. Figures are added in the same manner as to the *Doppeldominant*: 1, 3, 5 or I, III, V to the upper right for the upper dominant, lower right for the under dominant, and to the left for the tonic, as seen in example 23.[12]

The chord at a) in example 23 consists of the third of the tonic (e), third of the dominant (b), and third of the subdominant (a). The chord at b) is

Example 23. *Dominanttonikaklänge* and Their Symbols

composed of the minor third of the tonic (e♭), major third of the upper dominant (b), and root and third of the minor under dominant (f–a♭). By adding the parallel and leading-tone-change chords other complicated structures result. With this system Erpf was able to analyze exerpts from the works of Schönberg.[13]

Other theorists who used the Riemann symbols for chord combinations were Ernst Kirsch *(Wesen und Aufbau der Lehre von den harmonischen Funktionen,* 1928) and Friedrich Neumann *(Synthetische Harmonielehre,* 1951).

92   RIEMANN'S THEORY OF HARMONY

Sven Emanuel Svensson (1899–1960), an important theorist and musicologist at the University of Uppsala, Sweden, was another disciple of Riemann. I was told that Svensson taught a dual-functional system based on Riemann and his own *Harmonilära* (1933) to generations of musicology students. His article, "Vårt tonsystem och dess temperaturer" [Our tonalsystem and its temperament], uses the Riemann Arabic and Roman numerals to indicate intervals above and below a given prime.[14] The *Musik in Geschichte und Gegenwart,* article "Svensson," states that his writings on theory are interesting and original. This applies less to his *Harmonilära,* based on Riemann's function theory, and more to his articles on melodic analysis *(Quintspannung)* and to his interval-chord-rhythm method, whereby the dissonant intensities of the various intervals and chordal interval combinations can be objectively represented.

RIEMANN SIMPLIFIED

According to Seidel, the textbooks in use today based on functional harmonic theory—the books of Grabner and his students, Hugo Distler and Wilhelm Mäler—have little in common with Riemann except for the symbols and terminology. Grabner's textbook, *Handbuch der Harmonielehre: Praktische Anleitung zum funktionellen Tonsatz* (1944), is organized in the same sequence of material as Riemann's *Vereinfachte Harmonielehre* and *Handbuch der Harmonielehre.* One recognizes immediately that it is a monistic method, major and minor receiving the same treatment. The three primary functions of tonic, dominant, and subdominant and their symbols are the same as Riemann's. The secondary chords, Riemann's parallel clangs and leading-tone-change clangs, are renamed the under-third clangs and over-third clangs *(Unterterzklänge* and *Oberterzklänge).* He uses the same symbols for the parallel clangs (Tp, Sp, Dp), but Riemann's leading-tone-change clangs are renamed *Gegenparallelklänge* (Tg, Sg, Dg). The modulations are diatonic, avoiding the vast possibilities of far-reaching modulations of *Vereinfachte Harmonielehre.*

Grabner's student, Distler, published his harmony method in 1940, a method similar to that of his teacher. According to Imig, the most widespread function symbols in use today are those of Mäler, another student of Grabner.[15] In opposition to Riemann and Grabner, he distinguishes between major and minor tonality through large and small letters. This letter designation was also used by Dietran Schubert and Wilhelm Keller.[16]

RIEMANN'S SUCCESSORS 93

The Dissemination of the Chord and Function Symbols

Imig's *Systeme der Funktionsbezeichnung in den Harmonielehren seit Hugo Riemann* (1970) covers in encyclopedic detail Riemann's chord and function symbols (pp. 5–119) and then traces them throughout the harmonic systems of his successors (pp. 120–265). According to Imig, the symbols most commonly borrowed from Riemann have been the three primary functions T, D, S, the parallel clangs, the *Zwischendominante* (secondary dominants), and in a few cases, the leading-tone-change symbols. In addition to those theorists already mentioned, others can be listed: Richard Eidenbenz, Hans Joachim Moser, Schönberg, Hugo Kauder, Georg Capellen, Joseph Achtelik, and Franz Marschner.[17] The table of symbols in figure 12, from Imig's *Systeme der Funktionsbezeichnung* (p. 163), presents the function symbols of most of the above-mentioned theorists in both major and minor, along with those of Riemann. Imig also mentions a number of other theorists who have used certain concepts of the function theory in their step theories: Rudolph Louis and Ludwig Thuille, Gustav Bumcke, François August Gevaert, Gustav Güldenstein, Hugo Kaun, Wilhelm Klatte, and Bruno Weigl.[18]

Imig also traces Riemann's *Klangschlüssel* in jazz. The following commonly used jazz symbols are a type of *Klangschlüssel* in the sense of Riemann's: C = c–e–g; Cm = c–e$^\flat$–g; C6 = c–e–g–a; C7 = c–e–g–b$^\flat$. Augmented and diminished chords use the + and ° signs (C+ and c°).

Alfred Baresel (*Jazz-Harmonielehre* [1953]) even applies the symbols S, T, D, Tp, Sp, Dp. The primary chord symbols are used in figuring the circle of fifths:[19]

g$^\flat$+	d$^\flat$+	a$^\flat$+	e$^\flat$+	b$^\flat$+	f+	c+	g+	d+	a+	e+	b+	f$^\sharp$+
S6	S5	S4	S3	S2	S	T	D	Ð2	Ð3	Ð4	Ð5	Ð6

The chord symbol, Ð $^7_3$, is an E major seventh chord with omitted third.

A few examples will show that some of Riemann's concepts are also common in publications on the American continent. The secondary dominant principle is found in Walter Piston's *Harmony* (V of IV, V7 of III) and in William Christ, et al., *Materials and Structure of Music* (V7/ii, V$^6_5$/IV). The method of indicating inversions with Arabic numerals 3, 5, and 7 is found in Carolyn A. Alchin's *Applied Harmony* ($^{iii}_3$ = first inversion, $^{IV}_5$ = second inversion). The method used by the Royal Conservatory of Music of Toronto, widespread in Canada, uses a variation of the latter method (Ia, Ib, Ic = root, first inversion, and second inversion).

	in C - Dur					in a - Moll:				
Riemann:	°S	S	T	D	$D^{3>}$	$S^{m<}$	°S	°T	°D	D+
Grabner:	°S	S	T	D	°D	+S	°S	°T	°D	D
Distler:	$S^>$	S	T	D		S^+	S	T	D°	D+
Eidenbenz:	°S	°Sv	T	D	Dv	°Sv	°S	°T	Dv	D+
Kirsch:	oS	S	T	D	oD	+S	oS	oT	oD	+D
Neumann:	°S	+S	+T	+D	°D	+S	°S	°T	°D	+D
Maler Keller Schubert	s	S	T	D	d	S	s	t	d	D
Schonberg:	sd	SD	T	D	v	SD	sd	t	v	D
Erpf:	D_o	D_+	+T	D+	D°	D_+	D_o	oT	D°	D+
Bumcke:		U	T	D						
Kauder:		+G	+T	+D			-D	-T	-G	
Karg-Elert:	c	C	T	D	d	d̦	Ɑ	λ	Ɔ	ɔ
Capellen:	L_o	L	M	R	R_o	L	L_o	M_o	R_o	R

Figure 12. A Comparison of the Primary Function Symbols of Riemann and His Successors

These latter symbols were apparently borrowed by the RCMT from English writers such as Charles H. Kitson (*Elementary Harmony* [1920]) and C. H. Pearce.

All of Riemann's symbols cannot be traced here, but this is sufficient to show that his influence has had a far-reaching effect.

MAX REGER

Riemann recognized the importance of analysis as a background study for all musicians. That the numerous projects in analysis of the Beethoven piano sonatas and the Bach preludes and fugues have not attained much notice is due, according to Grabner, to the rigid, dualistic manner of theorizing, from which even his student, Reger, turned away.[20] Reger was a composition student of Riemann's at Sondershausen and Wiesbaden. Riemann's approach to teaching composition began with the analysis of masterworks and proceeded with attempts at imitating the originals. In spite of Reger's rejection of Riemann's methods, he recognized the significance of the theories for practical analysis and used them in his own teaching and writings. Grabner, a student of Reger's, states that Reger's entire theoretical outlook stems directly from Riemann. Reger's small book *Beiträge zur Modulationslehre* (1903) was printed ten times and translated into French and English by 1917. The outer form of his theory of modulation is clearly Riemann's concept of the change of meaning of tonal functions.

Grabner also recognized the value of Riemann's system of analysis, especially the function theory as a replacement for the older step theory:

> The illogical step theory, above all, the deficiency of its chord symbols to present a clear perception of tonality, caused me to attempt to make Riemann's system accessible in a general, easily understandable type of monistic practice.[21]

He explains that the untenability of the dualist system and Riemann's complicated presentation has prevented a general recognition of the system. He retains the function symbols, but removes the Roman numerals associated with the opposite minor concept. The complicated terminology of chord progressions is also removed.

HEINRICH SCHENKER

Although Schenker does not admit learning anything from Riemann, some of his most important concepts are too close to Riemann's to be overlooked. However, he denies the natural origin of the minor triad and claims that the minor mode arises from the same principle as major. The most natural of all relationships, the fifth-relationship, is retained; only the third is different. The minor system is artificial: "The minor mode springs from the originality of the artist, whereas the source, at least, of the major mode flows, so to speak, spontaneously from nature."[22]

Schenker's attitude toward the Renaissance church modes is similar to Riemann's. They were unnatural systems and defective in respect to our major and minor. In fact, he gives instructions to the readers of "old scores" to add sharps and flats wherever possible to make the "old music" as much like major and minor as possible. He further states that the church modes "were nothing but experiments . . . in theory as well as in practice," [23] which contributed to the eventual understanding of the two main systems.

There is some similarity between Riemann's three tonal functions of tonic, dominant, and subdominant and Schenker's *Stufen*.[24] The *Stufen* (scale-steps) are those structural chords which have definite functional purpose, around which other nonfunctional chords revolve. It is a higher and more abstract unit than the triad. The *Stufen* are identical with those ascending series of fifths which brought about the rising fifth-relationship. The tonic is the progenitor chord. The order of higher fifth-relationships above the tonic is that of dominant, supertonic, submediant, mediant, and leading tone. The subdominant, by contrast, is found by the process of inversion—by returning through the series of fifth-related steps and going one step beneath tonic. How close this is to Riemann's derivation of the under dominant! Schenker's most important *Stufe* is the dominant, the most closely related step above tonic. He infers that the next important *Stufe* is the subdominant due to its position directly beneath the tonic as an inverted dominant. This is seen in his discussion of the authentic cadence when he states that the two dominant chords encircle the tonic for a satisfying close. The IV–V–I, or its variation, V–IV–I, can occur anywhere within the phrase as well as at the end. The subdominant *Stufe* is not replaced by the supertonic in the ii–V–I cadence, for this movement is only a modification of the IV–V–I progression.[25] The tonic system, then, is represented by a root tone and five other tones determined by the rising fifth-relationship and by the under dominant located a fifth below tonic, but the most important are the two dominant *Stufen*. The origin of Schenker's system of *Stufen* might well have been Riemann's tonal system of tonic with its upper and lower dominants. Although Riemann includes only one upper fifth-relationship and Schenker has five, it should be remembered that Riemann accepted root relationships of fifths as being perfectly natural.[26]

In the psychological implications of consonance and dissonance Riemann compares consonance to the repose found only in the tonic chord. Dissonance is movement away from the tonic to other chords. The same applies to modulation. Modulation from the home key is movement to a state of dissonance that can only be resolved by the eventual return of the home key and to the tonic chord. Herein lies the epitomy of Schenker's mature theories found in *Der freie Satz* (1935). For Schenker the greatest unifying force is tonality; by tonality he means that tone or sound which governs the entire piece. This tone consists of a fundamental tone and its first five partials, reduced to a major triad, and called clang. This clang is never changed by modulation; the background tonality remains the same. Composition is, therefore, the *Auskomponierung,* or unfolding of the clang. The unfolding is the process of changing the natural clang through artistic means into a horizontal position of succession. Tonality is maintained by the various transformations of the triad. This transformation involves two concepts, that of space as applied to the vertical triad in simultaneity and that of time as applied to the clang in succession. These two concepts are manifest in the *Urlinie* and the *Bassbrechung.* The *Urlinie* is a purely inner melodic descending line which fills in the spaces of the clang. The *Bassbrechung* is the fundamental bass line composed of a fundamental arpeggio whose function is purely harmonic. These two voices form the *Ursatz,* the background tonal structure of the composition.[27] The term *harmony* refers to the functional *Stufen* which occur on three different levels in the composition: background, middleground, and foreground.[28] *Counterpoint* refers to the motion in more than one voice that fills in the spaces between the *Stufen* of the *Ursatz.*[29] This filling in creates a foreground in which new and distant chords are conceived. Modulations are only foreground action. The *Ursatz* is nature's gift; foreground is man's use of that gift. The *Ursatz* as developed by Schenker appears to be an enlargement of the Riemann psychological concept that a composition is a journey from the state of consonance of the tonic center through the dissonant lands of other chords and keys, but constantly referring back, and eventually coming to rest in the consonance of the home chord.

PAUL HINDEMITH

Hindemith, like Schenker, rejects the undertone series as a basic for minor harmony: "It seems to me repugnant to good sense to assume a force capable of producing such as inversion."[30] The major triad, he states, is given to us freely by nature, but nature gives no hint of the minor triad. Hindemith, then, uses overtones as the basis for his system of music, from which he obtains neither the major nor the minor scale, but a twelve-tone chromatic scale. The first seven tones of this chromatic scale correspond perfectly to Helmholtz's relationship of tones (C–c–g–f–a–e–e♭–a♭). This series of twelve tones, called Series I, is used as the basis for understanding the connection of tones and chords, the ordering of harmonies, progressions, and accordingly, the tonal progression of compositions."[31] Compare this statement to the one given by Riemann having to do with relationships of the same level:

As the principal tone of a chord is related to its accessory tones . . . , and as the tonic chord of a key is related to the accessory chords . . . , so the principal key of a piece is related to the accessory keys which occur in it. . . .

Thus the fundamental laws of chord succession, as well as the succession of keys (Modulation) may be deducted from the extension of these simplest musical conceptions, consonance and dissonance.[32]

In Hindemith's chapter on melody we find that the degree progression of melody is based on the same laws that rule tonal progressions. The melodic degree progression points out the more important notes of the melody, drawn mainly from the harmonic content of the melody. It may be interesting to compare statements by Riemann, Schenker, and Hindemith in relation to melodic progression. Riemann says: "Chordal progressions (also melodies, since they exhibit the principle of chordal progression in its simplest form) are heard much like one hears the relationship of chords to a main *Klang*."[33] Schenker is more specific and closer to Hindemith's ultimate melodic degree progression.

Nature as well as art is satisfied if the course of a melody offers to our ear the possibility of connnecting with a certain tone its fifth and third, which may make their appearance in the melody by and by. . . . The harmonic element thus has to be pursued in both directions, the horizontal as well as the vertical.[34]

Hindemith's melodic degree progression is a series of chord roots found in the melodic line, placed in succession:

In order to set up the degree progression of a melody we shall inclose in a dotted bracket . . . the notes which can be heard without effort as a harmonically related group. In general these groups will form broken triads with nonchord tones. . . . We now extract the roots of the harmonic groups of a melody . . . and place them in succession.[35]

The rules of chordal progression are practically the same for all three theorists. All three agree that root relations of a fifth are the strongest because of the relationship of the first overtone. Third-related chords come next, followed by relationships of the second. Hindemith adds that root relations of the tritone are the weakest of all. He then demonstrates how his twelve-note series (Series I) governs the progression of larger harmonic sections. The roots "which support the burdens of larger harmonic groupings may be called *degrees,* and their succession in accordance with the demands of Series I the harmonic *degree-progression*."[36]

All three theorists speak of modulation in two different senses. In one sense it is a change of key or tonic and in the second, seen on a wider scope, it is a movement away from the tonic into other regions of varying relationships to the original tonic, to which it will eventually return. It is interesting to see how nearly alike the wording is in Schenker's definition of tonicalization and Hindemith's definition of modulation. Schenker says:

Not only at the beginning of a composition, but also in the midst of it, each scale step [Stufe] manifests an irresistible urge to attain the value of the tonic for itself as that of the strongest scale step. If the composer yields to this urge of the scale step . . . I call this process tonicalization.[37]

Hindemith speaks of modulation in the following manner:

Every tone seeks an importance greater than that which it has simply as a tone: . . . it seeks to become the . . . tonal center of a degree progression. When we yield to this tendency, when we allow one tone to usurp the place of another as tonal center of a degree progression, we are modulating.[38]

In the wider sense of the term modulation, Riemann speaks of a movement into dissonance from tonic repose. Schenker, in his later writings, defines composition as a history of the tonic Klang.[39] Modulation is not a change of tonic; it is only foreground action, or the unfolding (Auskomponierung) of the clang through artistic means. Hindemith also speaks of the over-all tonality:

The tonal centers of all the tonalities of a composition produce, when they are connected without the inclusion of any of the intervening tones, a second degree progression, which should be constructed along the same lines as the first one, built of the roots of all the chords. Here we see the full unfolding of the organizing power of Series I. The entire harmonic construction of a piece may be perceived in this way: against one tonal center chosen from among many roots are juxtaposed which either support it or compete with it [sic]. Here, too, the tonal center that reappears most often, or that is particularly strongly supported by its fourth and its fifth, is the most important. As a tonal center of a high order it dominates a whole movement or a whole work.[40]

ERNST KURTH

The amount of influence of Riemann on Ernst Kurth (1886–1946) is difficult to determine. In Kurth's works, especially Musikpsychologie (1931), there are numerous references to Riemann, some in agreement, but many in disagreement. Most references are in regard to psychological concepts, that being the most important aspect of Kurth's writings. He claims that although some of his early ideas on Tonvorstellungen were much similar to Riemann's, they were worked out independently. His book, Grundlagen des linearen Kontrapunkts (1917), had already gone to press when Riemann's "Ideen zu einer 'Lehre von den Ton-vorstellungen,' " was published. Denecke, in his book *Die Komposi-tionslehre Hugo Riemann, historisch und systematisch dargestellt* (1937) in the chapter entitled "Die Wirkung Riemanns auf seine Nachfolger" [The influence of Riemann on his successors], discusses some of Kurth's views on the psychology of music as they are presented here.

Kurth rejects Riemann's function theory in favor of the step theory and also denies the dual system in the outward sense.[41] Yet, he has a psychological explanation for the dual concept. Instead of defining major and minor as opposite chord forms, he explains them as being two op-posing active factors of the same harmonic tonicity, or expansive power [*Spannkraft*]: "The minor represents a tendency to balance the tonicity of the major, which, however, tends toward the opposite side to an analogous tonicity." Nevertheless, he adds that the minor chord is not seen as a "disturbance of the major chord, but both chords represent op-positely directed deviations from the same state of absolute rest."[42] The chordal repose found in the major and minor chords is only relative on ac-count of the latent tension of the leading tone of the third. Kurth defines major and minor opposition in a similar manner in his work, *Grundlagen des linearen Kontrapunkts*:

The natural feeling of rest in the major chord . . . experiences a diversion in the sense of an upwardly directed expansion. . . . Likewise, in the minor chord (as in the major) the two thirds amalgamate into a complete chordal consonance; . . . however, in the minor chord the expansion is directed downward.[43]

A detailed definition of this energetic major-minor relationship is found in Kurth's book, *Musikpsychologie*:

With regard to the condition of tension in the chord, the dualistic ascending and descending tendencies are centralized in the major and minor antithesis. . . . The minor triad of the same root (not Riemann's upper fifth) is the opposite form. The c minor triad, in contrast to the major triad, signifies a modification of the character of the third, which in reference to the natural form of the triad, is comprehended as having the suggestion of a striving downwards (alteration of e to eb).[44]

Also, the major-minor key system is, according to Kurth, a system of dynamic, energetic movement:

Basically, harmony is the transformation of tension. The opposition of major and minor is based on the difference of the third. The altering of the third of a triad is primarily not a change of chord, but is only an emotional effect.[45]

Kurth, therefore, arrives at a completely different interpretation of har-monic dualism than Riemann. Comprehending music as an expression of energetic tension, he proceeds from forces which lie behind the outward musical manifestation. Riemann, on the other hand, holds to pure musical factors and seeks to derive the major and minor chords from the overtones and undertones.[46]

Kurth also gives a psychological explanation for consonance and dissonance. In the widest sense consonance is associated with feelings of rest, dissonance with tension. This is, of course, similar to Riemann's views.[47]

In the essays "Ideen zu einer 'Lehre von den Tonvorstellungen' " and "Neue Beiträge zu einer Lehre," Riemann seeks for the sources of the psychological values of music (melody, harmony, rhythm, meter). "Musical hearing is not only a passive endurance of the effects of the sound waves; it is a highly developed activity of the logical functions of the human intellect."[48] Kurth also emphasizes the "activity" upon which is founded the concept of melodic hearing. He states:

Tonal concepts depend not only on objective tonal material, but also on the art of subjective conception. Even with larger tonal phenomena such as melody, chords, forms, etc., it is an activity of the imagination. Individual components are selected, others are suppressed, and others even added. . . . Although *Vorstellung* is to be comprehended as an "act" and not as a passive reflected perception, it appears to be aimed at greater connections, which first is influenced by the concept of the individual tones. While I was realizing these ideas in music theory, and while they were coming forth from my theory of counterpoint, especially in the basic concepts of melody, Hugo Riemann's "Ideen zu einer 'Lehre den Tonvorstellungen' " appeared. . . . The works came forth completely independent of each other.[49]

For Riemann, musical hearing is the understanding of the musical substance by means of confirmation of logical functions. Kurth, on the other hand, urges a process whereby musical occurrences are conceived as a process of physical tension:

Musical listening, the experience of an art work, is not essentially an involvement of the ear or an activity of harmonic logic. It is a process of psychical suspension being carried along with the primeval energetic motion.[50]

Kurth adds his opinion that the idea of *Tonvorstellung* is not adequate for explaining the process of musical events:

Riemann, in the first essay on *Tonvorstellungen* correctly designates the capability to read ahead ["reading the score at a concert with the eyes one line ahead"] as "one of the greatest wonders of human gifts."[51] But one can see that the concept of *Tonvorstellung* is no longer adequate and must be replaced by the idea of unity of motion [*Bewegungseinheit*].[52]

Frankly, I fail to see that the gift of reading ahead is any greater than many other marvelous wonders of which the human intellect is capable. In conclusion, it is quite evident that Riemann's harmonic theories are still very much alive today. In fact, the growing number of publications reveal a revival of interest in that theorist. I sincerely hope that my first goal—a comprehensive presentation of Riemann's theory of harmony—has been satisfactorily attained. Hopefully, it will also prepare and equip the reader, both in understanding and interest, for the reading of Part II of this work—*Riemann's History of Harmonic Theory, A Translation of Die Harmonielehre,* Book III of *Geschichte der Musiktheorie im IX.–XIX. Jahrhundert.*

NOTES

1. Imig, *Systeme der Funktionsbezeichnung in den Harmonielehren seit Hugo Riemann,* p. 135.

2. *Ibid.*

3. Hermann Grabner, *Die Funktionstheorie Hugo Riemanns und ihre Bedeutung für die praktische Analyse* (Munich: Otto Halbreiter, 1923), p. v.

4. *Die Musik in Geschichte und Gegenwart,* s.v. "Riemann, Hugo."

5. Hugo Riemann, "Consonance and Dissonance," pp. 26–27.

6. Paul Schenk, "Karg-Elerts polaristische Harmonielehre," in *Beiträge zur Musiktheorie des 19. Jahrhunderts,* pp. 133–162.

7. *Ibid.,* p. 153.

8. Imig, *Systeme der Funktionsbezeichnung,* p. 124.

9. Schenk, "Karg-Elerts polaristische Harmonielehre," p. 162.

10. Denecke, "Die Kompositionlehre Hugo Riemanns," pp. 86–87.

11. Imig, *Systeme der Funktionsbezeichnung,* pp. 212–218.

12. *Ibid.,* p. 215.

13. Denecke, "Die Kompositionslehre Hugo Riemanns," p. 87.

14. Sven E. Svensson, "Vårt tonsystem och dess temperaturer," in *Svensk Tidskrift för Musikforskning* (1950–51), pp. 152–186.

15. Imig, *Systeme der Funktionsbezeichnung,* p. 122.

16. Hugo Distler, *Funktionelle Harmonielehre* (Kassel und Basel: Bärenreiter, 1940); Wilhelm Mäler, *Beitrag zur Harmonielehre* (Leipzig: Lückhardt, 1931); Dietran Schubert, *Satzlehre* (Wolfenbüttel: Möseler, 1960); Wilhelm Keller, *Handbuch der Tonsatzlehre,* 2 vols. (Regensburg: Bosse, 1957–1959).

17. Richard Eidenbenz, "Dur- und Moll-Problem und Erweiterung der Tonalität" (Ph.D. diss., Zurich, 1927); Hans Joachim Moser, "Funktionslehre," in *Musiklexikon,* 4th ed. (Hamburg: Hans Sikorski, 1955); Arnold Schönberg, *Die Formbildenden Tendenzen der Harmonie* (Mainz: Schott, 1957); Hugo Kauder, *Entwurf einer neuen Melodie- und Harmonielehre* (Vienna: Universal-edition, 1932); Georg Capellen, *Fortschrittliche Harmonie- und Melodielehre* (Leipzig: C. F. Kahnt Nachfolger, 1908); Josef Achtelik, *Der Naturklang als Wurzel aller Harmonien, Eine ästhetische Musiktheorie* (Leipzig: C. F. Kahnt, 1922); Franz Marschner, *Die Klangschrift, ein Beitrag zur einheitlichen Gestaltung der Harmonielehre* (Vienna, 1894).

18. The pertinent publications of these authors are listed in the Bibliography.

19. Imig, *Systeme der Funktionsbezeichnung,* pp. 133–134.

20. Grabner, *Die Funktionstheorie Hugo Riemanns,* p. 3.

21. *Ibid.,* pp. v–vi.

22. Heinrich Schenker, *Harmony,* trans. Elizabeth Mann Borgese, ed. Oswald Jonas (Chicago: Chicago Press, 1954), p. 52.

23. *Ibid.,* p. 59.

24. *Ibid.,* pp. 138–153.

25. *Ibid.,* pp. 38–39, 216–224.

26. Hellmut Federhofer, "Die Funktionstheorie Hugo Riemanns," pp. 183–190. Federhofer does not attempt to show any influence of Riemann on Schenker. Rather, he proceeds to show how Schenker's step theory is superior to Riemann's function theory.

27. Heinrich Schenker, *Der freie Satz,* 2d ed. (Vienna: Oswald Jonas, 1956), Pt. I, p. 39.

28. Allen Forte, "Schenker's Conception of Musical Structure," *Journal of Music Theory* 3, no. 1 (April 1959): 1–30.

29. Adele T. Katz, "Heinrich Schenker's Method of Analysis," *Musical Quarterly* 21 (1935): 311.

30. Paul Hindemith, *Craft of Musical Composition,* p. 78.

31. *Ibid.,* p. 56.

32. Riemann, "The Nature of Harmony," pp. 30–31.

33. See this study, p. 218.

34. Schenker, *Harmony,* pp. 133–134.

35. Hindemith, *Craft of Musical Composition,* p. 183.

36. *Ibid.,* p. 143.

37. Schenker, *Harmony,* p. 256.

38. Hindemith, *Craft of Musical Composition,* pp. 148–149.

39. Schenker, *Der freie Satz.*

40. Hindemith, *Craft of Musical Composition,* p. 151.

41. Ernst Kurth, *Musikpsychologie* (Hildesheim: Georg Olms, 1969), p. 197.

42. Kurth, *Die Voraussetzungen der Theoretischen Harmonik* (Bern: M. Drechsel, 1913), p. 122.

43. Kurth, *Grundlagen des linearen Kontrapunkts* (Bern: M. Drechsel, 1917), p. 84.

44. Kurth, *Musikpsychologie,* p. 214.

45. Kurth, *Romantische Harmonik und ihre Krise in Wagners "Tristan"* (Hildesheim: Georg Olms, 1968), p. 179.

46. Denecke, "Die Kompositionslehre Hugo Riemanns," p. 85.

47. *Ibid.,* p. 87.

48. Riemann, "Ideen zu einer 'Lehre,'" p. 11.

49. Kurth, *Musikpsychologie,* p. 46.

50. Kurth, *Romantische Harmonik und ihre Krise,* p. 8.

51. Riemann, "Ideen zu einer 'Lehre,'" p. 4.

52. Kurth, *Musikpsychologie,* p. 95.

PART II

Riemann's History of Harmonic Theory:
A Translation of Die Harmonielehre,
Book III of
Geschichte der Musiktheorie
im IX.–XIX. Jahrhundert

CHAPTER VII

Gioseffo Zarlino and the Discovery of the Dual Nature of Harmony

THE harmonic triad was almost identified by a number of contrapuntal theorists, especially after the middle of the fifteenth century. However, the term itself first appears in *Le Istituzioni harmoniche* (1558) of Gioseffo Zarlino, the subsequent chapelmaster of St. Marks in Venice. In Chapter XXXI, Book III of this work, which established the imperishable fame of its author as a theorist, the following is clearly stated:[*1]

The essential substance of polyphonic composition is not to be found in the variety of the consonances created by the two parts, but rather, in the characteristics of the two possible forms of harmony. These two types of harmony are distinguished by the position of the third which divides the fifth either harmonically or arithmetically. All of the diversities and perfections of harmony depend upon the distinction of these two formations:

The third and fifth or their inversions are the only elements of composition, and the ear desires no other sound between or beyond these intervals, nor any distinctly different from them.

Chapter XV of Book I of the *Istituzioni* states that all the designated consonances are contained within the proportions 1:2:3:4:5:6,[*2] and the simultaneous sounding of the six tones corresponding to these numbers effects the most beautiful of harmonies (*Opere* I: 33). Zarlino does not at first clarify the fact that the chord produced by six strings whose ratios correspond to the numbers 1–6 is a minor triad, but instead supposes that he can use these numbers in reference to the major triad, as is commonly done. Actually, in order to obtain a major triad from string ratios the numbers 2, 3, 4, 5, and 6 are assigned to the new tones successively above the fundamental, as Marin Mersenne correctly understood *(Harmonie universelle, I. Livre des consonances,* p. 98). Zarlino means:

	Major triad			Minor triad
C	= 1	and not:	1 = g′	
C:c	= 2:1		2 = g	
C:g	= 3:1		3 = c	
C:c′	= 4:1		4 = G	
C:e′	= 5:1		5 = E♭	
C:g′	= 6:1		6 = C	

Nevertheless, the corresponding relationship between the two series is clear to him even from the beginning. Zarlino doubtlessly means all inversions by the term *Replicate*—the third and fifth below the fundamental, or the fundamental above the third and fifth. Otherwise, it would be inconceivable for him to reduce the entire essence of harmony to these two intervals (third and fifth). His explanation that "all harmony directly exhibits either the harmonic or the arithmetic order or their likenesses" can mean only that, e.g., e–g–c $(\frac{1}{5:6:8})$ belongs just as much to the harmonic series as does c–e–g $(\frac{1}{4:5:6})$, and e–a–c (8:6:5) just as much to the arithmetic series as does A–c–e (6:5:4) In Chapter XXX of Book I (Opere I:30) he places both series in juxtaposition:

EQVALITA
et
Principio dell'Inequalità

		Proportiono di equalita		
1	Subdupla		Dupla	1
2	Subsesquialtera		Sesquialtera	2
3	Subsesquiterza		Sesquiterza	3
4	Subsesquiquarta		Sesquiquarta	4
5	Subsesquiquinta		Sesquiquinta	5
6	Subsesquisesta		Sesquisesta	6
7	Subsesquisettima		Sesquisettima	7
8	Subsesquiottava		Sesquiottava	8
9	Subsesquinona		Sesquinona	9
10	Subsesquidecima		Sesquidecima	10

The *Dimostrazioni harmoniche,* which appeared in 1571, proves beyond doubt that Zarlino had a perfectly clear conception of chordal structures which differ from each other only by their inversions. His presentation demonstrates that he also meant the same thing in the *Istitu-zioni*. Regarding the proof of all the consonances within the *Senario*,*3 he states (*Opere* II: 102, *Proposta* XI) that one can assume him to have discussed even those intervals of the series that he has not particularly mentioned (e.g., the tenth and others). He also mentions the fact that the *Senario* contains either the actual *(in atto)* or the potential *(in potenza)* ratios of the elements of all the conceivable consonances. On page 87 (*Ragion.* II, *Defin* XVII), he emphatically states that even though the minor sixth actually lies outside the *Senario* it exists potentially within it and is therefore a consonant.*4 The ratio for the minor sixth is of course 8:5, with the 8 lying outside the *Senario,* but since the 8 is only a replica of 4 and 2, the minor sixth is still potentially within the *Senario*.

The identity of all vertical chord structures in relation to their inversions is thus positively established, and Zarlino's statement that all varieties of harmony are based on the unanimity of the third proclaims that there are no fundamental harmonies beside the major and minor chords.

I have on frequent occasions called attention to the fact that Zarlino and later theorists—Francisco Salinas, Rameau, Tartini, etc., and in our day, Moritz Hauptmann—do not distinguish two kinds of the thirds, but make use of only one proportion of the third (5:4) as the constitutive element of the minor harmony as well as of the major harmony. Zarlino firmly asserts that in the major triad *(Divisione harmonica)* the major third lies below, while in the minor triad *(Divisione arithmetica)* the major third is the higher interval. He also characterizes the major third as "joyful" *(allegro)* and the minor triad as "mournful" *(mesta)* and discusses the importance of varying the two types of harmony in order to obtain diversity of character: "Too many successive minor chords would give an excessively melancholy color to the composition. For that reason (!) the minor triad seems to reduce in some degree the perfection of the harmony." *5

It would be difficult to determine whether Zarlino did or did not discover the antithesis of the harmonic and arithmetic series independently. There is a possibility that—with the help of some Venetian well versed in languages—he may have become acquainted with the Arabian *messel* theory which, contrary to the traditional Pythagorean system, produces all the consonances through the arithmetic division of the string (into twelve equal parts) rather than through the harmonic division. This, of course, includes the intervals of the major and minor third as well as of the major and minor sixth.6 In my *Studien zur Geschichte der Notenschrift* (pp. 77–85) I endeavored to explain successfully the *messel* theory, which had been effectively translated from Mahmud al-Schirazi's "Durrat al taj" by Raphael Kiesewetter (*Die Musik der Araber* [1842]) with the help of v. Hammerpurgstall, a student of oriental languages. I have also attempted to purge it of all original misunderstandings in order that we might have reference to a competent interpretation. However, the *messel* theory is probably much older than the fourteenth-century theorist Mahmud al-Schirazi and his teacher Ssaffieddin Abdolmumin ("Schereffije"), since El Farabi's attempt (*circa* 925) to introduce the Greek music system to the Persians is said to have failed because the Persians already possessed a highly developed system. This was, undoubtedly, the *messel* system. Although the pursuit of these ideas lies outside the scope of my work, it should be mentioned that the Arabs knew the consonance of the third (5:4) long before Zarlino.

The most signficant work of the Spaniard Francisco Salinas, *De musica libri septem* (Salamanca, 1577), provides a valuable complement to Zarlino's writings. He discusses the significance of the *Senarius* in its twofold function: first, the relationship of the whole to its aliquot parts ($1:1/2:1/3:1/4:1/5:1/6$), and second, the relationship of the simple to the multiple ($1:2:3:4:5:6$). He also contrives an interesting diagram in which all the consonant ratios within the *Senarius* can be conveniently observed:

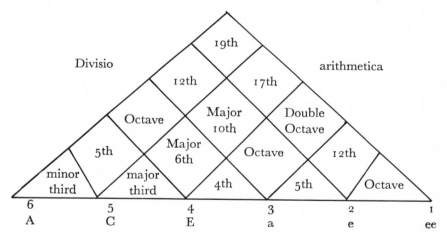

He omits an analogous illustration of the ratios of the *divisio harmonica* which produces the same intervals in inverse order and exhibits only the series with the following six tones:

60		30	20	15	12	10
A		a	e	aa	#cc	ee

He explicitly states that there are no consonant ratios beyond the six (except, of course, the octaves of those already found within the *Senarius*).*7 He finds the *divisio harmonica* (the major chord) much more pleasing than the *divisio arithmetica* (the minor chord).*8

Salinas also perceives that the octave occupies a superior place among the intervals because its involution yields no dissonance. He offers a philosophical explanation for this notable psychological fact, which is neither better nor worse at clarifying the problem than those conceived so far (see my *Musikalische Syntaxis* [1877], p. 10, and *Katechismus der Musikwissenschaft* [1891], pp. 94 ff).9 Concurring with St. Augustine, Salinas sees the *principium a quo* of all consonances in the unison as in the number one, and in the *principium per Quod* in the octave as in the number two.*10 With the identity of the tones of the octave accordingly settled, he uses the octave to prove the consonance of the minor sixth, and in general to show the synonymy of all the harmonic intervals which are related by inversion (fourth = fifth, third = sixth).*11

Salinas, a man of keen intellect, is not content with knowing that the series of harmonic ratios stop with the number six; he must also discover the reason. He submits the following: as the two perfect intervals, the fifth and its complement the fourth, arise from the harmonic division of the superior interval of the octave, so also the two imperfect consonances, the major third and its complement the minor third, arise through the harmonic division of the fifth, and within the octave the minor and major sixths are complements of both thirds respectively. A further division can only come from the major third, since the minor third cannot be considered (nor can the harmonic division of the fourth). This division yields the large whole tone 8:9 and its complement the small whole tone 9:10. The large whole tone cannot be divided according to the principle of harmonic division (16:17:18) because the difference between the fourth and the major third already yields the next smallest interval, the diatonic half step 15:16, just as the difference between the fifth and the fourth yields the whole tone 8:9. The chromatic half tone 25:24, however, arises from the difference between the diatonic half tone and the large whole tone. Inasmuch as smaller intervals are not used in melodies, it is self-evident that theory stops at the number six, while the seven and all higher numbers are not considered: *12

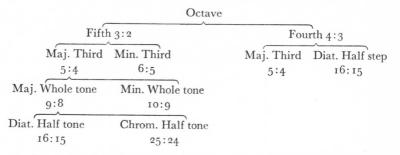

Zarlino writes his observations on the epoch and the dissemination of the newly established modes. His statements (*Istituzioni* IV, cap. 14) agree almost word for word with Heinrich Glarean's innovation increasing their number to twelve. The new modes are C G c (its plagal GG C G) and a e a' (its plagal E a e). Zarlino, however, logically places the *Ionius* before the *Dorius,* and the *Aeolius* after the *Mixolydius,* bringing about a completely different numbering of the church modes, which he regularly employs:

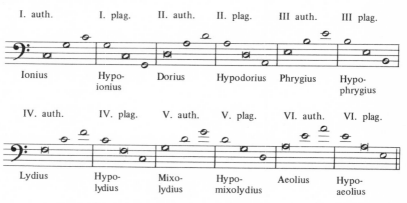

Although this method of numbering the church modes is undoubtedly logical and successful, it conflicts with the traditional method. Salinas, therefore, illustrates a useful way to uphold and preserve the old system. To the eight former modes he adds the *Aeolius* with its plagal as nine and ten and the *Ionius* with its plagal mode as eleven and twelve, bringing about the following scheme:

However, he also accepts Zarlino's method of numbering and calls special attention to it as being superior, since the series of six final tones as well as the *sociales* correspond to a normal hexachord:

C D E F G a   (Finals)
GG A B C D E   (Lowest notes of the
plagal modes)

Andreas Werckmeister (*Musicae mathematicae Hodegus curiosus* [1687]) names those who used Zarlino's numbering: Giovanni Artusi (*L'Artusi overo delle imperfettioni della moderna musica* [1600–1603]), Sethus Calvisius (*Exercitationes musicae duae* [1600]), Johann Lippius (*Synopsis musicae* [1612]), Heinrich Baryphonus (Pipegrop, *Pleiades Musicae* [1615]), and others. Heinrich Grimmius, in the long epistle to Baryphonus in which he gives careful consideration to the *seriem numerorum*, explains why the *Ionius* should be the first mode. Conrad Matthaei also writes about these dispositions (*Kurtzer, doch ausführlicher Bericht von den Modis musicis* [1652]), as do other writers.

Orazio Tigrini, whose *Il compendio della musica* (1588) is dedicated to Zarlino, adheres to the old method of numbering because it is better known *(piu familiare)*. He also states that Zarlino gave this numbering in the *Istituzioni*, which is an error. I will spend no further time on this work, since according to the confession of the author "the flowers of its garland have been picked from Zarlino's garden." Incidentally, however, Book IV contains quite reasonable explanations of various kinds of contrapuntal manipulations.

The *Institution harmonique* of Solomon de Caus (1615) is interesting in some details but lacks any real value. He follows Zarlino blindly in the numbering of the modes (Part II, Chapters X–XXII, devotes a chapter to each mode from the first [C–g–c] to the twelfth [E–a–e]). De Caus calls the fifth step of the authentic modes and the fourth step of the plagal modes the *dominante*.[*13] This is probably the first authentic appearance of the term although not wholly with its later meaning. Another notable detail from De Caus is his pointing out of the great value to composers of knowing the organ or spinet *(espinette)* (p. 29). The organ keyboard sketches divide the notes at f (F–E, f–e, ff–ee, fff–eee). Also, this book of only forty-seven folios contains some noteworthy remarks about musical instruments.

We cannot examine here Zarlino's and Salinas's contributions to instrumental practice wherein they show the various possibilities of temperament (see my *Katechismus der Musikwissenschaft*, pp. 36 ff). I shall only point out again that Zarlino endeavors to divide the octave into twelve equal parts. Unequal temperament was never an end in itself; the intent was to come as near as possible to equalizing the half steps.

Throughout the following period Zarlino was regarded as the unquestioned authority in contrapuntal theory. In music theory he is the true representative of the Venetian school—one of the great lights beside the esteemed organists Claudio Merulo, Andrea Gabrieli, and Giovanni Gabrieli, to whom musicians from Germany, France, the Netherlands, and England came in order to complete their musical training (Hans Leo Hassler, Jan P. Sweelinck). The development of theory was not continued after Zarlino's time. He, like Bach, lived on the edge of two great eras, and was the master of both: the old—precise and inclusive, the new—clearly moving ahead. With the establishment of the figured bass around the time of Zarlino's death, speculative theory fell into ill repute, and, except for a few congenial thinkers such as Salinas, his great knowledge of the essence of harmony remained for his and for future generations a sealed book not to be opened for one and one-half centuries. On the other hand, his version of contrapuntal theory continued in high esteem because it was written in the mid-sixteenth century during the golden age of polyphony. It was reliably regarded as classic in an era aware of having departed from the *stile osservato*—an era seeking its salvation in breaking away from time-honored traditions (the seventeenth-century masters of the Palestrina style were as classical for their time as are present-day composers who hold fast to the traditions of the Haydn-Mozart-Beethoven period).

We should not expect to find anything new in Zarlino's teachings on counterpoint. Rather, *Le Istituzioni harmoniche* (1558) with its commentary the *Dimostrazioni harmoniche* (1571) was in its time in a position similar to that of the *Speculum musicae* of Normannus Muris two hundred years earlier,[14] with this difference: the period of the *Nuove musiche,* to which Zarlino appeared as the representative of conservative principles, began only after Zarlino's death in 1590. Yet, much can be found in these writings that shows great independence. They reveal a thriving golden age, distinguished from the preceeding eras by its standardized practices.

Zarlino's classification of consonances is also new.*[15] Chapter VIII, in Book III of *Le Istituzioni harmoniche* is entitled "Full-Sounding and Empty-Sounding Consonances." The full-sounding consonances "are those the ear hears as strongly distinguishable tones." The fifth sounds fuller than the octave if one considers that the notes of the octave sound more nearly alike. Consequently, except for the octave (!), the further away the tones of the intervals are from being consecutive in the natural series (the *divisione harmonica* and the *divisione arithmetica*) the emptier is the sound when expressed with the smallest possible numbers. Empty, then, are the so-called compound intervals, whose quotients are not formed from members which directly follow one another, such as 5:3, 8:5, 3:1, and so on.

The term *Soggetto* ("subject") is also new, at least as a technical term. Zarlino uses it to denote the part which is derived independently of the others and around which the other voices are composed, whether it be freely invented or borrowed from some other source (*Istituzioni* III, cap. 26).*16

Zarlino handles dissonances in much greater detail than his predecessors did. He defines consonance as the substance of harmony but perceives dissonance as being merely accidental: dissonance is the foliation of consonance.

The first of the old contrapuntal rules (to begin a composition with a perfect consonance) immediately furnishes Zarlino with the opportunity to demonstrate his intellectual superiority over his predecessors. He agrees with Gaffurius that the rule should not be unconditionally binding.*17 It should also be permissible to begin with an imperfect consonance. He then, however, makes the following modifications: when the voices begin singly one after the other the first vertical interval formed by the two voices may be any consonant (!), but always observe that the beginning note of each voice must stand one to another in the relationship of a perfect consonance or a perfect fourth (!!), especially when it concerns the two main tones of the mode (the final and its fifth). With the canon the rule may be handled more freely; that is, the beginning tone of each voice may also stand one to another in the interval of any imperfect consonance.

We can hardly agree with the sharpness of the prohibition of parallel consonances Zarlino extends to the imperfect consonances (*Istituz. harm.* III, cap. 29). After discussing the old prohibition that harmony can only result from the union of diverse elements, he introduces the unfortunate idea that thirds, sixths, and tenths should not progress in parallel motion using the same sized steps. Rather, one voice should move by a whole step and the other by a half step, or the first interval should be a major third and the second a minor third, and so on. Thus, a new rule arises from theoretical speculation which is, unfortunately, at variance with the practice of the masters: the forbiddance of two major thirds, two minor thirds, two major sixths, two minor sixths, and so forth, in direct succession:*18

These successions must all be wrong because in each case both voices move by a whole step instead of one of the voices moving by a half step, from which arises everything good in music, and without which all harmonies and modulations are harsh and inharmonious. Of course, the defectiveness of parallel imperfect consonances is less than that of perfect consonances because the latter are closer to unity. Therefore, two minor thirds or two major sixths in parallel succession are more tolerable (!), but such movement is never permissable when the voices leap:

Because of the extraordinary authority enjoyed by Zarlino, it is conceivable that even such a subtly invented rule as this could be handed down over a long period of time by theorizing epigones. For example, the same rule is also found in *Le Istitution harmonique* (1615) of Salomon de Caus in Chapter VI, Part II ("The imperfect consonances should be written so that like intervals neither ascend nor descend in parallel motion").[19] Werckmeister *(Hodegus curiosus)* also explains the rule, though less radically:

Although the interval of a minor third moving parallel by leap of a minor third up or down to another minor third will not be readily approved by the more strict present-day composers, it may, nevertheless, be permitted in order to present a melancholy effect, e.g.:

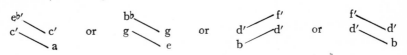

On the other hand, the following progressions are very bad:

In Chapter XXX, Book III of the *Istituzioni* Zarlino mentions cross relation when it occurs between the first note of one voice and the second note
of the other voice as another reason for the majority of these prohibitions.[*20] The intervals to be avoided in voice leading (diminished and
augmented octaves, diminished and augmented fifths, and the tritone) are
also to be avoided when they are divided between two voices (!). The
subtlety of such distinctions appears to be carried to the extreme in the
remark that cross relations are less offensive when a half step is implied in
the movement of one of the voices:

The progressions a) and b) are considered tolerable because the movements
of a minor third (g–[a]–b♭, d–[c]–b) imply a half step! However, Zarlino
recommends that such progressions ought to be avoided—also c), d), and
e). Still, he allows the intervals of the diminished fifth and the tritone,[*21]
and in polyphonic compositions of more than two parts he dispenses with
the strict observance of his rules.[*22]

The most important chapter contributing to the theory of voice leading
is Chapter XXXVI, Book III of the *Istituzioni,* "Rules regarding the Progression of Consonances in Similar Motion."[*23] This chapter may indeed
be considered the genuine codification of the present-day teachings condemning "hidden fifths and octaves," although the chapter still allows
much which is forbidden in our day by the theorists of "strict composition." The following sentence appears at the beginning: "When perfect
consonances of different sizes are placed one after another in similar motion one voice should progress stepwise while the other leaps":

(Movimenti
supportabili)

Here again Zarlino unfortunately goes into too much detail to prove his
theory that such descending progressions as b) and c), above, are better
than the ascending progressions. The reason given is "because the slower
vibrations of the deeper tones are easier to grasp" (?!). The four examples

arranged according to their value are b), c), a), and d). Although Zarlino readily admits that common practice does not bother with such sophistry, he advises that such progressions be applied sparingly in two-part composition.

Yet, by stressing these four cases as being allowed, all other progressions of perfect consonances in similar motion (namely, those wherein both voices leap) are now strictly forbidden, for example, even those at b) :

Criticism is due in other cases of restrictions in compositional procedures where an imperfect consonance progresses in similar motion to a perfect consonance.*24 The leap of both voices from an imperfect consonance to a smaller perfect consonance is forbidden, as well as movement in similar motion of a sixth to a fifth with one voice moving stepwise (N.B.) :

(Movimenti vietati)

N. B.   N. B.

But he also admits that experience, the master of all things, sets such observations aside whenever these progressions are not unpleasant to the ear!

Progressions in similar motion ascending from an imperfect consonance to a smaller perfect consonance*25 are permitted when the higher voice moves stepwise (except, of course, 6–5) :

(Movimenti supportabili)

but not:

The progression from an imperfect consonance to a larger perfect consonance*26 is also permitted, ascending as well as descending, when one voice moves by a step, with the further restriction that a progression to the octave demands the half step in one voice:

Even the movement from a perfect to an imperfect consonance is qualified. The movement to a larger imperfect consonance is allowed only when one voice moves by a step or, at most, by a minor third b) :*27

Such movements as the following are also ruled out:

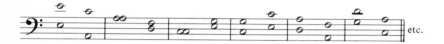

On the other hand, the progressions by leap from the fifth to the third, and from the third to the fifth, are explicitly permitted when the upper voice leaps a third and the lower voice leaps a fifth.*28 Zarlino admits that the leap of a major third at b) sounds somewhat harsh but permits it because composers seek desirable effects through the use of these progressions:

Wholly in keeping with Zarlino's ratiocinations is his statement that the progression $g \nearrow b$ should be especially gay because "the faster vibrations of $c \nearrow g$ the higher tones are more sonorous" (in this case they are no less intelligible!). Moreover, Zarlino guards against the reproach of incompleteness (as to what is forbidden and allowed), arguing that it is impossible to enumerate and explain all the possible combinations.

Later theorists dared to lay aside only a few of Zarlino's many prohibitions, although their arguments for not discarding more were often unconvincing. The entire modern theory of "strict composition," or "contrapuntal theory," as it was called to distinguish it from the newly developed "figured-bass theory," was based definitively on Zarlino as the greatest theorist of the age of Palestrina. For example, B. C. Masson, a distinguished French theorist of Rameau's time, places at the conclusion of his *Nouveau traité des règles pour la composition de la musique* ([3rd edition] 1705) a table of the possible interval progressions marked as follows: *b bon* [good], *m mauvais* [bad], *p passable*. I have included a few of those marked *m* (i.e., prohibited), and a few marked *b*:

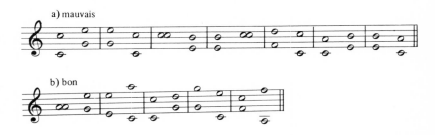

It is hardly necessary to point out that the decisive factors are similar and contrary motion. Only a very few examples of similar motion are marked *b,* and only a very few in contrary motion are censored with an *m*.

The *Gradus ad Parnassum* (1725) of the Viennese *Kapellmeister* Johann Joseph Fux, translated into German by Lorenz Mizler in 1742 (Italian, 1761; French, 1773; English, 1791) and regarded up to the present day as the "classical formulation of the strict vocal style," may be considered a clarification and abridgment of Zarlino's teachings. The essential contents of the work can be reduced to a few sentences. Fux himself sums up the voice leading rules at the end of Book I (p. 42):

1) A perfect consonance proceeds to another perfect consonance by either contrary or oblique motion.
2) A perfect consonance may proceed to an imperfect consonance by all three types of motion.
3) An imperfect consonance proceeds to a perfect consonance by either contrary or oblique motion.
4) An imperfect consonance may proceed to an imperfect consonance by all three types of motion.

This can be said even more concisely: "A perfect consonance (unison, fifth, and their octave equivalents) cannot be approached by similar motion." This is, indeed, an obvious improvement over Zarlino, insofar as a multitude of separate restraints are replaced by an easily remembered general rule. It also considerably simplifies the materials of instruction. Unfortunately, the practice of composers did not conform to this precept; for even Palestrina and Orlando Lasso—especially esteemed by Fux as authorative—did not respect the rule. Already familiar to us from Glarean (see Riemann, *Geschichte der Musiktheorie,* 2nd ed., p. 364) is Fux's advice against using the major sixth as a melodic interval (p. 53) : "Saltus sextae majoris in contrapuncto, in quo compositionis genere amnia cantui facillima esse debent, prohibitus est." Although this principle is very sensible (insofar as the third performs the service of the sixth), it too remains unconfirmed in the literature.

Granting that the significance of Fux as a theorist has been highly exaggerated, yet it cannot be denied that he performed a great service. At a time when the musical laws were becoming ill-defined through the influence of operatic style, he pointed out a simple, singable voice leading as the essential basis without which esthetic values could not be obtained by even the most effective means of expression.

The five species of counterpoint made universally known because of the *Gradus ad Parnassum* are: [29]

1. Two notes against one.
2. Three notes against one.
3. Four notes against one.
4. Syncopation.
5. Free counterpoint.

Although this by no means constitutes an ineffective arrangement for study, the number of species could be just as effective reduced or increased. The normal treatment of dissonance was fully established long before Fux. Considering that the *Gradus ad Parnassum* (1725) appeared three years later than Part I of Bach's *Das Wohltemperierte Klavier,* he might not ignore the point of view that the *Gradus* was outdated at the time of its publication. It was beyond Fux's capacity to provide a key to the understanding of Bach's harmonic art. On the contrary, the application of Fux's rules to Bach's works leads to a completely distorted judgment of them. Only the harmonic theory developed from the figured bass, embraced by Fux with little affection, gradually reveals that complete mastery which is the essence of Bach's art. For that reason, Fux's attempt to turn back to pure contrapuntal theory seems basically anachronistic. This judgment appears all the more valid with reference to the contrapuntal

teachings of Heinrich Bellermann (*Der Kontrapunkt* [1862]) who re-
nounces the modern tonal system and demands a complete return to the
modal system of the fifteenth century. All of the archaisms made ridiculous
by Mattheson almost two hundred years earlier are seriously being taught
again, and the salvation of musical art is sought in the hollow imitation of
a past age—an age surpassed in spite of all its beauty.

   With surprising tenacity Zarlino holds fast to the rule which had prevailed in various forms from the time of Marchettus of Padua (see my
Geschichte der Musiktheorie [2nd ed.], p. 135) that an imperfect consonance moving to a perfect consonance should be of the size most nearly
approximating that of the perfect consonance (*Istituzioni* III, cap. 38).
The motion, of course, may be oblique as well as contrary (!) : *30

(Minor third)   (Major sixth)   (Major third)

(Minor sixth)   (Major third)   N. B.   N. B.   etc.

(Apparently, Zarlino does not notice that a rule of such broad applications
would render impossible a number of progressions previously allowed.) Because of Zarlino's reputation these rules which had been extremely useful
in the thirteenth and fourteenth centuries for indicating the semitones by
accidentals, were dragged on by the traditions of theorists in their all-too-
general form. For example, Pietro Pontio states in his *Dialogo ove si tratta
della theoria e prattica di musica et anco si mostra le diversità de' Contraponti et canoni* (1595) that the minor third may move only to the
unison (in contrary motion to the tenor) or to the minor sixth (! over a stationary tenor), and the major third only to the perfect fifth (in contrary
motion) or to the major sixth (in oblique motion). This was the prevailing
practice.*31 Nonetheless, these observations in the alternatives they provide are excellent, inasmuch as they produce consonant harmony by connecting the minor third to the minor sixth and the major third to the major
sixth:

$$\left(\begin{matrix} \text{g–c, a–d} \\ \text{e} \quad \text{f} \end{matrix} \right)$$

Zarlino strongly opposes the following sensible statement of Franchino Gaffurius: "The rule that the major sixth must proceed to the octave is valid only at cadences" ("che l'andare dalla sesta maggiore all'ottava si dovea osservare solamente nelle cadenze"). Zarlino also strictly forbids the movement of the minor sixth to the octave and of the major sixth to the perfect fifth.*32 Corrections are always possible by adding accidentals *(chorde chromatiche et enharmoniche)*. However, other progressions are possible for the minor sixth (to imperfect consonances):

In two-part writing Zarlino rigidly adhers to cadences on the octave or unison (*Istituzioni* III, cap. 29) even though the rule is often broken by men of little taste ("che questa regola d'alcuni di non molto giudizio sia stata poco osservata"). But except for beginnings and endings he advises that octaves and unisons be avoided wherever possible (*Istituzioni* III, cap. 41).

The chapter, "Practical Introduction to Simple Note Against Note Counterpoint" (*Istituzioni* III, cap. 40), contains some excellent observations:

> Above all, the student should study note-against note-composition long and diligently, because this type is essentially the most difficult (owing to the fact that it is strict). He should attempt ever new improvements on his counterpoint and then choose that which seems the best out of the many possibilities; those which otherwise appear worthwhile should be laid aside for another time.*33

To write as many different counterpoints as possible (in the same style) to the same *cantus firmus* without choosing a particular one from among them, is excellent advice even today for those who believe in doing their best. Also valuable is the advice to try placing the counterpoints which were written above the *cantus firmus* underneath it and compare them as preliminary exercises in double counterpoint.

Unfortunately, it is impossible in this history of music theory to continue discussing the remaining parts of Zarlino's theory of composition in such detail. This author alone would take up all the space at my disposal. But considering that the basic instructions for connecting intervals, which have already been covered, are fundamental for all advanced lessons in practical composition, there is no need for doing so. It will be sufficient to

summarize the rules for treating dissonance; these rules do not differ essentially from those of Zarlino's predecessors.

Zarlino completely forbids dissonance in note against note counterpoint.
Chapter XLII, Book III of the *Istituzioni,* which is dedicated to diminished
counterpoint, permits passing-stepwise *(per grado)* dissonance only on the
weak beat (the second of two ♩ , the second and fourth of four ♩). When a
leap appears in a series of minims, the note preceding the leap as well as the
one following should be consonant, since due to the leap a dissonance
would be intolerably noticeable.*34 Dissonance on the strong beat is allowed only in the form of the syncope (in connection with the value of the
following weak beat). In attempting to explain the good effects of syncopated dissonance,*35 Zarlino uses for the first time the term *suspension,*
by which it came to be commonly known in later times: "In the syncopation the voice becomes stationary *(se tiene salda)* and a kind of delay
*(suspensione)*36 or holding back *(faciturnita)* takes place during the production of the tone." Zarlino also tries to explain that dissonance is
tolerable because it is concealed. He eventually perceives, however, that a
prepared dissonance is not only inoffensive but even quite acceptable, because after it the consonance sounds so much more pleasant. Thus, by
referring to the intensifying of sensation through contrast he is well on the
way to recognizing that syncopation is not a concealment but a preparation—an expressive representation of dissonance.

In resolving the dissonance of the syncope*37 Zarlino requires a
descending stepwise movement of the syncopated tone:

But he also lists a number of strange resolutions of the dissonance, namely:

a) The resolution of the second to the unison, which is good if one of the
voices moves a half step;

b) The resolution of the fourth to the diminished fifth (!) followed by a major
third, which will give no bad effects whatever, even though the dissonance does
not resolve into a consonance;

c) The resolution of the ninth into the octave, if afterwards one voice [the
lower] moves downward a step and one voice [the upper] leaps down a fifth or up
a fourth:

He concludes that normally the new note resulting from the descending resolution of the dissonance should be held no longer than the dissonance itself (therefore, half as long as the syncopating note). Neither should the note of resolution be tied to another consonance; i.e., a consonant syncope must not be formed, but the voice must either ascend by leap or step. If it does syncope, another dissonance should be introduced.*38

This should be sufficient to give an idea of Zarlino's teaching methods. Naturally, he gives the already familiar warning to avoid faulty parallels by detaining one of the voices with a short pause, or by using a light figurative note to cover them adequately (*Istituzioni* III, cap. 48). In addition, he advises against long pauses between short notes (cap. 50). Chapter LI gives detailed instructions for cadence formations.39 Of course, Zarlino considers the addition of accidentals unnecessary, because wherever the voice which descends stepwise does not move by a half step (!) the ascending voice must do so. (This is so self-evident that even the uncultured country folk who sing without music put in the semitones!) *40

Zarlino also recognizes that the cadential bass in two-part writing may descend by a fifth or ascend by a fourth, but he warns against the frequent use of these cadences because they are more suitable in compositions with more than two parts.*41 In two-part writing they should be avoided at final cadences and ought to be used only generally in canons and under other constrained conditions. However, these instructions can be considered more as counsel than as rules ("piu tosto conseglio che precetto"). He calls cadences which have the fifth (in two-part writing) improper cadences *(impropriamente)*. Other rare applications are called *Cadenze stravagante* or evaded cadences *(fuggir la Cadenza)*. The third book of the *Istituzioni,* Chapter LV, discusses imitation. Chapter LIV is concerned with the canon *(Fuga obligata)* and free fugal style *(Fuga sciolta,* but only the *Ricercar* rather than the not-yet-developed fugue).42 Chapter LVI treats double counterpoint at the twelfth and tenth.

Although we have long known from the actual literature that the era in which three-part writing prevailed was definitely over by the middle of the sixteenth century, we find this fact first mentioned in theory by Zarlino

(Chapter LVIII).*43 The individual voices of four-part composition—four parts were considered normal by this time—are compared to the four elements (bass-earth, tenor-water, alto-air, soprano-fire). The significance of the bass as the fundamental is fully recognized, and the characteristic features of its position are clearly distinguished (slower movement, further distance from the other voices). The tenor has completely lost its regimental position, but is still nominally regarded as representative of the mode and should "cadence correctly." The soprano has become the main voice to carry the melody, as well as the main representative of ornamentation and affection. It is also no longer considered an error (Chapter LIX)*44 when the tenor does not end on the final of the mode. On the other hand, the bass must always take the final at closes. It appears that composers still hold fast to the practice of beginning with the tenor, as a modest survival of its earlier lordliness, followed in order by the soprano, the bass, and the alto.*45 Nevertheless, the observance of this order is certainly not obligatory in free composition.

Zarlino has evidently taken a huge step beyond Glarean in the perception of the true essence of harmony. By contrast, Zarlino's precepts for simple counterpoint are conservative, influenced in part by the prevailing concepts of Gaffurius. The rules given in the *Istituzioni,* Book III, Chapter LVIII, for the placement of the bass and alto according to the interval between the tenor and soprano, e.g., the unison, third, fourth, fifth, sixth, and octave, explicitly require the customary tables of the Muris-Vitry epoch, even though Zarlino dictates the thicker harmony than that of the earlier composers. Actually, the inclination to measure Zarlino's historical significance by his presentation of contrapuntal theory is unfortunate. In this area he is merely a truly learned teacher endowed with the capacity to give a broad presentation of the contemporary system. He cannot, however, be spared the reproach of obstinate pedantry and shrewd but untenable reasonings. The reason for his true greatness lies in his discovery of the fundamental meaning of the triad consisting of the prime, third, and fifth, and in his discovery of the mathematical basis of the dual nature of harmony. In fact, harmonic speculative theory has its beginning in Zarlino's *Le Istituzioni harmoniche,* and its continued expansion refers repeatedly back to his work. Of course, the teachings of Zarlino and his intelligent student Salinas concerning the theory of the meaning of harmony disappeared after 1600, completely hidden by a half-mechanical treatment of chords which was averse to all speculation and served only the practical side of music. However, we would hardly be mistaken if we discovered the figured bass to be the first fruits of Zarlino's newly sown seeds. Not only does their closeness in time suggest such a thought, but the characteristic figured-bass habit of considering the intervals of the third and fifth self-evident when the designating figures are lacking also appears to have its roots in Zarlino's theories. It is indeed strange that intervallic duality—the distinction between the ascending harmonic and descending arithmetic series—was abandoned at that time. It is equally strange that two hundred years later Rameau's new thoretical embarkations into harmonic meaning were completely overlooked by Friedrich Wilhelm Marpurg, Kirnberger, and other prominent authorities, while only the schematic superposing of thirds found general understanding and a following.

However, as soon as theory began to entrench itself and look beyond the practical needs of the accompanists toward the establishment of universally applicable rules of musical performance, the pressing need to interpret the minor triad as the opposite of the major triad arose again, and the long-forgotten Venetian master was gradually brought back again into esteem. Rameau, Tartini, Hauptmann, and all of us today are indebted to Zarlino.

APPENDIX

FOOTNOTE 1: (*Tutte l'opere* [1589] I: 222): "La varietà dell Harmonia.... non consiste solamente nella varietà delle Consonanze, che si troua tra due parti; ma nella varietà anco delle Harmonie, la quale consiste nella positione della chorda, che fà la Terza.... Onde, ouero che sono minori et l'Harmonia che nasce, è ordinata, ò s'assimiglia alla proportionalità, o mediatione Arithmetica; ouero sono maggiori et tale Harmonia è ordinata, ouer s'assimiglia alla mediocrità Harmonica: et da questa varieta

dipende tutta la diversità et la perfettione delle Harmonie. Conciosiache è necessario (come dirò altrove) che nella Compositione perfetta si ritrouino sempre in atto la Quinta et la Terza ouer le sue Replicate; essendo che oltra queste due consonanze l'Udito non puo desiderar suono, che caschi nel mezo, ouer fuori de i loro estremi, che sia in tutto differente et variato da quelli...."

FOOTNOTE 2: "Delle proprieta del numero Senario et delle sue parti; et come tra loro si ritrova la forma d'orgni consonanze musicale."

FOOTNOTE 3: "Il Viola: 'Non havete gia fatto mentione alcuna dell'Hexachordo minore: ne della Diapason col Semiditono: et di molte altre Consonanze, che si pongono ne i Contrapunti,' Allora soggiunsi: Quando hò fatto mentione de tutte quelle Consonanze simplici che si possono porre in atto e che nascono secondo l'ordine naturale dei Numeri harmonici, imaginatevi, chi'io habbia fatta anco mentione die ciaschedun'altra Composta- et di tutte quelle, che nascono da un ordine accidentale.... Percioche... tra questi termini, che vi hò mostrato.... si ritrovano tutte le parti del numero Senario- le quali contengono in atto et in potenza tutte quelle Consonanze, che si può l'Huomo imaginare, che possano servire alla Musica."

FOOTNOTE 4: "Ancore che tra le parti del Senario non vi sia la forma dell'Hexachordo minore in atto: tuttavia per esservi.... in potenza (e consonante)."

FOOTNOTE 5: (*Opere* I: 221): "Ma perche gli estremi della Quinta sono invariabili et sempre si pongono contenuti sott'una istessa proportione (lasciando certi casi ne i quali si pone imperfetta), pero gli estremi della Terza si pongono differenti tra essa Quinta, non dico pero differenti di proportione ma dico differenti di luogo; perioche (come ho detto altroue) quando si pone la Terza maggiore nella parte graue l'Harmonia si fa allegra et quando si pone nell'acute si fa mesta. Di modo che dalla positione diuersa delle Terze, che si pongono nel Contrapounto tra gli estremi della Quinta (ouuer si pognono sopra l'Ottava) nasce la varieta dell'Harmonia.... Io non dico gia che'l Compositore non possa poree due divisioni Arithmetiche l'una dopo l'altra; ma dico, che non dee continuare in tal divisione lungo tempo perche farebbe il concento molto maninconico. Ma il porre molte divisioni Harmoniche l'una dopo l'altra non porra mai dar noja.... Quell'ordine ch'e Arithmetico ouer s'assimiglia alla proportionalita Arithmetica si longtana un poco dalla perfettione dell'Harmonia."

FOOTNOTE 7: (Lib. II. cap. 12. p. 61): "Et quo clarius Senarii virtus elucescat non solum in eo omnes formae consonantiarum simplicium inveniuntur singulis ejus partibus ad proximas et immediatas comparatis.... sed quaecunque pars ad totum ipsum et ad quamcunque ejus partem comparata consonantiam facit simplicem aut compositam, ut non tantum in sex primis simplicibus sed etiam in sex primis (cum aequa) multiplicibis inveniantur, in tripla sicut in sesquialtera, in quadrupla sicut in dupla, in quintupla sicut in sesquiquarta et' in sextupla sicut in tripla et sesquialtera. Neque ultra sextuplam in proportione septupla consonantiam inveniri, sicut neque in sesquisexta ultra sesquiquintam.... Sciendum est, intervalla nunc secundum Arithmeticam divisionem disponi nunc secundum Harmonicam. Divisione Arithmetica aequales esse differentias ac spacia, inaequales vero proportiones.... Telem autem divisionem in primo Senario reperiri satis et praecedenti figura liquet. Quod autem eaedem consonantiae inter sex primos Denarios Harmonice dispositae inveniantur: ita ut proportiones majores collocatae sint in numeris majoribus minores vero minoribus id omne sequens ostendit descriptio."

FOOTNOTE 8: (Page 63): "Et mirum est quanto suaviorem efficiant auribus concentum hae consonantiae, sic Harmonica medietate divisae, quam Arithmetica ut in priori chorda dispositae sunt."

FOOTNOTE 10: (Page 63): "Unisonantia quatenus principium est a quo omnes consonantiae originem trahunt, quemadmodum unitas est principium a quo omnes numeri derivantur, et aequa proportio mater est omnium proportionum. Deinde Diapason quae potest etiam dici principium consonantiarum per quod: quemadmodum D. Augustinus vocat in numeris unitatem principium a quo et binarium principium per quod; neque enim putat binarium esse numerum quia non habet principium medium finem...,. Dupla proportio etiam poterit dici proportionum principium per quod: Quia in binario ad unitatem collocato reperitur, et omnes proportiones eam aut dividunt ut superparticulares aut multiplicant ut multiplices."

FOOTNOTE 11: (Lib. II. cap. 25. p. 90): "Inter duo diapason extrema ita dispositae sunt consonantiae ut quae ad alterum eorum sit Semiditonus ad alterum Hexachordum majus esse reperiatur et quae Ditonus Hexachordum minus, et quae Diatessaron Diapente. Ex quibus elicitur Semiditonum et Hexachordum majus ejusdem proper esse naturae, quoniam eadem est vis extremorum.... quod idem deprehenditur in Ditono et Hexachordo minori, unde prope similem concentum autibus efficient. Et multo manifestius experimur Diapente et Diatessaron esse tamquam germanas gemellas eodem partu editas e Diapason et solum quantitate differre."

FOOTNOTE 12: (Lib. II. cap. 24. p. 63): "Ex excessibus numque consonantiarum intervalla minora oriantur necesse est.... ut ex excessu Diapente ad Diatessaron oritur tonus in proportione sesquioctava, et differentia Diatessaron ad Ditonum Semitonium majus in sesquidecimaquinta, ex excessu Ditoni ad Semiditonum Semitonium minus in sesquivigesimaquarta. Sed ex excessu Semiditoni qui est in sesquiquinta, ad intervallum sive consonantiam quae nascitur ex sesquisexta nullum oritur intervallum minus ad harmoniam aptum."

René Descartes, *Compendium musicae,* "De octave: Ex jam dictis elicimus omnes consonantias ad tria genera posse referri: vel enim oriuntur ex prima divisione unisoni, illae quae octavae appellantur et hoc est primum genus; vel 2° oriuntur ex ipsius octavae divisione in aequalia, quae sunt quinta et quarta, quas ideirco consoantias secundae divisionis vocare possumus; vel denique ex ipsius quintae divisione quae consonantiae sunt tertiae et ultimae divisionis tres esse dumtaxat numeros sonoros 2, 3, et 5."

FOOTNOTE 13: "Et quant a la note comprise entre le Diapason dite d'aucuns mode nes Note Dominante, on la fera ouir souvent, a celle fin de suivre la nature de la (!) mode."

FOOTNOTE 15: (*Istit. harm.* III cap. 8): "Quali Consonanze siano più piene et quali più uaghe. La onde chiamano più piene quelle Consonanze, le quali hanno maggior possanza d'occupar l'Udito, con Suoni diuersi; per il che si può dire, che la Quinta sia più piena della Ottaua; perchioche li suoi estremi occupano maggiormente et con più dilleto l'Udito condiuersi Suoni, che non fanno gli estremi della Ottaua; i quali sono equisonanti, et s'assimigliano l'un l'altro. Di modo che lasciando da un Canto essa Ottaua, tutte l'altre si dicono esser più piene l'una dell'altra, in quanto l'una hà maggior forza di contentare l'Udito; si come sono quelle, che sono più uicine al loro principio, et hanno maggior perfettione de tutte l'altre. Si che de qui si può cauare una Regola; che tutte quelle, che sono di maggior proportione sono più piene; lasciando (come ho detto) da un Canto la Ottaua et le Replicate anco.... Et tanto più sono uaghe quanto più si partono dalla semplicita, della quale i nostri sentimenti non molto si reallegrano; poiche amano maggiormente le cose composte che le semplici et s'accompagnano ad altre consonanze." (*Istit. harm.* I. cap. 16): "Dico adunque che Consonanza o Intervallo semplice e quello che pigliati li minimi termi della sua proportione in tal modo sono ordinati che non possono riceuere tra loro alcun termino mezano che diuida tal proportione in più parti, essendo che sono sempre l'un dall'altro distanti per l'Unita."

FOOTNOTE 16: "Il Soggetto d'ogni composizione musicale chiamarsi quella parte sopra la quale il compositore cava l'inventione di far l'altre parti della cantilena, siano quante si vogliano. Et tal Soggetto puo esser in molti modi, prima può esser inventione propria... dopoi può essere, che l'habbia pigliata dall altrui compositioni, accomodandolo alla sua cantilena, et adornandolo con varie parti et varie modulationi: come più gli aggrada, secondo la grandezza del suo ingegno. Et tal Soggetto si può ritrovare de più sorti, perchiocche può essere un Tenore, overo altra Parte di qual si voglia cantilena di Canto fermo, over di Canto figurato, overo potranno esser due, o più Parti, che l'una seguiti l'altra in Fuga, o Consequenza...."

FOOTNOTE 17: (*Istit. harm.* III. cap. 27): "Che le Compositioni di debbono comporre primieramente di Consonanze et dopoi per accidente di Dissonanze: Et benche ogni Compositione et ogni Contrapunto et per dirlo in una sola parola, ogni Harmonia si componghi di Consonanze principalmente, et primieramente ... la Dissonanza fa parer la Consonanza, la quale immediatamente la seque più dilettevole." (Cap. 28): "Quando la parte del Contrapunto incomincierà à cantare insieme con la parte del Soggetto, allora si potrà incominciare per una delle Perfetta già dette: ma quando per maggior bellezza et leggiadria del Contrapunto; et anco per maggior commodita, li Musici facessero, che le parti non incominciassero à cantare insieme; ma l'una dopo l'altra con l'istesso progresso de figure, o note: che detto Fugo, o Consequenza; il quale rende il Contrapunto non pur dilettevole; ma etiandio artficioso; allora potranno incominciare da qual Consonanza vorranno, sia perfetta, ouero imperfetta: percioche intrauengono la Pause in una delle parti. Si debbe però osservare, ch almeno i Principij dell'una et dell'altra parte habbiano tra loro relatione ad una delle nominate Consonanze perfette, ouer d'una Quarta; et cio non sarà fatto fuori di proposito: consionsia che si viene à incominciate sopra le chord estreme, ouero sopra le mezane de i Modi sopra i quali è fondata la Cantilena; che sono le lor chorde naturali, ouero essentiali.... Et questo credo io, che intendessero gli Antichi, quando dissero, che nel principiare i Contrapunti si douesse dar principio ad una della Consonanze perfette; la quale Regola non è fatale, o necessaria: ma si bene secondo il uoler di colui, che la compone. Quando adunque uorremo incominciate alcuno Contrapunto in Fuga, o Consequenza, lo potremo incominciare per qual si voglia delle Perfette, ouero Imperfette, et per quarta anche: non che le parti incomincino à cantare per questa consonanz: ma dico per Quarta rispetto al principio del Soggetto, con la parte del Contrapunto, o per il contrario;... Et cosi osservaremo la Regola data, di cominciar per una della Consonanze perfette; facendo incominciar le Parti a cantare insieme in una Terza maggiore.... Ne possono queste due parti generare cosa alcuna di tristo all'Udito...."

FOOTNOTE 18: "Conciosiache molto ben sapeuano, che l'Harmonia non può nascere, se non da cose tra loro diuerse, discordanti et contrarie; et non da quelle che in ogni cosa conuengono. La onde se da tal uarietà nasce l'harmonia; sarà dibisegno, che nella Musica, non solo le Parti della cantilena siano distanti l'una dall'altra per il grave et per l'acuto: ma etiandio che le loro modulationi siano differenti ne i mouimenti: et che contenghino uarie Consonanze, contenute da diuere proportioni.... Quando

fussero poste in tal maniera che non facessero euidentemente alcuna Dissonanza tra
le parti, tuttauia farebbono udire un non so che di tristo che dispiacerebbe.... Et ag-
giungeremo a uuesto che per le regioni gia dette non si debbe anco porre due o più
Imperfette consonanze insiemen ascendenti o discendenti l'una dopo l'altra
senz'alcun mezo come sono due Terze maggiori due minori due Seste maggiori anco
et due minori.... Consiosiache non solo si fa contra quello c'ho detto delle Perfette ma
il loro procedere si fa udire alquanto aspro per non havere nella lor modulatione de
parte alcuna l'intervallo del semituono maggiore, nel quale consiste tutto il buono
nella Musica et senza lui ogni Modulatione et ogni Harmonia e dura aspra et quasi
inconsonante.... Et cio nasce anco conciosiache tra le parti ouer tra le uoci delle due
Terze maggiori et delle Seste minori non si troua la Ratione harmonica il che fa che
siano alquanto piu triste delle altre come piu oltra uederemo. Laonde dobbiamo som-
mamente avertire ch'in ogni progresso ouer modulatione che fanno le parti cantando
insieme almeno una di quelle si muoua o faccia l'intervallo del Semituono maggiore
potendolo fare.... La qual cosa si havera facilmente quando le Consonanze si porrano
l'una dopo l'altra che siano diuerse di speci come dopo la Terza o la Sesta maggiore si
porra la Minore o per il contrario, et dopo la Terza maggiore si porra la Sesta minore
ouero dopo questa si porra quella et dopo la Terza minore la Sesta maggiore,
similmente dopo la Sesta maggiore la Terza minore. Ne ui e maggior ragione che più
ne vieti il porre due Perfette che due Imperfette consonanze immediatamente l'una
dopo l'altra, percioche le prime sono consonanze Perfette, tuttauia ciascuna
dell'Imperfette si ritrova esser perfetta nella sua proportione.... conciosiache non
sono tanto consonanti quanto sono le Perfette.... due Terze minori.... ascendenti ouer
discendenti per grado, similmente due Seste maggiori si potranno supportare.... ma
quando le parti si mouessero per salto allora per niun modo porremo due o più simili
ascendenti o discendenti l'una dopo l'altra."

FOOTNOTE 20: "E ben vero che due parti ch'insieme ascendono et habbiano un
mouimento che contenga il semituono tanto in una quanto nell altra per che sian
tollerate dall Udito per cagione de i moveimenti fatti per cotali Semituoni come sono
quelli del primo luogo della Diapason superflua et della Semidiapent.... Et anchora sia
minor male il ritrouarlo per relatione tra due modulationi che udirlo nella modulatione di una parte; tuttavia quel male istesso che si ode in una parte sola si ritroua
diuiso tra due et e quella istessa offesa dell Udito. Questi intervalli adunque che nel
modulare non si ammettono, si devono schivare nelle Cantilene di maniera che non si
odino per dette relationi tra li parti, laquel cosa verra fatta, quando le parti si potranno mutar fra loro con Intervalli harmonic proportionati contenuti nel genere
diatonica, cioè quando da una voce della parte graue potra ascender alla sequente
della parte acuta per un spatio legitimo et cantabile et cosi per il contrario, ma non
gia quando tra le parti di qual si voglia Compositione tra quattro uoci al detto modo
non si udira la ratione de i detti Intervalli...."

FOOTNOTE 21: "Nondimeno potremo usare alle volte la Semidiapente in una istessa
percussione et ciò faremo, quando immediate da essa veremo al Ditono.... Ne
solamente sarà lecito usare la Semidiapente; ma il Tritono anco alle volte.... (E ben
vero che torner a meglio usar la Semidiapente che 'l Tritono).... quelle parti
c'haveranno la Semidiapente ovvero il Tritono debbono havere primieramente avanti
essa.... senz'alcun mezo una Consonanza sia poi perfetta over imperfetta."

FOOTNOTE 22: "È vero che nelle compositioni de più voci molte volte è impossible di poterli schivare et di non incorrere in simili intrichi."

FOOTNOTE 23: "Quando si vorra porre due Consonanze perfette l'una dopo l'altra avertiremo, che movendosi l'una per salto l'altra si muova per grado, perciocche allora si potrà passar dalla maggiore alla minore come dall'Ottava alla Quinta et per il contrario senz'alcuna offesa del Udito.... E ben uero ch'e molto più lodeuole quando le parti discendono insieme nel graue perciocke allora necessariamente i Mouimenti loro si fanno tardi et tanto più e lodeuole quanto più sono graui, perche per la Tardita si comprende facilmente la diversita delle specie. Il che non cosi facilmente si comprende ne i suoni acuti nati dalla uelocita de i mouimenti conciosiache tendono quasi ad una simiglianza massimenente quando le parti ascendono insieme dalla Perfetta minore alla Perfetta maggiore. Ma perche queste cose non sono hoggidi considerati da i Prattici, essendoche pongono tali passagi ne i lor Contrapunti senz'alcuno auertimento, pero dico solamente, che non si debbono usare spesse fiate ne i Contrapunti a due voci, concoisia che dal Senso sono maggiormente compresi di quello che sarebbono se tali mouimenti si ritrouassero in una Cantilena a piu voci, perciocke allora la diuersita de mouimenti che farebbono le parti tra loro et la loro moltitudine non lasciarebbono udire ne questi ne altri simili."

FOOTNOTE 24: "Ne anco e cosa lodeuole che si oda ne i Contrapunti due parti che ascendino insieme da una consonanza maggiore che sia di specia Imperfetta ad una minore che sia Perfetta et facino i loro mouimenti per salto cioe per piu d'un grado, oueratmente due parti che ascendino o discendino insieme per detti mouimenti da una consonanza contenuta da una proportione maggiore sia perfetta ouero imperfetta ad una che segue sia perfetta come dalla Terza all'Unisono et della Decima all'Ottava, perciocke sempre dara qualche noia alle purgate orecchie. Ne anco torna bene il por la Sesta auanti la Quinta quando le parti ascendino o discendino insieme; ancora che l'una si muovi per grado et l'altra per Salto....

"Quando poi siano grati questi movimenti all'Udito, l'Esperienza maestra della cose per uia del senso ce lo manifesta, essendo che la Natura ha in odio le cose senze proportione et senza misura et si diletta de quelle c'hanno tra loro conuenienza."

FOOTNOTE 25: "Per il contrario adunque sara lecito il porre una Consonanza maggiore che sia imperfetta avanti una minore che sia perfetta quando le parti ascenderanno delle quali l'una cioe l'acuta ascendi per grado et la graue per salto."

FOOTNOTE 26: "Stara anche bene che da una Consonanza imperfetta minore si uada ad una perfetta maggiore ascendendo la parte graue per grado et l'acuta per salto, ouer discendendo l'acuta per grado et la grave per salto. Si concede etiandio che dalla Consonanza imperfetta che sia minore di proportione della seguente si uadi all'Ottava, quando insieme ascendono ouer discendono le parti; pur che una di esse faccia il Mouimento per grado et tal Mouimento sia d'un Semituono maggiore."

FOOTNOTE 27: "E concesso etiandio il venire dalla Consonanza perfetta all'imperfetta quando le parti ascendono ouer discendono insieme, pur che l'una di esse si muova per grado et la Consonanza imperfetta sia di maggior proportione della perfetta. E lecito etiandio por due Consonanze l'una dopo l'altra che faccino tra due parti il mouimento di salto, pur che l'una di esse si muova per un Semiditono."

FOOTNOTE 28: "Si puo ancora con mouimenti di salto por due parti ne i Contrapunti che insieme ascendino o discendino, quando la parte acuta discende per una
Terza et la graue per una Quinta et si viene della Terza alla Quinta ouer per il
contrario si ascende dalla Quinta alla Terza et l'una delle parti cioe la graue ascende
per una Quinta et l'acuta per una Terza..."

"E ben uero che quando una de loro facesse il moto per Ditono massimamente
discendendo che tali mouimenti si potranno schivare, percioche 'l procedere in cotal
modo e alquanto aspro come l'esperienza ce lo manifesta. Ma l'ascendere dalla
Quinta al Ditono si concede percioche le parti procedono per alcuni mouimenti i
quali non solamenti sono sopportabili ma anco molto dilettano, essendo che sono
molto sonori."

FOOTNOTE 30: "Et cio dobbiamo osservare non solo quando le parti della cantilena
fanno contrarii movimenti ma etiandio quando una di esse non si movesse dal proprio luogo et l'altra ascendesse o discendesse per salto di due gradi."

FOOTNOTE 31: (Pages 74–75): "Vedono che fatta la Terza minore si passa alla
Sesta minore e cosi parimente fatta la Terza maggiore alla Sesta maggiore, quali
movimenti sono e regolati e moderni.... Siche questa Terza minore havra duoi moti
soli, uno all'Unisono e l'altro alla Sesta minore."

FOOTNOTE 32: "Accoicche con facilita si osservi questa Regola che qualunque volte
si vorra procedere dalla Consonanza imperfetta alla perfetta di fare che almeno una
delle parti si muova con un movimento nel quale sia il Semituono maggiore tacito
overo espresso. Et per consequite tal cosa giovera molto l'uso delle Chorde
chromatiche et dell'Enharmoniche."

FOOTNOTE 33: "Debbe adunque il Musico etiandio cercar di variar sempre il suo
Contrapunto sopra un sogggetto et potendo far molti passaggi eleggera quello che
sara it migliore che li tornera piu in proposito et che fara il suo Contrapunto piu
sonoro et miglio ordinato et lasciera da un canto gli altri."

FOOTNOTE 34: "Quando adunque tra molte Minime se ne ritrovasse alcuna che non
procedesse per grado non sara mai lecito ch'ella sia dissonante anzi l'una et l'altra de
due figure che faranno tal grado si debbono porre consonanti.... percioche per tal
separatione la Dissonanza si fa tanto manifesta ch'a pena si puo tolerare."

FOOTNOTE 35: "Si potra nondimeno porre la prima parte della battuta che sia
dissonante quando sara la seconda minima d'una Semibreve sincopata del Contrapunto percioche la prima parte di tal figura sara posta senza dubbio nel levar la
battuta e la seconda nel battere et tal Dissonanza si potra supportare, percioche nel
cantar la Semibreve sincopata si tiene salda la voce e si ode quasi una suspensione o
taciturnita che si trova nel mezo de la percussione dalla quale nascono i suoni e per
essa si discernono l'un dall'altro et consiste nel tempo, onde l'Udito quasi non la
sente perche da lei non e mosso di maniera che la possa comprendere pienamente per
non esser da lei percosso et anco per la debolezza del mouimento che si scorge in essa,
perche manca della percussione che lo move. La onde la voce allora nel perseverar
della Sincopa perde quella vivacita c'hauea nella prima percussione di modo che fatta
debole e essendo percossa de un movimento piu gagliardo d'un altra voce forte che

si muove da un luogho all'altro con piu gagliardo mouimento nella quale e nascosta la
Dissonanza sopra la sua seconda parte, tal Dissonanza a pena si ode essendo anco che
prestamente ce ne passa. Et se pure il senso e da qualche parte offeso e dopoi rag-
guagliato per tal maniera dalla Consonanza che succede senz'alcun mezo che non
solamente tal Dissonanza non li dispiace ma grandemente in lei si compiace, perche
con maggior dolcezza et maggior soavita fa udire tal Consonanza. Et questo forse
aviene perche Ogni contrario maggiormente si scopra et si fa al sentimento piu noto
per la comparatione del suo Opposto."

FOOTNOTE 36: René Descartes, *Compendium Musicae* (1618) "De ratione com-
ponendi et modis: Syncopa fit, cum finis notae in una voce auditur eodem tempore
cum principio unius notae adversae partis, ut videre est in exemplo

posito ubi ultimum tempus notae B dissonat cum nota C quod ideo forte quia manet
adhuc in auribus recordatio notae A cum qua consonabat et ita se habet tantum B ad
C instar vocis relativae in qua dissonantiae perferuntur, immo etiam harum varietas
efficit ut consonantiae, inter quas sunt sitae, melius audiantur, atque etiam attentionem excitant; cum enim auditur dissonantia BC, augetur exspectatio et
judicium de suavitate symphoniae quodammado *suspenditur* donec ad notam D sit
perventum, in qua magis auditui satisfit et adhuc perfectius in nota E cum qua post-
quam finis notae D attentionem sustinuit nota F illico superveniens optime con-
sonat.... Praeterea advertendum auditui magis satisfieri in fine per octavam quam per
quintam, et omnium optime per unisonum.... quia in fine spectare debemus ad
quietem quae major reperitur in illis sonis inter quos est minus differentia vel nulla
omnino ut in unisono. Non solum autem haec quies sive cadentia juvat in fine, sed
etiam in medio cantilenae hujust cadentiae fuga non parvam affert delectationem
cum scilicet una pars velle videtur quiescere, alia autem ulterius procedit.... quod
autem attinet ad contrapuncta illa artificiosa ut vocant, in quibus tale artificium ab
initio ad finem perpetuo servatur, illa non magis arbitror ad Musicam pertinere quam
Accostica aut retrograda camina ad Poeticam."

FOOTNOTE 37: "Ma non si debbe giamai por la Prima parte della Semibreve che sia
dissonante siz poi sincopata e si dee avertire per ogni modo due cose, la prima che
dopo la Dissonanza segua una Consonanza a lei più vicina, la seconda che 'l
mounimento il quale fara la parte della sincopa debbe sempre discendere, et esser di
grado, et non ascendere. Onde potra esser utile questa Regola: Quando la
Dissonanza sara posta nella seconda parte della Semibreve sincopata, la quale sara
una Seconda, allora dopo lei accomodaremo ottimamente la Terza che le e più uicina.
Cosi ancora quando in essa Sincopa sara posta la Quarta si fara il medesimo. Alla
septima poi se le accompagnera la Sesta percioche le e più vicina. Similmente si
potrebbe dir delle Replicate come della Nona dopo la quale si accompagna la Decima

et della Undecima che riceve la Decima.... Si potra anco alle volte (come costumano fare i buoni Musici non senza suo gran commodo) dalla Seconda sincopata uenire all'Unisono et cio quando le parti sarano ordinate in tal maniera che l'una faccia il mouimento di Tuono et l'altra di semituono. Usaremo etiandio la Quarta sincopata dopo la quale segue senz'alcun mezo la Semidiapente et dopo questa immediatamente segue la Terza maggiore percioche la Semidiapente e posta in tal maniera che fa buono effetto, essendoche tra le parti non si ode alcuna trista relatione. Sogliono ancora i Prattici usar di porre la Nona quando dopo essa si viene all'Ottava per contrarii mouimenti et l'una delle parti ascende per Quarta o discende per Quinta et l'altra discende per grado."

FOOTNOTE 38: "Si de pero osservare.... che quella Figure la qual segue la Dissonanza et discende non sia legata ad un altra Consonanza cio e che non faccia un'altra sincopa, che sia tutta consonante ma che di due cosa sia l'una: ouer che tal Figure la qual sara sempre di valor de la meta di quella che contiene la sincopa ne habbia un'altra dopo si sia qual si voglia la quale discenda o pure ascenda per grado o per salto, ouero chella siz legata ad un'altra figura che sia simigliamente dissonante et che tra loro facciano un'altra Sincopa."

FOOTNOTE 40: "Et cio si potra simpre fare in ciascun luogo senza porre il segno ♯ della chorda chromatica per far dell'Intervallo del Tuono un Semituono imperoche in quella che la penultima Figura et 'utimlla si toua il mouimento che ascene semprde s'intende esser collacato il Semituono, pur che l'altra parte non discenda per simile intervallo.... Perche s'udirebbe un'Intervallo minore d'un Semiditono che sarebbe dissonante. Ma la Natura ha provisto in simil cosa, percioche non solamente i periti della Musica ma anco i Contadini che canto senz'alcuna nota, procedono cantando a questo modo per l'Intervallo del Semituono."

FOOTNOTE 41: "Oltra queste due sort di Cadenza, ue n'e un'altra terminata per Ottava over per Unisono la qual si fa quando si pone le seconde Figure.... distanti tra loro per un Ditono facendo discendere la parte grave per un salto di Quinta overo ascendere per quello di Quarta et ascendere la parte acuta per grado, come si vede.... Ma perch queste Caedneze non si usano molto nelle Compositioni de due voci, conciosiache l'ascendere per i mostrai salti et lo descendere anco e proprio dalla parte gravissima di alcuna compositione composta a piu voci."

FOOTNOTE 43: "I Musici nelle lor cantilene sogliono il piu delle volte Quattro parti, nelle quali dicono contenersi tutta la perfettione dell'harmonia, et perche si compognono principalmente de cotali parti, pero le chiamano Elementali della compositione alla guisa di quattro Elementi.... Si come 'l Fuoco nutrisce et e cagione di far produrre ogni cosa naturale che si troua ad ornamento et a conservatione del Mondo cosi il Compositore se sforzara di far che la parte più acuta della sua cantilena habbia bello, ornato ed elegante procedere di maniera che nutrisca et pasca l'animo che ascoltano. Et sicome la Terra e posta per fundamento de gli altri elementi cosi l'Basso ha tal proprieta che sostiene stabilische fortifica e da accrescimento all'altre parti, consiosiache e posto per Basa et fondamento dell'Harmonia, onde e detto Basso quasi Basa et sostenimento dell'altre parti. Ma si come averebbe quando l'Elemento della Terra mancasse (se cio fusse possibile) che tanto bel ordine delle cose reuinarebbe et si quastarebbe la mondona et la humana Harmonia, cosi quando 'l Basso mancasse tutta la cantilena si empirebbe di confusione et di dissonanza et ogni cosa andarebbe in ruina. Quando dunque il Compositore componera 'l Basso della sua compositione procedera per mouimenti alquanto tardi et separati alquanto over lontani piu di quelli che si pognono nell'altre parti, accioche le parti mezane possino procedere con movimenti eleganti et congiunti et massimamente il Soprano, percioche questo e 'l suo proprio. Debbe adunque esser il basso non molto diminuito ma procedere per la maggior parte con Figure d'alquanto piu valore di quelle che si pongono nell'altre parti et debbe esser ordinato di tal maniera che faccia buoni effetti et che non sia difficil a cantare et cosi l'altre parti si potranno collocare ottimamente ne i proprij luoghi nella cantilena. Il Tenore.... e quella parte che regge e governa la Cantilena et e quella che mantiene il Modo o Tuono nelquale e composto.... osservando di far le Cadenze a i luoghi proprii et con preposito."

FOOTNOTE 44: "Ma si debbe anco avertire che quantunque il basso possa alle volte tenere il luogho del tenore, et cosi l'una dell'altre parti quel dell'altra, nondimeno si de fare, che 'l Basso finisca sempre sopra la chorda regolare et finale del Modo sopra 'l quale e composta la cantilena et cosi l'altre parti a i lor luoghi proprii percoiche da tal chorda haveremo a giudicare il Modo. Et se bene il Tenore venisse a finire in altra chorda che nella finale questo non sarebbe di molto importanza, pur che si habbia proceduto nella sua modulatione secondo la natura del Modo della Cantilena."

FOOTNOTE 45: "I Musici costumano di dar principio alle lor Compositioni il piu delle volte per il Tenore et dopoi ponogno il Soprano alquale aggiungono il Basso et ultimamente l'Alto.

NOTES

1. (*Tutte le opere* [1589] I: 222): "For the variety of harmony . . . consists not only in the variety of the consonances which occur between the parts, but also in the variety of the harmonies, which arises from the position of the sound forming the third. . . . Either this is minor and the resulting harmony is ordered by or resembles the arithmetical proportion or mean, or it is major and the harmony is ordered by or resembles the harmonic.

On this variety depend the whole diversity and perfection of the harmonies. For (as I shall say elsewhere) in the perfect composition the fifth and third, or their extensions, must always be actively present, seeing that apart from these two consonances the ear can desire no sound that falls between their extremes or beyond them and yet is wholly distinct and different from those that lie within the extremes of these two consonances combined." [Strunk, *Source Readings in Music History,* p. 242.] [The asterisk by the footnote number indicates that the footnote is given in its original language in the appendix at the end of the chapter. Material which this translator has added to the footnotes is enclosed in brackets.]

2. "Some properties of the *Senario* and of its parts, and how among them can be found the form of every musical consonance."

3. "Il Viola: 'You have not mentioned the minor sixth or the octave with the major third, and many other consonances which are used in counterpoint.' To this I replied that when I discussed all those simple consonances which can be used and that are brought forth according to the natural order of the harmonic numbers, you must assume that I also mentioned every different mixture and of all those that are born of an accidental order, . . . since between these ends I have shown you . . . all the parts of the *Senario* are found which contain in actuality and in potentiality all those consonances that are of use to music."

4. "Although the minor sixth is not apparent within the parts of the *Senario* it nevertheless exists as a potentiality."

5. (*Opere* I: 221): "But since the extremes of the fifth are invariable and always placed subject to the same proportion, apart from certain cases in which the fifth is used imperfectly, the extremes of the thirds are given different positions. I do not say different in proportion; I say different in position, for (as I have said elsewhere) when the major third is placed below, the harmony is made joyful and when it is placed above, the harmony is made mournful. Thus, from the different positions of the thirds which are placed in counterpoint between the extremes of the fifth or above the octave, the variety of harmony arises. . . . I do not go so far as to say that the composer may not take two arithmetical divisions one after another, but I do say that he ought not to continue in this division for long, since to do so would make the concentus very melancholy. But to take two harmonic divisions one after another can never give offense. . . . The order which is arithmetical or resembles the arithmetical departs a little from the perfection of harmony." [Strunk, *Source Readings in Music History,* pp. 242–243.]

6. The *messel* theory defines the interval by which the lower tone is expressed as a multiple of the higher tone (according to the string length). For example, the perfect fifth is expressed as M + 1/2, i.e., 1–1/2 times the length of the string which produces the higher note, the major third as M + 1/5, etc. [Also, see this study, pp. 40–41.]

7. (Lib. II. cap. 12. p. 61): "The excellence of the *Senario* might be seen also in that not only all simple consonant relations are contained therein when we take one after the other in succession . . . but furthermore, each relation is in a simple or composite consonant relation with the whole and with each of its components. Consonant relations obtain not only in the first six [proportions] but also in the multiples of the first six, in the proportion 3 as in the *sesquialtera* [3:2], in 4 as in duple [4:2], in 5 as in *sesquiquarta* [5:4], and in 6 as in *tripla* and in *sesquialtera*. Beyond the proportion 1:6 there is no more consonance (1:7 is not a consonance), nor is the *sesquisexta* a consonance beyond the *sesquiquinta*. . . . Please observe that I have ordered the intervals in arithmetic proportion as well as in harmonic proportion. In the arithmetic proportion the interval differences and spaces are equal, but the proportions are unequal. . . . Such an arrangement is easily found in the first *Senario,* and the figure above makes it clear. The principle that the same consonances are contained in the first six harmonic proportions leads to the conclusion that the major proportions are expressed by larger figures, the minor proportions by smaller figures; all this becomes clear by what follows."

8. (Lib. II. p. 63): "It is remarkable how much more pleasant are those con-

sonances that are thus derived by harmonic division, by comparison with those derived through arithmetic division."

9. Karl Stumpf did not solve the problem either. It first appeared that he may have had a pretext for a sharper distinction through his *Theorie der Verschmelzungsgrade*. But he admitted in his latest work, *Konsonanz und Dissonanz* (1898), that the difference of amalgamation of the octave and of all other intervals was at least as great as that of the consonances and dissonances—again that hope of finding a real solution to the problem.

10. (Lib. II. p. 63): "The unison is the source from which [*principium a quo*] all consonances originate, just as unity is the source from which all numbers are derived; and equal proportion is the mother of all proportions. Then the octave is that which can also be called the source of the consonances 'through which' [*principium per quod*]: just as D. Augustinus in numbers called unity the 'source from which,' and binary, the 'source through which.' He does not think that binary is a number because the middle principle does not have an end. . . . Duple proportion could be called the principle of proportions 'through which' because it is found in two parts located together near unity. All proportions are divided so that they are superparticular, or multiplied so that they are multiple."

11. (Lib. II. cap. 25. p. 90): "Between the two extremes [notes] of the octave the consonances are so placed that that [note] which is the minor third to one of them is found to be major sixth to the other; that which is major third to one extreme is minor sixth to the other; and that which is fourth to one is fifth to the other. From this it is found that the minor third and major sixth are almost of the same nature because the strength of the extremes is the same [the two intervals fill up the space of the octave]. . . . The same thing is found in the major third and the minor sixth, for which reason they make an almost similar concord to the ears. Thus, we learn much more clearly that the fifth and the fourth are, as it were, true twins, sprung from the same birth, and differ from the diapason only in quantity."

12. (Lib. II. cap. 24. p. 63): "For it is necessary that the minor intervals arise from the differences between the consonances. . . . Thus, the tone in a *sesquioctava* [9:8] proportion, results from the difference between the fifth and the fourth; and the greater semitone, in *sesquidecimaquinta* [16:15] proportion, from the difference between the fourth and the major third; and the smaller semitone, in a *sesquivigesimaquarta* [25:24] proportion, from the difference between the major third and the minor third. But from the difference between the minor third which is in a *sesquiquinta* [6:5] proportion and to the interval or consonance which results from the *sesquisexta* [7:6] proportion no smaller interval results suitable for harmony."

René Descartes's (Cartesius) comments in his *Compendium Musicae* (1618) are very similar. In the chapter, "The Octave," he states: "We deduce that all consonances belong to one of three categories: the first contains those consonances derived from the division of the unison and the octave; those of the second category are derived from the division of the octave itself into equal parts—fourths and fifths—and we can therefore call them consonances of the second division; finally there are those derived from the division of the fifth itself; the consonances of the third and last division." Following this is the famous statement: "There are only three interval members, to wit: 2, 3, and 5." Descartes calls the fourth the "unhappiest of all consonances" because it "must never be used in composition except accidentally and must be supported by other consonances." He produces very convincing proof for the close relationship of the sixth to the third, and the fourth to the fifth, and so on, in the covibration of the octave, which he presents in the follow-ing: "No sound is heard without its octave sounding audibly." He is quite cognizant of the oscillations of bodies related to the vibrating tone in the ratio of the upper (!) third or fifth and their octave equivalents: "I have proved this by experimenting with the strings of the lute (any other instrument whatsoever will do equally well). If we pluck one of its strings, the force of its sound will set in vibration all the strings which are higher by any type of fifth or major third." [Quotations from Descartes's *Compendium of Music,* pp. 16–27.]

Mersenne's *Harmonie universelle* (1636), especially the two *Livres des con-sonances,* is based on the same principle. Mersenne nearly discovered the phenomenon of overtones, since he made the degree of consonance dependent upon the strength of the sympathetic vibration of a string caused by the sounding of another vibrating string (*I. Livre des consonance,* Chap. XIII ff.). He sharply stresses the exceptional position of the octave among all the intervals (p. 58) and discusses in great detail why the complex of consonance is closed with the number 6. But he also reaches the remarkable conclusion that one could become accustomed to hearing the ratios 6:7, 7:8, and even 5:7 as being consonant. He points out on page 212 that intervals which have the relationship of inversions to each other are so much alike that even distinguished composers can interchange them. Mersenne exhibits the relationship of tones by using the series from the natural tones of the trumpet and takes as a basis the number of vibrations, rather than string lengths. By this method he concludes that the arithmetic series (1, 2, 3, 4, 5, 6) yields the major chord and the harmonic series (1, 1/2, 1/3, 1/4, 1/5, 1/6) yields the minor (pp. 94 ff). But he decides that since the first series yields the more perfect harmony it should be called the harmonic. Rameau (*Traité de l'harmonie* [1722], p. 18) cites this claim as that of a Mr. Desermes, the pseudonym under which the first *Livre des consonances* first ap-peared in 1627 as *Livre I. de la Musique théorique.*

13. "And regarding the note found within the *Diapason* [octave] called by some modern musicians the *Note Dominante,* the term will be heard frequently in order to follow the current trend."

14. [The name should be Johannes de Muris.]

15. (*Istit. harm.* III. cap. 8): "The consonances that are fuller and those that are empty. The sound waves called full are those consonances which have greater power of occupying the sense of hearing with diverse sounds. Thus, one can say that the fifth is fuller than the octave because its extremities occupy with more delight the ear with different sounds which the extremities of the octave do not make, for they are equal sounding and assimilate themselves one to the other. Therefore, except for the octave, all the intervals are said to be full, according to how well they satisfy the ear. Those which are closer to their source are more perfect than the others. From this a rule might be devised. All those consonances of major proportions are fuller, except as I have said, the octave and its compounds. . . . The others become more pleasing the further they depart from simplicity, this being something of which our senses are not very pleased, because they love more the complicated things than the simple ones, and they accompany themselves to other consonances." (*Istit. harm.* I. cap. 16): "I say, therefore, that a consonance or simple interval is that which takes the smallest limits of its proportion ordered in such a way that they cannot receive between them any middle ends which divide such proportions into more parts." (The major sixth is composite because it is divisible into 5:4:3; the minor sixth 8:5 = 8:6:5; 3:1 = 3:2:1; 4:1 = 4:2:1 and so on.) This evaluation is not

without contradiction inasmuch as on the one hand the intervals closest to unity (fifth, fourth) are mentioned as *pie piene*; on the other hand the empty *composte* are more pleasing.

16. "In every musical composition, what we call the subject is that part from which the composer derives the invention to make the other parts of the work, however many they may be. Such a subject may take many forms, as the composer may prefer and in accordance with the loftiness of his imagination: it may be his own invention; . . . again, it may be that he has borrowed it from the works of others, adapting it to his work and adorning it with various parts and various modulations. And such a subject may be of several kinds: it may be a tenor or some other part of any composition you please, whether of plainsong or of figured music; again, it may be two or more parts of which one follows another in consequence." [Strunk, *Source Readings in Music History*, p. 230.]

17. (*Istit. harm.* III. cap. 27): "Compositions should be made up primarily of consonances, and secondarily and incidentally of dissonances. And although every composition, every counterpoint, and in a word every harmony is made up primarily and principally of consonances . . . a dissonance causes the consonance which immediately follows it to seem more acceptable." [Strunk, *Source Readings in Music History*, p. 231.] (Cap. 28): "When the contrapuntal part begins with the subject one may begin with one of the perfect consonances already mentioned. But often, for greater beauty, contrapuntal charm, and greater convenience the composers do not make the parts begin together, but have one part begin after the other, using the same progression of figures or notes in imitation, thus rendering the counterpoint delightful and artistic. In this case they may begin with whatever consonant they wish, be it perfect or imperfect, since there are pauses occurring in one of the parts. However, one must observe that the beginnings of the voices have as a relationship between them one of the abovementioned perfect consonances or a fourth. This is not done without reason for one must begin with the octave or the fifth of the mode upon which the song is based, these being the natural or essential tones. . . . This, I believe, is what the ancients meant when they said that in the beginning of the counterpoint one must always start with one of the perfect consonances. This is neither inevitable nor is it necessary, but is preferred by the composers. Therefore, when we wish to begin counterpoint with imitation we can start with whatever perfect or imperfect interval we wish, including the fourth. I do not mean that the voices must begin to sing by this inverval—I say the fourth in respect to the beginning of the subject along with the contrapuntal part or to the contrary. . . . Thus, we will observe the rule given at the beginning, to have a perfect consonance between the beginnings of the two parts, but causing the voices to start singing together in a major third. . . . Thus, these two voices cannot possibly create anything that would be unpleasant to the ear. . . ."

18. "For they knew very well that harmony can arise only from things that are among themselves diverse, discordant, and contrary, and not from things that are in complete agreement. Now if harmony arises from variety such as this, it is not sufficient that in music the parts of the composition be at a distance from one another with respect to the low and the high; the modulations must also be varied in their movements and must contain various consonances, subject to various proportions. . . . For although these consonances, taken in this manner, would obviously cause no dissonance between the parts, a certain heaviness would be heard which would displease. . . . We add that, for the reasons already given, the composer ought not to

use two or more imperfect consonances one after another, ascending or descending together, without a mean, such as two major or minor thirds, or two major or minor sixths. . . . For not only do these offend against what I have said about the perfect consonances, but their procedure causes a certain bitterness to be heard since there is altogether lacking in their modulations the interval of the major semitone, in which lies all the good in music and without which every modulation and every harmony is harsh, bitter, and as it were inconsonant. Another reason for this bitterness is that there is no harmonic relationship between the parts or sounds of two major thirds or of two minor sixths, which makes these somewhat more dreary than the others, as we shall see later on. Thus, in every progression or modulation which the parts make in singing together we ought to take special care that wherever possible at least one of them has or moves by the interval of the major semitone. . . . This is easily managed if the consonances taken one after another are diverse in species, so that after the major third or sixth will follow the minor, or vice versa, or so that after the major third will follow the minor sixth, or after the latter the former, and after the minor third the major sixth, or in the same way after the major sixth the minor third. Nor is there more reason for forbidding the use, one after another, of two perfect consonances than of two imperfect ones, for although the former are perfect consonances, each of the latter is found to be perfect in its proportion. . . . [Thus, since it is forbidden to use two perfect consonances of the same species one after another, we ought still less to use two imperfect ones of the same proportion] seeing that they are less consonant than the perfect. But when two minor thirds, and similarly two major sixths, are used one after another, ascending or descending together by step, they may be tolerated, . . . But when the parts move by leap we ought by no means to use two or more similar consonances one after another, ascending or descending." [Strunk, *Source Readings in Music History,* pp. 233–237.]

19. "Les consonnantes imparfaites doibuent éstra composées ensemble de telle façon, que ceux qui ont mesme intervalle ne montent ny ne descendent ensemble."

20. "But when two parts ascend together and the one or the other makes a movement which involves the semitone, it seems that because of this movement they are tolerated by the ear, as are the first cases of the augmented diapason and the semidiapente. . . . And although it is not so bad to find this in the relationship between two modulations as to find it in the modulation of a single part, the same evil that was heard in the single part is now divided between two, and it gives the same offense to the ear. . . . Thus, in a composition for several voices, those intervals that are not admitted in modulation are to be so avoided that they will not be heard as relationships between the parts. This will have been done when the parts can be interchanged by means of harmonically proportioned intervals of the diatonic genus, that is, when we can ascend from the first sound of the lower part to the following sound of the upper, or vice versa, by a legitimate and singable interval. But this will not be the case when nonharmonic relationships are heard between the parts of the composition, whatever it may be, among four sounds arranged in the manner explained, for these cannot be changed unless with great disadvantage, as the intervals. . . . ." [Strunk, *Source Readings in Music History,* pp. 238–239.]

21. "We may sometimes use the semidiapente as a single percussion if immediately after it we come to the ditone. . . . And we are permitted to use not only the semidiapente, but in some cases the tritone also, as we shall see at the proper time. It will, however, be more advantageous to use the semidiapente than the tritone. . . . And we ought to take care that, in the parts involved, the semidiapente or

tritone is immediately preceded by a consonance, no matter whether perfect or imperfect." [Strunk, *Source Readings in Music History*, p. 240.]

22. "But in compositions for more than two voices it is often impossible to avoid such things and not to run into intricacies of this kind." [Strunk, *Source Readings in Music History*, p. 240.]

23. "When one wishes to use two perfect consonances consecutively, one voice should move by leap and the other by step. In this manner one can pass from a larger interval to a smaller, as from the octave to the fifth, and to the contrary without any offense to the ear. . . . It is quite true that it is more commendable when the parts descend together, since their motion necessarily becomes slow. They are very euphonious when they are low, because through the slowing down one easily comprehends the diversity of the species. But the higher sounds originating from a greater velocity of vibration are not as easy to comprehend because they have a closer similarity, especially when the parts ascend together from a smaller perfect consonance to a larger perfect consonance. But these things are not considered by present-day composers for they place such passages into their counterpoint without any caution. I can therefore only say that they should not use them too often in two-part counterpoint. Such movements would be better understood if they were found in a song with many voices because in such a case the variety of the movements would prevent the listener from hearing them or any other similar sounds."

24. "It is not commendable for both voices to ascend by leap from an imperfect consonance to a smaller perfect consonance. Truly, two parts ascending or descending by leap from a larger perfect or imperfect consonance to a smaller perfect consonance, such as from the third to the unison or from the tenth to the octave, will always give annoyance. Neither is it good to move in similar motion ascending or descending from the sixth to the fifth, even when one voice moves by step and the other by leap. . . .

"Nevertheless, experience, the master of all things, reveals to us when these movements are pleasant to the sense of hearing, for nature hates things without proportion and without rule and takes pleasure in those that have suitability in them."

25. "On the contrary, the ascending movement in similar motion from an imperfect consonance to a smaller perfect consonance wherein the upper voice ascends by step and the lower voice by leap is permissible."

26. "The ascending movement from an imperfect consonance to a larger perfect consonance is good when the upper voice leaps and the lower voice moves stepwise. Or in descending motion the upper voice will move stepwise, and the lower voice will move by leap. It is also permissible for a smaller imperfect consonance to move in similar motion to the octave, provided that one voice moves only by half step."

27. "The movement from a perfect consonance to a larger imperfect consonance is also allowed when the parts ascend or descend together, provided that one of them moves by step. Also, both voices may leap, provided that one moves by a minor third."

28. "Both voices may descend by leap from a consonance of a third to a fifth when the upper voice descends by a third and the lower voice descends by a fifth; or they both may leap upward from the consonance of a fifth to a third if the upper voice leaps by a third and the lower voice by a fifth. . . .

"It is true that the descending movement of a major third in one voice would better be avoided, for experience shows that it is rather harsh. But the ascent from the interval of a fifth to a major third is allowed because the parts proceed by means of some movements which are not only substantiated, but are very delightful, being that they are very resonant."

29. [The five species of Fux are not correctly designated here by Riemann. Fux lists them as follows:

1. Note against note.
2. Two notes against one.
3. Four notes against one.

4. Syncopation.
5. Free counterpoint

(Johann Joseph Fux, *Steps to Parnassus,* trans. Alfred Mann [New York: Norton & Co., 1943], pp. 27–139).]

30. "And this must also be observed not only when the parts move in contrary motion, but in oblique motion as well, one voice standing still and the other ascending or descending by a leap of two steps."

31. (Pp. 74–75): "From the minor third you must move to the minor sixth, and equally, from the major third to the major sixth, such movements being both orderly and modern. . . . Therefore, the minor third must move either to the unison or to the minor sixth."

32. "In order that this rule be observed the movement from an imperfect consonance to a perfect consonance should have a half step in the upper part. In order to accomplish this it is necessary to use chromatic and enharmonic tones."

33. "Consequently, the musician should always try to vary his counterpoint above a subject. He must then choose those passages that will better suit his purpose—those that will make his counterpoint more sonorous and better ordered—and leave out the others from a song."

34. "When, however, among many minims a few are found that proceed by leap, it should never be allowed that such minims be dissonant. Rather, both of the two notes which establish such a leap must be placed in consonance because by such a separation the dissonance becomes so obvious that it can scarely be tolerated."

35. "Nevertheless, one will be able to place the dissonance on the beat when it is the second minim of a syncopated semibreve. The first part of such a note will occur on the offbeat and the second on the beat. Such dissonance will be acceptable because in the singing the syncopated semibreve keeps the voice firm, and in the center of the percussion a certain suspension or taciturnity is heard, in which one tone is discerned from the other in time. The sense of hearing hardly notices this dissonance because it is not moved by it in such a way as to be fully comprehended. Also, the movement is perceived as being weak because it lacks the percussion by which the ear is stimulated. The voice then in preserving the syncope looses that vivacity that it has in the first percussion in such a way that it is made weak. But since the one strong voice, being struck by a motion more vigorous and moving from one place to another with more vigorous movement, conceals the dissonance in its second part, such dissonance being heard as painful quickly passes by. If then the sense is offended by some part and afterwards balanced by a following consonance, such a dissonance is not displeasing, but rather, is pleasant because the following consonance makes the hearing sweeter and with greater gentleness, and all this happens because the sentiment becomes more obvious through the comparison of its opposite."

36. René Descartes (*Compendium Musicae* [1618]), who is familiar with Zarlino's *Istituzioni* and quotes from it, also uses the expression *suspenditur.* He is, however, more logical than Zarlino insofar as he does not perceive the syncope as a

concealment of dissonance but, rather, stresses the dissonance itself. In the Chapter "About Composition and the Modes" he states: "A suspension occurs when one hears the end of a note in one voice together with the beginning of a note in the opposing voice:

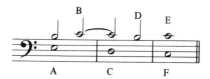

One can see this in the example above, where the last beat of the note B is dissonant with the beginning of the note C. This can be tolerated because the memory of the note A, with which it was consonant, is still in the one's ear. The same relationship and dependent state exist between B and C, a situation in which dissonances are tolerable. Their variety even has the effect of making the consonances between which they are located sound better and more eagerly anticipated. For while the dissonance BC is being heard, our anticipation is increased, and our judgment about the sweetness of the harmony is suspended until we come to the note D. The end of note D holds our attention and the note F now following produces a perfect consonance, an octave. . . . It is noteworthy, too, that the ear is more satisfied by an octave than by a fifth as final concord and is satisfied most of all by the unison. Not that the fifth is very unpleasing as a consonance, but at the end we demand repose, and that is to be found to a higher degree between those pitches between which there is the smallest difference or none at all, as in the unison.

"Not only this effect of repose but a full cadence is necessary at the end of a composition. During the course of a composition the avoidance of such a cadence has a charming effect. This occurs when, so to speak, one voice seems to wish to rest while another voice proceeds further. . . . Other elaborate contrapuntal devices, as they are called, also can contribute a great deal when they occur in parts of compositions. Such tricks, however, when they are used from beginning to end of a composition, have as little to do with music, I believe, as acrostics or palindromes with poetry." [Descartes, *Compendium of Music,* pp. 50–51.] Please pardon me for using such a long quotation. It is regretful that such a perceptive thinker did not write more about music, and that the *"rationes subtiles"* which he drew from his premises *"inter prigrinandum evanuerunt."* It must be especially regretted that he did not put into writing his statements regarding the normal succession of intervals, of which he was of the opinion that they might be *magis plausibles* [more believeable] than those of Zarlino (as seen a few pages earlier).

37. "The first part of the semibreve should never be dissonant, but the second part is syncopated. One is also cautioned of two things: after the dissonance a consonance follows closely, and the movement that makes a part of the syncope must always descend stepwise, and never ascend. The following rule should be very useful: when the dissonance of a second is placed on the second part of the syncopated semibreve, the semibreve resolves downward into the third. Moreover, when the fourth is used with the syncope, it will do the same. The seventh will be followed by the sixth because it is closer. This also applies to the ninth, which

resolves into the tenth; and to the eleventh, which is followed by the tenth. . . . The syncopated second might also resolve to the unison (as the good musicians customarily do with great ease). The parts will then be ordered in such a way that the one moves by a whole step and the other by a half step. We might also allow the diminished fifth to come after the syncopated fourth if the major third follows immediately after, considering the diminished fifth is placed in such a way that the bad relation is not heard. Again, practicing musicians are accustomed to resolving the ninth into the octave, after which through contrary motion one voice ascends a fourth or descends a fifth, and the other part descends by step."

38. "However, one must observe . . . that the descending note which follows the dissonance should not be bound to another syncopating consonance. The note following the syncope should always be half the value of the syncope. The next note may descend, or even ascend by step or leap, or the resolution may be bound to another figure that is similarly dissonant and which also makes a syncope."

39. [Chapter LIII, not Chapter LI.]

40. "One need not use the chromatic sign to change the interval of a tone into a semitone because the semitone is always used in the ascending movement between the penultimate and the final note, provided that the other voice does not descend by a similar interval. . . . An interval smaller than the semiditone would thus form a dissonance. But Nature has provided something similar, for, not only do the musical experts sing by means of the interval of the semitone, but the country people who sing without notes also sing this way."

41. "Besides these two kinds of cadences there is another ending for octaves and unisons. . . . From the interval of a major third the lower part descends a fifth or ascends a fourth and the upper part moves stepwise. . . . But these cadences are not used much in two-part compositions because of the huge leap in the one part. It is found to be more proper in the lowest part of compositions having more voices."

42. [Chapter LII, not Chapter LV, and Chapter LI, not Chapter LIV.]

43. "The musicians are generally in the habit of setting their songs in four parts, in which they say all the perfection of harmony are contingent. And because there are four such parts they call them the elements of composition, in comparison to the four elements. . . . Just as fire nurtures and causes the production of every natural thing that is found to adorn, and is a conservative in the world, so the composer finds that the upper part of his composition is to be beautiful, ornamented, elegant, and to proceed in such a way as to nourish and feed the souls that listen. And as the earth has been placed as foundation of the other elements, so the bass has such a property that sustains, stablilizes, fortifies, and augments the other parts. Through the bass the foundation of the harmonies is secured, and it becomes the support of all the other parts. Therefore, when the composer writes the bass of the composition he will proceed with movements somewhat slow and rather separated, or farther separated from those that are placed in the other parts in order that the middle parts, and especially the soprano because this is his own, can proceed with elegance and with related movements. Therefore, the bass must not consist of small intervals but must proceed for the most part with leaps of longer intervals than those that are placed in the other parts and must be ordered in such a way that it makes a good effect. But it must not be difficult to sing, and the notes of the other parts must be placed excellently into the exact places of the song. The tenor is that part which rules and governs the melody and maintains the mode in which the piece is composed . . . making the cadences at the exact places and with purpose."

44. "But one must be aware that the bass may also at times exchange places with the tenor, and so also may the other parts exchange places. The bass, therefore, always terminates in the mode in which the work is composed with the other parts at their exact places because from the final chord we decide the mode. When the tenor finishes on a note other than the final of the mode it should not be considered very important, for it proceeds according to the nature of the mode of the melody."

45. "Composers customarily begin their compositions with the tenor, followed by the soprano, to which they add the bass, and lastly the alto."

CHAPTER VIII

The Disintegration of Solmization: The Figured Bass

URING the course of the sixteenth century a noticeable change in the conception and apperception of polyphony gradually took place. Instead of the voices being composed successively as melodies to be sung together (still prevalent in the fifteenth century), the harmonies (chords) which were consequently created by the simultaneous movement of the voices came more and more into consideration. The listener as wel as the composer became increasingly more interested in the structure and progression of harmony. The first allusions to this seem to be found in the popular songs set note against note, which reach back at least into the fifteenth century. There is a definite basis for the assumption that dance music was sung and played in a similar manner, with simple chords, at an even earlier date. Evidence indicates only a gradual encroachment of the style of this folk music—so lowly esteemed as to scarcely be mentioned by the masters of the higher arts—into the sphere of real art music (see the *laici conductus* of Anonymus IV, in Riemann, *Geschichte der Musiktheorie* [2nd. edition], p. 206). An artistic treatment of the dance, which we find already developed into real chamber music in Germany by 1600 (variation suites of Peurl, Schein and others), may have been the means of transition. Of secondary importance is organ music, which quickly blossomed during the course of the sixteenth century and began to take on a chordal character because of its close connection as an accompanimental medium to sacred vocal music.

As a natural result of this revolution the didactics of solmization were gradually abandoned. Solmization, as the inclusive formative concept, proved increasingly to be an obstacle in a harmonic complex. For example, two different notes of a chord could have the same solmization syllable, such as E–b = MI–MI, F–b♭ or F–C = FA–FA; or a note and its octave could be placed together with two different syllables, such as E G B E = MI SOL MI LA, wherein MI LA is the octave and MI MI is the fifth! In

Germany, the Netherlands, and England, where the alphabetical letters continued to be used (because of the organ tablatures) to name the notes (A B C D E F G) solmization never became as deeply rooted as it did in the Romanic lands. But even in these countries such inconsistencies could not continue to be ignored.

Toward the end of the sixteenth century the impulse to do away entirely with solmization resulted in the establishment of the six Guidonian syllables on the notes C D E F G A, with the addition of a seventh syllable on B.

F. Sweertius (*Athenae belgicae* [1628], p. 320) accredits the Netherland composer Hubert Waelrant with having begun this sensible reform.*1 The addition of the syllable SI to the note B, which is attributed to him, and the retention of the other six syllables for the notes C D E F G A gradually found universal acceptance. The same writer also testifies that Waelrant proposed other, completely different names besides these for the seven steps, namely: BO CE DI GA LO MA NI for C D E F G A B. But strangely enough, these new syllables were at first most widely used in Belgium, suggesting that they were presented earlier than SI, and not at the same time. But Ludovico Zacconi, an even earlier writer than Sweertius, testifies in his *Practtica di musica,* Part II (Lib. I. cap. 10 [1622]), that Anselm von Flandern, another Dutchman and a member of the Bavarian court, was responsible for adding SI for B and BO for B♭ to the Guidonian syllables. It appears, therefore, that Sweertius subsequently gave to his former teacher, Waelrant, credit belonging to Anselm von Flandern. Mersenne (*Harmonie universelle* [1636], in the sixth book [not denoted as such], *Livre des consonances,* p. 342) mentions a Sieur Le Maire as the innovator of mutationless solmization, with ZA for B.2 He prefers this to a system which had abandoned the solmization syllables in favor of BO CE DI GA LO MA NI, which he refers to on page 50 of Book I as being widespread. Apparently, this ZA is of a later date and is only recommended by Mersenne because it leaves the older names as they were. However, in the preface of the *Harmonie universelle,* Vol. II, he states that other names for the seven syllables (BI CI DI NI SI BA and ZA) were evidently proposed by several people at the same time.*3 In France Sieur Granjan, municipal secretary of Sens, initiated the practice of always solmisating with UT on C and using MI on E and B (!) (Fétis does not mention this Granjan.) Some such establishment of the six Guidonian syllables, with the double use of MI, could very well have been the beginning of the reform. The use of BI for B was introduced by Erycus Puteanus (*Modulata Pallas* [1599]). Adriano Banchieri proposed BA in his *La Cartella musicale* ([2nd edition] 1610), and according to Caramuel de Lobkowitz (*Arte nueva de musica* [1644]) the Spaniard Fr.

Pedro de Urenna suggested NI about 1620. Daniel Hitzler (*Newe Musica* [1628]) suggested that new syllables be developed from the musical alphabet (1A, Be, Ce, De, mE, Fe, Ge). Proposals for the syllable SI[4] first appeared in the works of Sethus Calvisius (*Exercitatio musica tertia* [1611])[5] and Guillaume-Gabriel Nivers (*La gamme du Si* [1646]). Earlier, in the *Compendium* (1594) Calvisius had advocated BO CE DI GA LO MA NI.[6]

For an entirely different reason (i.e., because UT is an unfavorable syllable for the practice of solfège) the syllable DO began to be used about 1670 in Italy, as first reported by G. M. Bononcini (*Musico prattico,* [1673]).*[7] In conclusion it should also be noted that the famous acoustician Joseph Sauveur used the syllables PA RA GA SO BO LO DO for c d e f g a b for scientific purposes, but with the adjustment of other vowels (a, e, ε, i, o, u, ɤ) for the seven parts (*Merides*) into which he divides the whole tone (see Sauveur's *Mémoires* in the *Histoire de l'Academie Royale des sciences* in Paris, of 1700–1713, in which proof of the overtone series is also found).

Johann Mattheson (*Das Beschützte Orchestra* [1717]) was the last to write about solmization.

The thoroughbass could not have originated much earlier than 1600, since it can hardly be supposed that such a convenient expedient for compositional practice would remain unnoticed by theorists for a longer period. The existence of the thoroughbass is traceable only to the year 1595, in the title of Adriano Banchieri's *Concerti ecclesiastici (aggiuntovi nel primo choro la spartitura per sonare nel organo comodissima).* Unfortunately, I have not been able to obtain an example of these songs with thoroughbass, which appear to be lost.[8] It is highly probable that Jacopo Peri's *Dafne,* as well as Giulio Caccini's *Euridice,* had a figured bass, and since Emilio del Cavaliere's oratorio, *Anima e di corpo,* published in 1600 by Al Guidotti, had a figured bass, it appears that the inventor of the thoroughbass will never be identified. It is not likely that the origin of the *stile rappresentativo* can ever be attributed to one great innovator, for such a person would surely have been crowned with glory.*[9] It would be more reasonable to assume that this abbreviated manner of indicating harmonic progressions through numbers over a bass line had developed gradually in the practice of the Italian organists, suddenly gaining universal attention when the monodists began to use it in their music.[10]

Many of the earliest works with thoroughbass betray an origin in which the thoroughbass is not represented by just one independently moving voice. Rather, it is a continuous row of the lowest sounding tones throughout the entire musical work, many such tones without any figures, some with incomplete figures. Banchieri calls such a bass which passes from one voice to another a *Basso seguente*. ("Ecclesiastiche Sinfonie dette Canzoni in aria francese per sonare et contare et sopra un *Basso seguente* concertare entro l'organo" [Op. 16 (1607)]. Nevertheless, the bass in the first *Concerto nell'organo* of this work is a real continuo.) The comments in the preface concerning the *Basso seguente* give the option of putting the entire piece either in score or tablature.*[11] It may be realized on a keyboard instrument only, without voice parts, or performed by the organ with voices and other instruments, in which case the *Basso seguente* should be played without any modification, but with fullness and emphasis. At first sight this gives the impression that the organist should do nothing with it. However, it probably means that the bass voice itself should not be varied or embellished when the chordal accompaniment is self-evident. The fully laid out *Bassi seguenti* of Rauerij's great *canzoni* collection (Venice [1608], four–sixteen voice *canzoni* of G. Gabrieli, C. Merulo, G. Frescobaldi, L. Luzzaschi, G. Grillo, T. Massaini, and many other famous Italian organists of the time), as well as Frescobaldi's *Canzoni da sonar* of the year 1628 and other works of the time employ figures whenever the compositions have more than one part. (The term *Basssi seguenti* is applied to this special type of thoroughbass, described as follows: as long as the descant is performed singly only its notes should be played, but when the alto enters, its notes should also be added, and so forth. Consequently, independent notes should not generally be played; "accompaniment" should be used only in connection with the lowest voice.)

We might well assume that the *Bassi seguenti* is the original form of the thoroughbass, inasmuch as its purpose was at first to enable the organist, after studying the music, to support the chorus with prehensible harmonies without having to look at the complete score *(Intavolierung)* of all of the actual voices with their passing tones and other embellishments. Moreover, it enabled the organist to cover the eventual omission of individual parts with his accompaniment. In this we can see a foreshadowing of the future use of the organ accompaniment (keyboard instruments, *chitarrone,* and so on) as a harmonic support for the melody when it stands alone at the beginning or within a work. The gradually growing awareness of the significance of the bass as the foundation of musical composition can be sufficiently substantiated in the preceding chapters. The unrealized accompaniment—amounting to only a figured- or unfigured-bass line—did not at all suddenly become predominant because of the awareness that it would work. There was ample opportunity throughout the entire century to learn this. Even earlier it had been considered self-evident; in the arrangements of polyphonic *lieder* for soprano and lute the sixteenth century possessed a rich and highly treasured literature of accompanied monody.

The new outcry was much more: a declaration of war against counter-point—a deliberate contempt for the highest achievements of the great era of polyphonic music! Songs with only one melodically executed voice and additional supporting accompaniment were no longer to be merely an expediency or an inferior substitute. On the contrary, in such songs music should be much more capable of developing expression than in polyphonic pieces wherein "one voice confines, checks, and suppresses the others."

New ideas arose which, first kindled in Italy, soon enflamed the entire musical world—ideas for effecting a resurrection of the music of the ancients in its imagined splendor. The old world would be buried and a new one recalled to life. In 1594, the same year of Palestrina's and Orlando Lasso's death, the *stile rappresentativo* was born with Jacopo Peri's *Dafne,* and during the following few years spread throughout the world. Of course, the new schemes were at first thin and formless, but due to the sound disposition of the Italians they soon acquired musical vitality. Before the close of the century melody was reinstated, giving the lie to the originators of the style, who had scorned not only counterpoint, but melody too. Their reforms were also completely revolutionized. Counterpoint came into esteem again, but it had irretrievably lost its absolute monarchy and henceforth had to put up with the joint rule of harmony. Practical composition was immeasureably expanded into new musical spheres. At first it flourished in all the different forms of accompanied vocal music (opera, oratorio, cantata). From here the principle of accompanied monody was transferred to pure instrumental music (sonata, for a solo instrument [violin!] with figured bass, or for a small ensemble of varied instruments such as were used in concert, with accompaniment only for filling). Meanwhile, the polyphonic style, which had remained wholly conservative or only partly changed, was cultivated by the masters who adhered to the old music. Nevertheless, they could not remain uninfluenced by the wholesome effect of the new ideas. (The aftermath of the Palestrina style became the *stile osservato,* with both styles, contrapuntal and homophonic, finally amalgamating in the art of Bach and Handel.) However, our discussion is concerned less with practical music than with the direction into which musical theory was compelled.

First, it can be well substantiated that the thoroughbass, whose origin was entirely nontheoretical and was throughout purely practical in nature, became the vehicle for musical composition. But fortunately, we must also acknowledge the fact that the thoroughbass performed an inestimable service in the development of theory.

From the time of the *Ars discantus secundum* of Johannes de Muris to Zarlino's *Le Istituzioni harmoniche,* there existed schematic tables (which grew continually, but became ever less clear), containing all the existing interval combinations used in compositions of three and more parts. In view of this we may conclude that the thoroughbass stems, in practice, directly from these tables. More specifically, it is a clarification of the most detailed aspects of composition for the performer or reader of the thoroughbass part!

The desire to be able to read faster induced the first composers who used the new figures to make a number of practical reductions. The most important such reduction was to leave unmarked the most frequently appearing chordal formation—that consisting of the third and fifth above the bass. Zarlino had presented sufficient grounds, theoretically, for such an abbreviation. I would, therefore, like to show a causative connection between Zarlino's theory and the thoroughbass, even though due to the figured bass his ingenious definition of the essence of major and minor harmony fell completely into oblivion. (In fact, speculative theory made no progress during the seventeenth century, subsisting almost until Rameau's time on the achievements of the Ramos-Zarlino period.)

For the sake of avoiding an overaccumulation of signs (in order to achieve the greatest possible facility in reading) the specific sizes of intervals (major, minor, and so on) were not indicated in the thoroughbass figures. The numbers 2, 3, 4, 5, 6, 7, 8, 9 [10, 11, 12, 13] signified only the second, third, and continuing, above the bass note. The scale, determined by the key signature (which already had a respectable number of possibilities as a result of the rapidly increasing number of transpositions through signatures of two, three, or four sharps or flats), relieved the figured bass of the responsibility of indicating whether the intervals were major or minor, diminished or augmented. Only when the scale, designated by the key signature, did not contain the desired note did the figures have to show a flat, sharp, or natural, which then indicated the respective raised or lowered note, just as it appeared in the actual notation. The figures, however, did not generally show whether the intervals were major, minor, diminished, or augmented, since they were supposed to be an abbreviated notation rather than a kind of theoretical explanation.

The first positive result of the establishment of the thoroughbass was the development of a number of concepts whose terminology depended directly on the figures—terms which were easy to remember and ever of practical value. It must be admitted that indicating the triad—the most important of these concepts—by a lack of figures gives no clue as to how it received its name.[12] However, it can be shown that from the very beginning there was the inclination to violate this rule of figuration. The "diminished triad," which occasionally appears in all the keys, was marked when it was actually intended by an additional sign, which was in reality redundant (flat by the 5, a diagonal stroke through the 5, and so on). But this is proof that even from the beginning of the figured bass, composers distinguished the consonant triad (major or minor) to a certain degree from all other harmonies. Additional tendencies to add such theoretical distinctions to the figured-bass notation are continually demonstrable (e.g., the addition of superfluous sharps and flats to show the size of the third where it is already indicated by the key). Apart from these small inconsistencies the sole exemption of the (consonant) triad from any figures already signifies a very important advancement and a future gain from a general point of view for the inner logic of chordal connection. The consonant triad comprises a whole series of different interval combinations over one bass note in the same tonality:

All these and many other three-, four-, or more part structures are indiscriminately included in the concept of the "triad on C," which is meant in the appearance of the note C without figures.

The earliest instructions for thoroughbass playing give no allusions to any new means of fostering theoretical understanding. The *Avvertimento* to Caveliere's *Anima e di corpo* simply states that[13]

the small numbers placed over the notes of the instrumental basso continuo indicate the consonant or dissonant intervals corresponding to the numbers, such as 3 the third, 4 the fourth, and so on. When a sharp (♯) is placed before or under the figure, the interval should be chromatically altered; likewise, the flat (♭) retains its usual meaning here. A ♯ without a number over the note always signifies the major tenth [etc.].

The *Avvertimento* to Peri's *Euridice* is even more meager:[14]

A sharp by the 6 over the bass note indicates the major sixth . . . a flat demands the minor third or tenth, and the sign is valid only for that one note by which it is situated, even when several notes follow one another on that self same step.

Banchieri's figured basses also correspond to these rules. Perhaps the missing basso continuo of his church concertos of the year 1595 contain instructions for realizing the figured bass.*[15]

The Augsburg organist Gregor Aichinger, perhaps the first German composer to make use of the thoroughbass, is supposed to have had an explanation of the figures prefacing his *Cantiones ecclesiasticae 3 et 4 voc. cum basso generali et continuo ad usam organistarum* (Dillingen, 1607). Unfortunately, I have not had the privilege of seeing them.[16]

Ludovico Viadana's ten rules in the preface of Book I of his *Cento concerti ecclesiastici a 1, 2, 3, et 4 voci con il basso continuo per sonar con l'organo* (Venice, 1602) are, of course, instructions for the organist, but nothing is said concerning the figures (Viadana makes use of only the sharp and the flat for the third).

On the other hand, Agostino Agazzari has left us a valuable, detailed interpretation of the thoroughbass figures under the title "Discorso del sonare sopra il basso con tutti li stromenti" in his *Sacrarum cantionum,* Op. 5, Book II (Venice, 1608). In section 16 it states:[17]

> The practice of performing from a thoroughbass was established for the following reasons: (1) For the new style of recitative singing (and for composing in this newly discovered style) in which speech is imitated with one or several voices, as some distinguished men do it in the new arias, and as is customary today in the concerts in Rome. Moreover, neither figures (*spartitura*) nor a complete composition (all the notes to be sung by the voices in score) are necessary; a simple bass line thereby suffices (!). (2) For convenience, i.e., to alleviate in score reading the difficulty of keeping in view so many individual voices, which is especially troublesome when the occasion requires a sight reading performance. (3) In order to reduce the great quantity of compositional materials required for performance; for if an organist were required to perform all the works in score which were performed in one year in Rome by merely one church giving regular concerts, he would need a library larger than that of a doctor of law. This type of bass, therefore, came about for very good reasons, especially since it was not effective to play the same parts as they existed—not an instrumental reproduction of the composition, but an accompaniment to the songs.

The paragraphs 6–8, especially devoted to explaining the figures, are premised by the remark that whoever wishes to accompany well should understand counterpoint, possess the required technique for playing his instrument, and be capable of following aurally the movement of the voices (!). Where the figures are lacking, his rules for the accompaniment are not definite. Here, one must listen for the direction of the progressions within the composition. However, in order to accompany correctly and to avoid offense one must make use of the figures employed by the composer, by which the consonances and dissonances are indicated by numbers above the bass note, with ♯, ♭, ♮ (not meant in the same sense as our accidentals, except for the ♭ on the seventh degree), 5 6, 6 5, 4 3, 7 6, and so on, exactly in the correct succession.

(7) When the intervals belong to the key, accidentals are not necessary (!). Signs placed beside the note are valid for that note only; those placed above the note apply to the following note as well.

(8) All cadences—those within the piece as well as final cadences—require the major third. Some indicate this, others do not. It is better to do so.

Undoubtedly, the major third of the penultimate chord, not that of the final chord, is meant here:

That the final chord should be major had long been self-evident (see *Geschichte der Musiktheorie* [2nd edition], p. 355). This is how Michael Praetorius (*Syntagma musicum* III: 135 [1620]) explains it. He also agrees with Agazzari that it is better at cadences to indicate the accidental. Otherwise, the orgainst would not know what was intended, as the composer often has in mind the minor third, especially in fugal writing. Praetorius defines a cadence in the following manner:

In cadences the bass descends a fifth or ascends a fourth. On the other hand, when the bass ascends a fifth or descends a fourth, no cadence takes place. In this case a minor third must be used [in the penultimate chord] instead of the major third [of course, only when the minor third belongs to the scale]. It could be that the composer has written it this way for some particular reason, in which case the major third, of course, would not be used.

Naturally, the thoroughbass could be realized in various ways, as well as at different levels of complexity. Already, Praetorius (*Syntagma* III: 143) reprimands the practice of simply playing the bass line along with the composer's written-out voice parts as not fulfilling the objectives.[18]

In reference to these organists (who previously set only one or two voices to the thoroughbass) it is no longer customary to perform only one or two voices with the thoroughbass just as they are written. It would sound rather poor and bare if no additional middle voices were added by the organists or by performers of other fundamental instruments.

Following this are instructions for a full, independent chordal accompaniment: "Therefore, it is not necessary for the organist to play the
vocal lines just as they are to be sung; he should play only the basic harmonies." The example below in four full parts presents Praetorius's realization
of the thoroughbass:

One of the earliest methods for the thoroughbass is found in the preface
to Bernardo Strozzi's *Affettuosi concerti ecclesiastici,* from which
Praetorius draws in his *Syntagma* (III: 127 and 134). It is especially interesting that both Strozzi and Praetorius consider the figure 6 as self-
evident for all notes with a sharp (♯), as well as for the MI of the *Cantus
mollis,* i.e., for a:

In all these cases the 6 is intended even though it is not written in. If the
composer wants the fifth, he must expressly demand it by adding ♯5. In
view of this rapid development of the fixed usage of certain chords considered as self-evident for certain steps of the scale, Fétis's assumption
(*Biographie universelle,* articles "Campion" and "Delair") that the so-
called *Regula dell'ottava (Règle de l'octave)* was generally known in Italy
long before 1700 does not appear to be exaggerated! [19]

According to the corresponding opinions of the earlier authors, the correct accompanimental performance from a figured bass presumes
a knowledge and mastery of the rules of counterpoint. It requires that the
counterpoint be applied without reflection, not only while composing com-
fortably at the table, but also in reading at sight during the performance of
the piece in concert. It is clear that this type of accompaniment is really a
kind of regulation for the *contrapunto alla mente,* although not as much

for the singer, as supposed by Giuseppe Baini, as for the instrumentalist. The thoroughbass in the first music dramas was not intended for one single instrument such as the organ or klavier, but for an orchestra of a most diverse sort (see the preface to Peri's *Euridice,* and G. B. Doni's presentation of Monteverdi's orchestra, and so on). Church concerts were also soon accompanied by the entire orchestra from a thoroughbass. The individual player, however, according to the custom of the time, considered it his valid right to perform running passages and other embellishments occasionally as a soloist (see Praetorius's amusing report about the instrumental accompaniment of church vocal music). Even if Praetorius himself acknowledged that these occasions often amounted to absurdity, it is obvious that the thoroughbass was a means for preventing at least the clumsiest errors.

One should, above all, not forget that the prodigious development of organ building during the course of the sixteenth century (see Praetorius, *Syntagma* III: 113 ff) had gradually taught the value of octave doublings.[20] This knowledge is essential in order to avoid a completely distorted concept of the tonal quality of instrumental accompaniment with a figured-bass foundation, including vocal works performed completely by instruments, as well as sonatas, *canzoni,* and so forth for several melody instruments and figured bass. It is not yet definitely known how far back into the sixteenth century the custom of strengthening the vocal parts with instruments extends. This involved doubling not only at the same pitch, but also, in the manner of the 16' and 4' organ stops, in the lower octave (especially the basses) or the upper octave (especially the top voice). This custom may well, however, be even a few centuries older (!). Even the *Scholium* of the *Musica enchiriadis* already mentions a six-voice organum which includes instruments. Our knowledge of the situation at the beginning of the seventeenth century was quite accurate, thanks to the thoroughness of the Wolfenbüttel *Kapellmeister* Michael Praetorius. His remarks conform to those of G. M. Artusi (*L'Arte del contrapunto,* 1586–1589), that in double- and polychordal singing it is not only admissible but desirable to keep the bass parts of the different choruses in unison whenever they are singing at the same time (see *Geschichte der Musiktheorie im IX.–XIX. Jahrhundert* [2nd edition], p. 374). Following this Praetorius enlarges on the remarks of Artusi:

The octave must be treated reasonably and precisely. *Octavae in omnibus vocibus tolerari possunt, quando una vox cantat, altera sonat.* Generally, in concert arrangement . . . it is customary to add a discant violin to the upper octave in the lower choir where the cantus must be sung by an alto with three trombones or three bassoons.

Following this, Praetorius advises against doubling the alto at the octave with instruments when a vocal soprano is present; the possible parallel fourths would result in higher parallel fifths by means of the octave doublings:

> Some suppose they can be tolerated to some degree, to which opinion I cannot at this time consent. . . . And *hac ratione* this can be allowed in all the voices, and give no *nigratum sonom auribus,* if when the *Concentor humane voce* sings, the cornets, viols, flutes, trombones, and bassons play at the upper or lower octave. A few *Instrumenta simplicia,* especially the flutes, are always to be reckoned one or two octaves higher than the notes of the melody they are to play. In such cases this is nothing more than when many stops of various quality are played on the organ together in unison, octaves, super octaves, and also in the lower octaves at the suboctave and (as some call it) the contrabass. Therefore, a very splendid *Harmonium* results in *pleno choro* when there is a bass consisting of many instruments: a common or *Quarttrombone,* a chorus bassoon, or *Pommer Bombard,* which give the bass its correct tone. In addition there are other instruments which play at the contra-octave similarly to the organ: octave-*Posaune,* contra-*Fagott* or large double-Bombard, and the contrabass. These are used in the present day Italian concerts and are fully justifiable.

Here, the principle of the modern orchestra is very clearly presented. Apparently, much was learned from the organ, for their builders were far ahead of their time in theoretical awareness of the construction of voices in various blends and octaves. Venice is the cradle of orchestral octave doubling (Adrian Willaert, and the two Gabrielis) according to a further observation from Praetorius (p. 97):

> I have recently received word from Venice that the most eminent *Musici* in Italy assiduously use unisons and octaves in the *Ripieni* (that is, in *pleno choro*). Their special experience and practice show that such methods result in much greater strength in large churches where the choirs are quite a distance apart. [21]

One of the most essential features of the thoroughbass notation was its capacity to expose dissonance. A figure 2, 4, 7, 9, or 11 always meant a dissonant note and warned the performer to provide for it, and if it occurred on the strong beat, to properly prepare and resolve it (stepwise). Under such conditions the passing of the rules of composition over into the thoroughbass school could not fail to take place (M. Locke, 1673; F. Gasparini, 1683; A. Werckmeister, 1698; J. Boyvin, 1700; F. E. Niedt, 1710, etc.).

The very practical significance of the thoroughbass gave an entirely new direction to compositional rule making. Although many of the old contrapuntal rules with their often entirely untenable prohibitions dragged further on through the seventeenth century, the endless chord tables were finally abandoned. As substitutes for them concise instructions were prepared for quick assistance, in view of the various problems brought about by the figured-bass symbols.

The manner in which these practical aids were formulated by the accompanists may be shown by Gottfried Keller's *Rules for Playing a Thorow-bass,* which apparently was written before 1700 but was not published until 1707 as the *Complete Method for Attaining to Play Thorough Bass upon Either Organ Harpsichord or Theorbo-lute,* of the "late famous Mr. Godfrey Keller," appearing therefore as the posthumous work of a respected London teacher. In quoting from Keller's work, published in the appendix of William Holder's *Treatise of Harmony* (1731), I shall limit myself to the most important matters: [22]

1. On any note where nothing is marked, only 3, 5, 8 (common chords) are played in any position: 8   5   3
                                                                                                      5   3   8
                                                                                                      3   8   5

2. When the sixth (6) is given, the third and octave are self-evident. In four-part writing (full playing) the following rules for doubling are given:
   a) When the sixth is minor (flat): if the bass is low the sixth is doubled; if it is high, then the third is doubled.
   b) When the sixth (and third) is major (sharp), the bass is doubled:

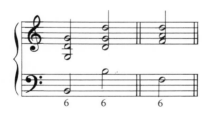

3. Whether the tonality is major or minor is not decided by the key signature at the beginning of a piece, but by the third; for if the third is major, the key is major; if the third is minor, then the key is minor.

4. All notes naturally sharp require the minor third (and sixth); all notes naturally flat require the major third (and sixth). (See Johannes Hothby's *principi* and *comiti* shown in *Geschichte der Musiktheorie* [2nd edition], p. 310).

5. Dissonances are prepared by concords and resolved into concords while one of the voices constituting the dissonances remains stationary (often, however, they are used in contrary motion).

6. The cadences, or full closes (when the bass rises a fourth, or falls a fifth), are

either the common cadence ($^6_4$ ♯), the six-four cadence ($^6_4$ $^5_♯$), or the great (or fullest) cadence (7 $^6_4$ $^5_3$ 7̣). In all these the fourth is resolved into the major (!) third and the octave into the minor seventh (!).

7. There is another cadence called the seven-six [suspension], which is counted as a half close. If the higher voice produces a whole tone it is never used as a final cadence because it does not satisfy the ear. When it ends one part of a piece it is to indicate a new tempo or the entrance of a new theme. [! We can see that the seven-six cadence, which was formerly regarded as perfectly satisfying, has been completely disposed of by the common cadence!] The sixth in this type of cadence can either be "sharp" or "flat"; according to whether the bass moves downward by a half or whole step, the soprano moves upward a whole or half step:

8. The bass seldom ascends or descends stepwise without one of the two notes having a sixth.

9. In so-called short cadences (when the bass ascends or descends twice stepwise to the final tone) two successive chords of the sixth are necessary:

[In the ascending examples b) and d) the $^6_5$ figures do not correspond to the text; Fétis's fitting opinion of Keller's *Rules* was that the examples were worse than the text].

The indications for using different figures [with a different bass note], which thereby produce harmonically equivalent chords from the same [upper] tones, are quite remarkable (p. 183), for they already contain the complete theory of chordal inversions.[23] The theory of inversion, then, was not accordingly discovered by Rameau without previous preparation; apparently, it was gradually brought to light in the practice of the cembalists:[24]

To make some chords easy to your memory you may observe as follows:

a) The triad ($\frac{8}{5}$) becomes a sixth chord ($\frac{8}{6}$) at the third above or sixth below. It becomes a six-four chord ($\frac{8}{6}$) at the upper fifth or under fourth.

b) The triad becomes a seventh chord ($\frac{7}{5}$) at the sixth above or third below. It becomes a chord of the second ($\frac{6}{4}$) at the seventh above or the second below.

c) The chord of the second ($\frac{4}{2}$) becomes a triad at the second (with a pure or diminished fifth according to the key). It becomes a sixth chord at the fourth or fifth below.

d) The augmented six-four-two chord over a flat note (c, f, and notes with flats) becomes a major seventh cord at the minor second below. It becomes a sixth chord at the augmented fourth above, or diminished fifth below.

e) The diminished seventh chord over a naturally sharp note (b, e, and notes with ♯) becomes a diminished triad at the third above or sixth below. It becomes a sixth chord at the diminished fifth above or at the augmented fourth below.

f) The $\frac{9}{4}$ becomes a $\frac{6}{5}$ on the second below (the fifth is perfect at the major second below and diminished at the minor second below). It becomes a $\frac{9}{7}$ at the third above or the sixth below.

g) The $\frac{9}{7}$ becomes a $\frac{9}{5}$ at the third below and a $\frac{6}{5}$ at the fourth below and fifth above.

h) Since the major seventh chord is unfortunately beyond recognition a designation is impossible (no example is given). However, it seems that instead of 3 5 7 either 2 5 7 or 4 6 7 should be given.

For comparision, the harmonic identity of the chords which were recognized and illustrated by Keller are shown below and are placed under the same letters:

Keller may have only had in mind the practical goal of having the accompanist immediately recognize that the notes for the right hand remain the same, notwithstanding a different bass progression and a change of figures; nevertheless, the undeniable outcome for the performer is a deeper view into the essence of inversion.

Keller's rules by which transpositions to all other keys can be accomplished with other clefs (p. 185) is perhaps the first of its kind:

However, it is questionable whether this is Keller's innovation, for it is also found in equal completeness at the close of Francesco Gasparini's *L'armonico practico al cimbalo* (4th edition, 1745), the earliest accessible edition. (However, according to Johann Nikolaus Forkel's table of contents the same subject is also discussed in the closing chapter of Gasparini's second edition of 1708. Forkel know nothing of the first edition [1683] of this work, which was reprinted continually up to 1802.)

The rules (p. 186 ff.) for preparing single dissonances (4, 7, 9, 2) by tying them to consonances (3, 5, 6, 8) are also remarkable because of their thoroughness. I shall pass over a number of otherwise excellent observations of Keller and just mention his remark that the figure 6 above a leading tone ("sharp") may be used with the diminished fifth, which attests to an already widely developed understanding of the significance of the chromatic secondary dominant-seventh chord.

Although Johann Mattheson of Hamburg was not a really significant theorist, his extensive knowledge and experience as well as his open-mindedness and integrity made him one of the greatest writers on music in the eighteenth century. For our purposes his *Das neu-eröffnete Orchestre* (1713) is particularly valuable. He enumerates the modern keys on pages 60–62:

The Italians and the contemporary composers no longer use the twelve modes. They use the new keys listed below:

1.	d	f	a	d minor
2.	g	bb	d	g minor
3.	a	c	e	a minor
4.	e	g	b	e minor
5.	c	e	g	c major
6.	f	a	c	f major
7.	d	f♯	a	d major
8.	g	b	d	g major

Although the above eight keys are obviously the best known and preferred, the following are nonetheless used and acceptable:

9	c	d#	g	c minor
10.	f	g#	c	f minor
11.	b♭	d	f	b♭ major
12.	d#	g	b♭	d# major
13.	a	c#	e	a major
14.	e	g#	b	e major
15.	b	d	f#	b minor
16.	f#	a	c#	f# minor

Whoever wants to know all the keys must also learn the following:

17.	b	d#	f#	b major
18.	f#	b♭	c#	f# major
19.	g#	b	d#	g# minor
20.	b♭	c#	f	b♭ minor
21.	g#	c	d#	g# major (misprinted g# minor)
22.	c#	e	g#	c# minor (misprinted c# major)
23.	c#	f	g#	c# major
24.	d#	f#	a#	d# minor

(In addition, see the "Characteristik der einzelnen Tonarten" [Characteristics of the individual keys], pp. 236–252, which, although not altogether enlightening, is in any case highly interesting. J. S. Bach himself was acquainted with the work, but he evidently refuted it in part with his *Das Wohltemperierte Klavier*.)

The following comment demonstrates to what extent the chromatic tones were still currently being designated in the mixed manner according to the custom of the German tablatures:

The symbols c#, d#, f#, and g# signify the notes lying a half step above c, d, f, and g, which are denoted by notes with sharps. If the desired note lies a half step below d, e, and g, then a flat must be placed before the notes ... (p. 99). The note c with a flat placed before it becomes b, b becomes b flat, a becomes g#, g becomes f#, f becomes e, and e becomes d# (!).

On the other hand Mattheson ably reorganizes old, outmoded rules. He regards as no longer valid the rule for beginning and ending with a perfect consonance (p. 100):[25]

Today such "antiquen harmonie" (c g c') would sound very bare because people have learned too well that a single third, especially when it is major, has a far greater effect and is more beautiful to the ear than all the fifths on earth (!!). For this reason accomplished composers do not double the *Tertiam majorem* because it has too sharp an effect on the ear.

(Heinichen also mentions this in his book *Der Generalbass in der Komposition* [1728], p. 142, footnote.) Of the formerly prohibited voice progressions Mattheson disapproves only of augmented fifths, fourths, and seconds (p. 111) : "The formerly forbidden leap of a seventh is presently one of our best embellishments." (!) He also has a liberal opinion of the *Mi contra Fa* (p. 112) : "Since it is not rigorously required in fully voiced works it is left mainly to the discretion of the composer." For example:

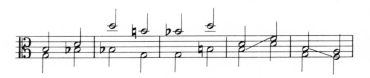

[p. 114] Our esteemed ancestors have given the following rules concerning the minor third: It should (1) seldom be used at the beginning, (2) never be used at the end, and (3) should be used sparingly in cadences. In my opinion all these rules are now no longer valid in galant (!) compositions, but their influence is still felt to some extent in the highly regarded traditional church style, especially in music for the organ. . . .

[p. 115] However, in the *Cantus mollis,* or wherever the minor third dominates, it [the major third] should never be used at the beginning . . . and for the final cadence this worthy tradition is only suitable for church and organ music, as everyone knows.

[p. 116] The fifth (it is said and written) should always be used more than the sixth at beginnings, endings, and throughout the piece. Unfortunately, this same sixth should not be used successively except in suitable cases. . . . However, nothing so simple and unproved as this can be said. At the present time, as has been said, the old consensus consisting of the fifth and the octave has been done away with completely and its vacuum filled with the third. Thus, in current usage it might be used occasionally at the beginning or in the middle, but at the end the fifth is not used because it is not appropriate. The third is used instead. The sixths have a much more pleasing and penetrating effect in the middle of a piece than the bare, pious fifths. . . . After this nothing is more beautiful than the fifth and sixth together, especially the *Quinta falsa,* a combination strictly forbidden by Bernhardi [Steffano Bernardi. *Porta musicale* (1615)] and other famous authors, even though in practice they are usually found without qualification to be completely free and suitable over each other in the middle of a piece as well as at cadences. One will not be greatly surprised by these and other great exceptions which violate such pretentious rules, or by clear-cut contradictions, if one understands that the tastes of our musical forefathers was very different from our own today.

In the handling of dissonance Mattheson devotes himself to those procedures which were finally breaking away from the old rules of counterpoint. He remarks (p. 136) "that a capable composer will know how to find new *Resolutiones* or *Syncopationes catachresticas* which cannot be specified." He says nothing whatever concerning "hidden" octaves and fifths. Only consecutive perfect fifths and octaves are forbidden, but even those with crossing of parts are "at times" permitted (p. 108).

In order to complete the picture of the new chordal theories developed from the figured bass by practitioners and regenerated by Rameau's speculative theories, we must still touch on G. A. Sorge's *Vorgemach* (1745–1747). This work, of course, appeared after Rameau's first publications, but it came forth without knowledge of them, as Sorge himself asserts. This could well have been concluded without his averment.

The work was published in the time when thoroughbass playing had reached the high point in its development—when the *Maestro al cembalo* was, so to speak, both conductor and concertmaster, and when no chamber or church concert, not even a song recital, could do without a skilled accompanist. The a capella style had almost completely gone out of fashion, and the first attempts at working out the artistic keyboard accompaniment which was to antiquate the figured bass a few years later were accomplished (J. S. Bach, Rameau). Studies in thoroughbass were therefore the "school of composition"; and composition itself, as an author of speculative theory has suggested, now appeared in the vestments of the thoroughbass. The title of Sorge's book is characteristic enough to be given in its entirety:

Vorgemach der musikalischen Komposition, or detailed, orderly, and competent instructions for present-day practice in the thoroughbass through which a *Studiosus Musices* may achieve a thorough knowledge of all the principles of composition and keyboard and the associated natural, aural, and artistic techniques, and consequently, not only learn to play the clavier as a good extemporaneous composer, but also to achieve important and thorough perfection in composition.

The scholarly organist in the employ of Count Reuss at Lobenstein has a thorough knowledge of the primary goals of the thoroughbass. However, he feels that he must extend the definitions of Mattheson and Mizler. Mattheson's definition (*Kleine Generalbassschule* [1735]) is as follows:

The thoroughbass is nothing more than bass notes with figures signifying a complete harmony, by which according to the rules a complete chord can be played on the keyboard or on some other instrument, and which can be used to support and to accompany an entire concert in exact harmony.

Mizler states (*Die Anfangsgründe des Generalbasses* [1739]):

The thoroughbass is a science based on the rules of composition, a harmony resulting from the nature of the given bass notes that are played and heard on appropriate instruments.

Sorge adds the following (p. 7) :

One would not be incorrect in calling the thoroughbass a concise concept of musical composition. It is true that the purpose of the thoroughbass is to function as a support and foundation. . . . Our sole aim is to show distinctly that a keyboard student by learning the thoroughbass . . . should consequently be able to play rather well *ex tempore* and in writing be able to establish a basis for learning and understanding all the rules of composition.

Within this program Sorge consolidates the theory of scales and points out the natural connection of consonances, which he verifies thrqugh the phenomenon of sympathetic vibration (p. 12), combination tones (p. 13), and overtones (p. 13). For "sympathetic tones" he cites Descartes's reference to the close relationship of tones which have the ratios of a major third and perfect fifth (p. 13). Above all he discusses in detail the *Trias harmonica perfecta* (major triad, pp. 13–16) and along with it the *Triad minus perfecta* (minor triad), the *Trias deficiens* (diminished triad), and Trias *superflua* (augmented triad), and even the *Trias manca*[26] ("major-diminished" triad of the thoroughbass system). The church modes are discussed in a short historical excursion (pp. 22–26). Then the twenty-four *Modi musici hodierni* from the final pages of Werckmeister's *Musicae mathematicae Hodegus curiosus* (1687) are explained. From the latter writing it is clearly seen that already before 1687 the terms *Dur-Dreiklang* and *Moll-Dreiklang* (major triad and minor triad) and *Dur-Ton* and *Moll-Ton* (major mode and minor mode) had become common among the German musicians.[*27] Sorge accepts Werckmeister's opinions and proposes the names *Modus Perfectus,* or *Modus masculinus* and *femininus.* Of course, Werckmeister himself already clearly predicts (*Musicae mathematicae* p. 125) that "these names will probably be retained because the terms have become so common." Sorge adds the following: "The naming is not really very important. It is more important that we correctly understand our two modes and learn to use them." Sorge already clearly recognizes that the major scale is composed of the elements of the three major chords (p. 28) :

We might also add that the *Trias perfecta,* by which our *Modus masculinus* begins and ends, is the basis and cause of these natural progressions, for a fifth stands above and below each member of this triad:

g	b	d
c	e	g
f	a	c

out of which our series of tones for the *Modi masculini* or *perfecti* arise, i.e.:

c   d   e   f   g   a   b   c

Sorge also calls the first note of the scale the *Finalis,* the third note the *Medians,* and the fifth note the *Dominans*—without any explanation, of course, since the terms are already in use.

He writes some short but excellent observations concerning the possible modulation (pp. 29 and 56) by which one can move from each major key in the system to the key of its second, third, fourth, fifth, and sixth, but with the limitations to those scales in which the triad on that respective step is common to both keys. The seventh degree is excluded with repeated references to how remarkable the number 7 is (the seventh overtone, dissonant seventh, and so on). Sorge compares the relationship of the relative modes to a marriage, while designating the variants (c minor–C major) as concubines (p. 30).

I can extract no more from these and other of his attempts to establish a connection of tones to one another. Moreover, this and the meaning of chords for the logic of composition are completely outside the scope of the figured-bass school. In Chapter XIII (p. 33),[28] however, Sorge oversteps the proper figured-bass theory and terminology, as the title "Vom Hauptakkord" shows:[29]

> The triad as described above usually doubles one of its tones *Sonum infinum* through a single, double, or triple octave. . . . The triad then consists of four-part harmony: (1) the bass or lowest part, (2) the major or minor third above the bass, either simple or compound [i.e., third, tenth, or seventeenth], and (3) the fifth above the bass, whether it be *perfecta, imperfecta,* or *superflua, simplex* (5) or *composita* (12, 19) !

Here again we encounter an accumulation of the most heterogeneous combinations of ideas—the characteristic of the thoroughbass school which so strongly retards the real theory. This aspect of the figured bass is concerned only with practical aspects and not the reasons behind them. Thus, Sorge is continually compelled to speak of the *Trias perfecta, imperfecta, deficiens,* and so on, as soon as he wishes to give a special rule.

Sorge has little to say about the many rules set up during the last flourishing of counterpoint prohibiting parallel movement of perfect consonances. However, he warns against frequent movement in similar motion from the third (and tenth) to the octave (p. 35). But earlier he remarks summarily (p. 34): "The concern over so-called covered octaves causes for the most part unnecessary difficulties, and it is not worthwhile for one to make much of them (!). It suffices for one to compose and to play well." He says nothing concerning covered fifths.[30]

Part II, published in 1746, discusses inversions of the triad—the sixth chord (with third in the bass) and the six-four chord (with the fifth in the bass). Whether this intelligible theory of chordal inversions was or was not conceived independently of Rameau must remain undecided. (In Part III Sorge expressly denies any acquaintance with Rameau's work.) It is certain that he discovered combination tones independently of Tartini, although later. He may have discovered this happy formula by himself, for even earlier we see the awareness of new perceptions gradually dawning.[31] In any case, the following deductions are his own (p. 68):

> That sixths spring from thirds is indisputable; if there were no thirds, then there would be no sixths. The minor sixth originates from the major third which is perfect, much more perfect than the minor third. . . . Therefore, the minor sixth is more perfect than the major sixth.

It would be difficult to express more precisely than is done in this sentence the complete change in the point of view regarding this interval which has taken place since the time of Franco of Cologne, for whom the minor sixth remained a real dissonance.

Sorge's attempt to prove that the six-four chord is less valuable than the triad is interesting, although not important to the subject (p. 108):

> One might think that the six-four chord would be more perfect than the triad from which it is derived, since its *Termini constitutivi* 3:4:5 are nearer to unity than 4:5:6. But it has already been mentioned that the sounds corresponding to the numbers 1, 2, 4, 8, et cetera, excel all others. The *Trias perfecta* can also be written 2:3:5 c–g–e′, or even 1:3:5 C–g–e′, but the six-four chord derived from it can produce no number under three. This is the reason why the major third 4:5 is more perfect than the fourth 3:4, because not only can it be seen as 4:5 but also as 2:5 and 1:5. On the contrary, the fourth with its *numeris radicalibus* cannot come under the number 3:4. No theorist, as far as I know, has made this observation.

(Werckmeister, however, had already come to the approximate conclusion in *Musicae mathematicae Hodegus curiosus,* p. 80.)

Also, Sorge's attempt to prove the consonance of the diminished and augmented fifth and fourth (pp. 120–21) should be considered an unfortunate consequense of the way the triad (with third and fifth) is left unfigured in the thoroughbass, for this leads to the establishment of three or even more degrees of consonance (!). The worthy J. F. Daube (*Generalbass in drey Accorden* [1756]) sharply opposes the extension of the consonance concept to the chromatically altered fifths and octaves (p. 10) (which opinion Mattheson also expresses):

> All these intervals are called consonant only because they are derived from consonances in name only, but they are no more consonant than any of the dissonances which stem from consonances and which are allowed to pass as con-

sonances. . . . The best arbitrator is the ear of those who understand very well, those who understand quite well, and the ignorant. An excessive number of true consonances in all types of melody can be more easily endured than only a small number of these false consonances which are related only nominally.

But it is again pure speculative theory when Sorge finds the source of all dissonance in the numbers 4:5:6:7 (the "natural" seventh chord). Here he is even more contiguous with Rameau than usual, deriving, as Rameau does, the diminished seventh chord from the minor ninth chord (pp. 347 and 379). This had already been done in Germany by Georg Philipp Telemann (*Evangelisch musikalisches Liederbuch* [1730]), who also had by this time established the eleventh and thirteenth chords. Fétis, who had a high regard for Sorge's *Vorgemach,* attributes to him the formation of independent chords not derived from consonant chords, but I do not really see why this should deserve any special merit. (I could not find anything like it anywhere in Sorge's work.) The *Vorgemach* is, in any case, one of the finest works among the harmonic theories having to do with the figured bass. However, it does not fully overcome the dilemma of working with two heterogeneous groups of concepts—the purely practical, which numbers the steps above the bass, and the purely theoretical, abstracted from the ratios showing the natural relationship of tones. Sorge's work does not arrive at a true apperception of the conflict since the practical side of the figured bass is still too important in the daily musical practice. Reflections on an adequate way to revive theoretical discussions of the figured bass could only ensue after accompanying from a figured bass had ceased, i.e., with the disappearance of the figures from the composers' scores.

In attempting to expose the theoretical aspects of the figured bass (aspects which reach back to its beginning), certain symbols must be regarded as redundant when the notes already belong to the scale, i.e., the ♯ (sharp) for the major third, the ♭ (flat) for the minor third, and ♭5 (flat five) for the diminished fifth. Rousseau's *Dictionnaire de musique,* article "Chiffres," lists a group of synonymous symbols (also reproduced in the *Encyclopedia methodique* [Paris, 1791] in the section prepared by Nicolas Etienne Framery and Guingené). The use of the diagonal stroke for lowering a note one half-step is especially noteworthy (5̸ instead of ♭5 for the diminished fifth, 7̸ instead of ♭7 for the lowered seventh). Sorge also used it (see also Sorge's account of the Telemann bow, 5̂, for the diminished fifth).[32] Today, as is well known, the stroke is applied only in the sense of raising, in which sense it is found, for example, in Heinichen's *Der Generalbass in der Composition* (1728), p. 112, in Johann Gottfried Walther's *Musikalisches Lexicon* (1732), David Keller's *Treulicher Unterricht im General-Bass* (1734), and others.[33] Apparently, Corelli introduced this extremely convenient symbol toward the end of the seventeenth century; it then came into general use through Bach and Handel. Its wide usage was already confirmed by Rameau in his *Dissertation sur les différentes méthodes de l'accompagnement* (1732) page 3:

> While the 2, 4, and 6 are generally stroked [⧸, ⧸, ⧸] for raising these notes in place of the sharp, the 5, on the contrary, is stroked to lower it in place of the flat. So many of our composers are of little accord in their treatment of the symbols, that while some stroke the 7 to replace the flat (!) others contradictorally do so to replace the sharp.

A superfluous stroke, such as a ⧸ over a d♭ in C major to clarify the augmented sixth reflects an unnecessary theoretical involvement. Of course, in a modern harmonic theory (after adequate agreement) it would not be called into question, but it does not belong to a thoroughbass intended for performance.

These and similar deviations from the basic principles of the thoroughbass, treated inconsistently by the various composers, gave Rameau the incentive to attempt to replace the thoroughbass with a new chordal notation that indicates the position of the harmony in the key.

APPENDIX

Footnote 1: "Is primo commentus est facilem canendi methodum ut nimirum supra UT RE MI FA SOL LA duae aliae nimirum SI UT superadderentur, quem cantandi modum non pauci probavere et ego in ea arte illo aliquando magistro sum usus. Idem quoque novorum appetens quam hic vides canendi formam adinvenit ut loco UT RE MI FA SOL LA reponeretur BO NI MA LO GA DI CE BO."

Footnote 3: "J'ajoute donc seulement que la méthode de chanter sans muances par le moyen de la 7e syllabe (BI, CI, DI, NI, SI, BA ou ZA), laquelle a ce semble été invent ou mise en pratique par plusieurs en mesme temps, a esté pratiquée in France par le sieur Gilles Granjan Maistre Escrivain dans la ville de Sens, dont la methode consistait seulement à prendre toujours UT en C solfaut."

Footnote 7: (Page 39): "S'averta che in vece della sillaba UT i moderni si servono di questa DO per essere più risonante." Gioseppe Frezza (*Il Cantore ecclesiastico* [1698], p. 12): "UT fu da Moderni cangiata in DO, forse per esser tra le vocali più sonora l'O che l'U (alcuni però non DO ma DU pronunciano, accioche che tutte le vocali abbian la sua nota)."

Footnote 9: (Peri, *Euridice* [1600], Preface, "Ai lettori"): "Prima ch'io voi porga benigni lettori queste Musiche mie ho stimato convenirsi farvi noto quello che m'ha indotto a ritrovare questa nouva maniera di canto, poiche di tutte le operazione umane la ragione debbe essere principio e fonte, e chi non puo renderla agevolmente dà a credere, d'aver operato a case. Benche del Sig. Emilio Del Cavaliere prima che da ogni altro ch'io sappia can maravigliosa invenzione si fusse fatta udire la nostra Musica su la Scena."

FOOTNOTE 11: "L'autore a chi legge. Queste Ecclesiastiche Sinfonie overo Canzoni alla Francese volendole sonare con tutte quatro le parti sopra l'istromento di tasto, si possono spartire et intavolare che reusciranno comode. Ma volendole concertare con voci et istromenti avertare l'organista favorirle sonando il Basso seguente senza alcuna alterazione ma con gravita et sodezza."

FOOTNOTE 15: (*Organo Suonarino*, p. 3): "Avertimenti alle guide del basso nell'organo. Volendo che quest'Organo Suonarino si renda utile et facile anco alli principianti Organisti e anco a quelli che hanno cognitione a gl'accidenti delle parti di mezo, haveranno per sicuro avertimento che gl'accidenti del ♭ molle et ♯ saranno collocati in tre positioni: 1° Quando sono avanti la nota, nell'istesso lougo servono a detta nota. 2° Quando sono una Terza avanti sopra la nota servono alle Terze et Decime. 3° Quando sono una Terza avanti sotto la nota servono alle Seste et Terzedecime.

FOOTNOTE 27: (Charles Masson, *Nouveau traité des règles pour la composition de la musique* [3rd ed., 1705], p. 9): "Les anciens se servaient du terme de Mode mais la plus grande partie des Modernes ont mis en usage celui de Ton en la place de celui de Mode à cause qui les différentes manières des Chants de l'Eglise s'appellent Tons. Mais enfin de faciliter les moyens de parvenir plus promptement à la Composition, je ne montrerai que deux modes, scavoir le Mode majeur et le Mode mineur: d'antant que ces deux Modes posez quelquefois plus haut et quelquefois plus bas renferment tout ce que l'Antiquité a enseigné et meme les huit Tons que l'en chants dans l'eglise excepte quelques uns qui se trouvent irreguliers. Il ne sera pas difficile de faire la différence du Mode majeur d'avec le mineur parce que le Mode majeur procède par la tierce majeure depuis la note Finale jusqu'a la Médiante. Ces deux modes ont chacun trois notes qu'on appelle cordes ou notes essentielles (*Finale, Mediante, Dominante*). Le mode majeur en general est propre pour des chants de joye et le Mode mineur est propre pour des sujets serieux ou tristes."

(Sebastien de Brossard, *Dictionnaire de Musique,* p. 49): "Cette manière d'etablir et expliquer etait supportable lorsqu'on ne se servait que des Cordes Diatoniques; mais depuis qu'un a pris l'usage de partager l'Octave in 12 demitones chromatiques, on a bientòt rejetté cette distinction des modes Authentiques et Plagaux. On a vu sensiblement qu'un Mode Plagal n'etait point absolument un veritable Mode, que ce n'etait tout an plus qu'une extensions de Mode Authentique et que tout Mode devait être Authentique. . . . Tout mode doit avoir trois Cordes qu'on appelle essentielles. . . . La Médiante enfin est celle qui partageant l'intervalle qui est entre la Dominante et la Finalle en deux tierces en fait aussi ce qu'on appelle la Triade ou le Trio harmonique . . . et comme des douze sons soit Chromatiques ou Diatoniques qui sont dans l'étendue de l'octave il n'y en a point sur lequel on ne puisse faire soit naturellement soit accidentellement une 3e majeure, il y a donc douze Modes majeurs; et comme il n'y a point sur lequel on ne puisse faire de même une 3e mineure, il y a aussi 12 Modes mineurs."

NOTES

1. "He first discovered an easy method of singing, such that above UT RE MI FA SOL LA two other [syllables], SI and UT are added. Many have tested this method of singing, and I myself once studied in this art with this man as my teacher. This same man, seeking for new things, devised the way of singing which you see here, so that in the place of UT RE MI FA SOL LA is substituted BO NI MA LO GA DI CE BO" (descending!).

2. [It is really the seventh book by actual count, but it is designated as the first book in the fourth treatise.]

3. "I add only that the method of singing without mutation by means of the seven syllables (BI, CI, DI, NI, SI, BA, and ZA), which seems to have been invented or put into practice by several people at the same time, was used in France by Gilles Granjan, municipal secretary of the town of Sens, whose method consisted of always placing UT on C."

4. [According to *Groves Dictionary*, 5th ed., s.v. "Solmization," the two letters of *Si* were suggested by the initials of "Sancte Ioannes," the last line of the Adomic verse from which the other solmization syllables were taken by Guido:

Ut queant laxis
*Re*sonare fibris
*Mi*ra gestorum
Fa mulituarum
Sol ve pol lu ti
*La*bii reatum
*Sancte I*oannes]

5. [*Die Musik in Geschichte und Gegenwart*, s.v. "Calvisius," gives the date of 1609 for the first edition and 1611 for the second edition.]

6. Also, see Gerbert's sketches of a history of the origin of mutationless solmization, *De cantu et musica sacra* II: 276–279.

7. (Page 39) "Please note that in place of the syllable UT modern writers use the DO in order to be more resonant." Giuseppe Frezza (*Il Cantore ecclesiastico* [1698]), a second, though somewhat later witness, reports (p. 12): "UT was changed into DO by the more modern composers perhaps because of the O being more sonorous among the vowels than the U. (Some, however, pronounce it DU rather than DO [!] in order that each note will have its own vowel.)"

8. Another work with thoroughbass before 1600 is Francesco Bianciardi's *IV libri di motete a 2, 3, 4 voci con l'organo* (1599 to 1608, according to Giuseppe Baini, *Memorie storico-critiche . .. Palestrina* I: 151). Banchieri reports in Part 7 of *La Cartella musicale* (1613) that Bianciardi is also one of the first to have written a method for playing the figure bass. [*La Cartella musicale* was published in 1610 as the second edition of *Cartella Ouvero Regole . . .* , not 1613, according to the *Riemann Musik-Lexikon*, 12th ed.]

[Riemann assumes that because the word *spartitura* appears in the title of Adriano Banchieri's *Concerti ecclesiastici* they had a figured bass. These works for two choirs, composed in 1595, have a *spartitura* composed of the bass on one stave and the soprano part on a stave above it. However, there are no figures (F. T. Arnold, *The Art of Accompaniment from a Thorough-Bass* [London: Oxford University Press, 1931], p. 7). In these unfigured basses the accompanist probably had to depend upon his ear to guide him, although the *cantus* line would be of great help. Banchieri's *Basso seguente* differs from Viadona's *Basso continuo* in two ways: (1) "It was unbarred, and (2) it was never independent, but always closely followed (hence, *seguente*) one or other of the voice parts." (*Ibid.*, p. 899.)]

9. Whether or not Peri's reference to Cavaliere in the preface to *Euridice* (1600) is of such like meaning is highly questionable. The preface "Ai lettori" begins: "Before laying before you, gracious readers, these my compositions, I have thought it fitting to let you know what led me to seek out this new manner of music, for in all human operations reason should be the principle and source, and he who cannot readily give his reasons affords ground for believing that he has acted as the result of chance.

"Although Signor Emilio del Cavaliere, before any other of whom I know, enabled us with marvelous invention to hear our kind of music upon the stage. . . ." [Strunk, *Source Readings in Music History,* p. 373.] Indeed, from all appearances, Peri is actually giving Cavaliere the honor of priority, but only for his particular type of monody, which is expressly different from that of the inventor of opera. Cavaliere might be considered the inventor of the solo song with figured bass, but the Florentines (Corsi, Peri, Caccini) must be designated the inventors of recitative. This is Baini's opinion (*Memorie storico-critiche* I: 132, n. 215), who had a high opinion of Cavaliere: "I consider Emilio de Cavaliere, a Roman noblemen, to be a great genius and one of the principle innovators of vocal music with instrumental accompaniment." Baini also voices the opinion that the thoroughbass resulted from the need of concealing the errors that arose through improvisatory singing. The *Contrapuntisti alla mente* had not only ventured to improvise a third voice to a two-part composition but were finally improvising a thirteenth voice to a twelve-part work. Since the added voice naturally collided here and there with the others, provisions were made (figured bass) whereby they had at least to some extent a concept of what was going on in the other voices, thereby not having to go about it haphazardly. Baini is responsible for evidence pointing to this type of origin. It may well have been the *Deshanteurs sur le livre* as well as the organ accompanists who influenced the production of such abbreviated scores. Also, Monteverdi distinguished the new style from the old as the "secondo prattica di musica" (1605).

10. [Riemann is right in assuming that the thoroughbass was not invented by any one person, but that the idea gradually developed in the practice of the Italian organists. According to the *Harvard Dictionary of Music,* 2d ed., rev., s.v. "Thoroughbass," it grew out of sixteenth-century improvisation methods. The earliest known description of this type is given by Diego Ortiz (*Tratado de glosas sobre clausulas y otros generos de puntos en la musica de violones* [1553]). In discussing the practice of improvising over a given bass he lists three ways the violone or bass Viol can play with the cembalo: (1) "Both players improvise. (2) A melody is played in an ornate form upon the Viol, while the Cembalo provides an accompaniment (over a given Bass) consisting of chords and also counterpoint suitable to the melody in question. . . . (3) A Madrigal, Motet or other piece for several voices (the examples given are in four parts) is put into 'short score' and played upon the Cembalo, while the Violist makes variations ('divisions') upon one or other of the parts, or even improvises a fifth part. The very significant recommendation is added that if the Violist selects the soprano part as the basis of his 'divisions' this part is best omitted on the Cembalo."] [F. T. Arnold, *The Art of Accompaniment from a Thorough-Bass,* p. 5; citing Ortiz, *Tratado de glosas sobra*

clausulas y otros generos de puntos en la musica de violones (Rome, 1553).] [The earliest known example of a bass separately written for organ (*bassus pro organo*) is a motet by A. Striggio of 1587 (Willi Apel, *Harvard Dictionary of Music*, s.v. "Thoroughbass," p. 746). Giovanni Croce's Motetti of 1594 for two four-part choirs have a *spartitura* (organ part) with both basses written out, one above the other with an occasional sharp and flat to indicate major and minor thirds (Arnold, *Art of Accompaniment from a Thorough-Bass*, p. 7)].

11. "From the author to the reader: If one wishes to play these *Ecclesiastiche Sinfonie* or the *Canzoni alla Francese* with all four parts at the keyboard, they can be divided and scored in an easy way. But if one wants to combine voices and instruments let the organist be aware that he should favor playing the *Basso seguente* without any alteration but with gravity and firmness."

12. Apart from Zarlino's and Salinas's terminology, which maintains a sharp distinction between major and minor (*Divisio harmonio* or *arithmetica*), the oldest authentic term for the triad (both major and minor), *Trias harmonica,* is by Johann Lippius in his three musical *Disputationen* (1609–1610) and in his *Synopsis musicae novae* (1612), p. 16: "In practica observa Triadem harmonicam" (!). The term *accorde perfetto* is found, for example, in the title of G. B. Doni's (died 1647) *In quanti modi si possa praticare l'accordo perfetto nelle Viole* (*Opera Tom. I.* 387). The corresponding French term, *accord parfait* (both major and minor in contrast to the chord of the sixth, designated as the *accord imparfait* [!] e.g., e–g–c, or e♭–g–c), had also been used, according to Rousseau (*Dictionnaire de musique,* s.v. "Accord") before Rameau's *Traité de l'harmonie* (1722). ("These names . . . had been given before any one knew of the fundamental bass.") The statement in Mersenne's *Harmonie universelle* even proves that this term was already commonly used during the first decades of the seventeenth century. (*I. Livre des consonances* [1636 or 1627], p. 213): "The one ordinarily (!) called the *Harmonie parfaite,*" the chord consisting of root, third, and fifth with any note doubled. Heinrich Albert states in the preface to Part II of his *Arien* (1640): "It is taken for granted (!) that all musical harmony, even that of a hundred simultaneously sounding voices, consists of only three sounds." (Mattheson echoes this in his *Das neu eröffnete Orchestre* [1713], p. 109: "And even if there were a hundred or more musicians in concert, all of them together could not bring forth any form of harmony other than these three tones.") Heinrich Albert also states, "Accordingly, wherever there are no figures or symbols, the fifth and third are to be played according to the tones that are naturally found in the piece." He does not use the expression *Dreiklang,* but it has, presumably, been in the German vernacular just as long as the term, *Trias harmonica,* which has been preferred in books since Lippius. Werckmeister simply used the Greek term *Syzygia* instead of *Akkord.* J.D. Heinichen (*Anweisung für den Generalbass,* p. 26 (1711) uses the terms *Akkord* and *Ordinarakkord* for the triad and gives three different positions in which the three primary chords of the thoroughbass can be played by the right hand in close position: 8 5 3 / 3 8 5 / 5 3 8

Incidently, Heinichen's *Anweisung* is especially recommended for those today who wish to make themselves thoroughly acquainted with the practice of figured-bass performance at the beginning of the previous century. The circle of fifths was established for the first time in the *Anweisung* (pp. 261 ff). This, in addition to Mattheson's direct stimulation (*Das neu eröffnete Orchestre*, p. 64), may well have influenced J. S. Bach to demonstrate the usefulness of all transpositions of the major and minor scales through his *Das Wohltemperierte Klavier*. In addition to Heinichen's *Anleitung*, Francesco Gasparini's *L'armonico pratico al cimbalo* (1683, and later editions [the first edition is 1708]) is particularly useful in those cases where the figures of the continuo are defective or incomplete, or even completely missing, as it unfortunately very often happens. Indications (p. 11) such as placing 5 6, 5 6, and so on, over a bass in long notes that continuously ascend stepwise, and (p. 20) placing 5 6 then 7 6, 7 6, and so on, over a bass in long notes continuously descending in stepwise motion, which give a closer look at the older chamber music, are very gratifying. The figures very often in such typical cases are of very little help.

In Gottfried Keller's *Rules for Playing a Thorow-bass* (1707) the English term *common chords* is already familiar ("in common chords which are the 3rd, 5th, 8th") for the comprising designation of third, fifth, and octave. In comparison, William Holder (*A Treatise of the Natural Grounds and Principles of Harmony* [1694]) was distressed for lack of a clear expression for what we call the consonant chord (p. 52, the 1731 edition): "So that the Unison, Third, Fifth and Octave or the Unison, Fourth, Sixth and Octave may be sounded together to make a compleat Close of Harmony: I do not mean a Close to conclude with (!), for the Plagal is not such, but a compleat Close, as it includes all concords within the compass of a Diapason."

13. "Li numeri piccoli posti sopra le note del basso continuato per suonare significano la consonanza o dissonanza di tal numero come il 3. terza, il 4. quarta e cosi di mano in mano. Quando il ♯ dieses e posto avanti overo sotto di un numero tal consonanza sara sostentata (!) et in tal modo il ♭ molle fà il suo effetto proprio. Quando il diesis posto sopra le dette note non e accompagnato con numero sempre significa decima maggiore" etc.

14. "Sopra la parte del Basso il diesis congiunto col 6 dimostra sesta maggiore . . . ed il bimolle della terza o decima minore, e non si ponga mai se non a quella nota sola dov'e segnato quantumque piu ne fussero in una medesima corda."

15. The *Organo Suonarino* (1607) designates (of course, as a private agreement with the reader of the book) that a sharp or flat directly before the note head refers to the bass note itself, but an accidental before the note head, but placed a third higher, refers to the third; a third below and before refers to the sixth (p. 3): "Direc-

tions for performing the organ bass: To make the playing of the organ useful and easy, not only for beginning organists but also for those who have some knowledge of the difficulties of the middle parts, all should be aware of the three positions in which the sharps and flats may be placed: (1) When they precede the note on the same level with it, they apply to the said note. (2) When they precede the note a third above it, they apply to the thirds or tenths above that note. (3) When they precede the note a third below, they apply to the sixths or thirteenths."

Frequently there is found in music printed during the early seventeenth century accidentals behind the note to which they belong. One sees how cautious he must be not to attribute things to authors they did not mean. Ambros makes an egregious blunder (*Geschichte der Musik,* Vol. IV: 437 [1878]) in that he considers the warning flat by the third in the tenor of a cadence by Banchieri to be a sign of depression:

Ambros has very little basis for his stern judgment of Banchieri. [The *Organo Suonarino* spoken of by Riemann here is apparently the second edition (1609) of the treatise *Conclusioni nel suono dell Organo* (1591).]

16. [According to L. U. Abraham (*Der Generalbass im Schaffen des Michael Praetonius und seine Harmonischen Voraussetzungen,* p. 29) such instructions do preface the compositions.]

17. "Il suonar il basso e stato messo in uso: 1° per lo stile moderno di centar recitativo e comporre in questo stile ultimamente trovato, imitando il ragionare con una o poche voci come sono l'arie moderne di alcuni valent'uomini e come al presente s'usa in Roma ne' concerti non e necessario far spartitura o intavolatura ma basta un basso. 2° per comodita e per liberarsi dall'incomodo di sonar d'intavolatura a veder tante parti, cosa incomodissima e molto più venendo occasione di consertar all' improviso. 3° per la quantita e varieta d'opere che si cantano fra l'anno in una sola chiesa di Roma dove si fa professione di consertare, bisognerebbe l'organista aver maggior libreria d'un legale, e perciò a molta ragione si e introdotto simil.basso, tanto più che si suona non deve far sentire le parti come stano mentre si suona per cantarvisi e non per suonar l'opera come sta."

18. For example, the realization of the *basso continuo* in the new edition of Georg Muffat's two collections of Suites (*Florilegium* I and II, in the *Denkmäler der Tonkunst in Oesterreich,* Vols. I, 2, and II, 2) is only a crib for musicians incapable of reading scores. It is not, however, a method on how a possible performance of the continuo might be accomplished. One may well agree with A. Adler's statement (*Monatshefte f. Musikgeschichte* [1898], p. 57) that a cappella compositions should preferably dispense with such "keyboard scores." But then one must, for the very same reasons, protest against the same things for orchestra compositions that use them in the same dilettantish way.

19. [See pp. 17–18.]

20. ["P. 113 ff" is incorrect; it should be p. 91 ff.]

21. [Praetorius is again quoting from Artusi.]

22. 1. "On any note where nothing is mark'd, common Chords are played.

2. "In sixes must be observ'd that when the bass is *low* and requires a natural flat 6th you must play two sixes and one third; if the bass is *high* and requires a natural flat 6th play two thirds and one sixth. If the 3d or 6th happens to be sharp instead of to [*sic*] sixes or two thirds play $\begin{smallmatrix}8\\6,\\3\end{smallmatrix}$ $\begin{smallmatrix}3\\8,\\6\end{smallmatrix}$ $\begin{smallmatrix}6\\3\\8\end{smallmatrix}$

Also in divisions [arpeggios] where a sixth is required, instead of two thirds, or two sixes play the same.

3. "All keys are known to be flat or sharp not by the flats plac'd at the beginning of a Lesson, but by the third above the key, for if your Third is flat the key is flat, if your Third is sharp the key is sharp.

4. "All sharp notes naturally require flat Thirds [*sic*] all flat notes require sharp thirds; the same Rule hold [*sic*] as to Sixes. B, E and A are naturally sharp notes in an open key; F, C and G are naturally flat notes in an open key.

5. "Discords are prepared by Concords and resolved into Concords which are brought in when a part lies still [and are sometimes used in contrary motion].

6. "There are three sorts of *Cadences* or full Closes, as when the Bass falls a 5th or rises a 4th, viz. the *Common Cadence,* the *6th and 4th Cadence* and the *great* or *fullest Cadence* [the examples are incorrect].

7. "There is another Cadence called the *7th and 6th* Cadence, which is counted as a *half Close* and if the 6th is flat is newer [*sic*] used for a final Close, because it does not satisfy the Ear, like as [*sic*] when the Bass falls a 5th or rises a 4th, 'tis often introduced in a piece of Musick as the Air may require; and when it ends any one part of a piece 'tis in order to begin a new Movement or Subject. The 7th and sharp 6th may be used for a final Close if the Design of the Composer requires it but 'tis very rarely done.

8. "Seldom two notes ascend or descend but one of them hath a Sixth.

9. "Now here follows an Example where two sixes are absolute [*sic*] necessary . . . because they are short Cadences instead of 7 6 mark'd."

23. Also, Andreas Werckmeister (1645–1706, organist [!] at Halberstad) (in *Musicae mathematicae Hodegus curiosus* [1687]) discusses specifically, fundamental chords and their inversions (p. 79): "Harmony consists of the union, not of like, but of unlike or diverse elements. As all consonances are of good effect, and please us because of their clearness, we try to arrange them in every possible order. Therefore we may take the Third, the natural position of which is above the ground-tone (this ground-tone, occupying the lowest position, being reckoned as the *root*) and use it instead of the ground-tone, which then appears as a Sixth above it; for if the Fifth or Third is not present in any combination, then the regular series of ordinal numbers has been departed from, and we have, as it were, a borrowed fundamental note." [Matthew Shirlaw, *Theory of Harmony,* p. 9; citing Werckmeister, *Hodegus curiosus,* p. 79.]

24. "To make some Chords easie to your memory you may observe as follows:

a) "A common Chord to any Note makes a $\begin{smallmatrix}8\\6\\3\end{smallmatrix}$ to the 3d above it or 6th below it. A common Chord makes a $\begin{smallmatrix}8\\6\\4\end{smallmatrix}$ to the 5th above it or a 4th below it.

b) "A common Chord makes a $\begin{smallmatrix}7\\5\\3\end{smallmatrix}$ to the 6th above it or a 3d below it. A common chord makes a $\begin{smallmatrix}6\\4\\2\end{smallmatrix}$ to the 7th above it or a 2d below it.

c) "A $\begin{smallmatrix}4\\2\end{smallmatrix}$ marked makes a common Chord to the note above it observing the 5th perfect or imperfect according to the key, as also an $\begin{smallmatrix}8\\6\\3\end{smallmatrix}$ to the 4th above it or 5th below it.

d) "An extream sharp $\begin{smallmatrix}4\\2\end{smallmatrix}$ marked on a flat Note makes sharp [sic] $\begin{smallmatrix}7\\5\\3\end{smallmatrix}$ on the half Note below it as also a sharp $\begin{smallmatrix}8\\6\\3\end{smallmatrix}$ to the sharp 4th above it or flat 5th below it.

e) "The flat 5th and extream flat 7th marked on a sharp Note makes ♭$\begin{smallmatrix}8\\5\\3\end{smallmatrix}$ to the 3d above it or the 6th below it as also a $\begin{smallmatrix}8\\6\\3\end{smallmatrix}$ to the flat 5th above it or sharp 4th below it.

f) "The 4th and ["or" is incorrect] 9th mark'd is the $\begin{smallmatrix}6\\3\end{smallmatrix}$on the whole Note below it and the ♭$\begin{smallmatrix}6\\5\\3\end{smallmatrix}$ on the half Note below it as also the $\begin{smallmatrix}7\\3\end{smallmatrix}$ to the 3d above it or 6th below it.

g) "The 9th and 7th mark'd is the $\begin{smallmatrix}9\\5\\4\end{smallmatrix}$ on the 3d below it and the $\begin{smallmatrix}6\\3\end{smallmatrix}$ to the perfect 4th below it or the 5th above it ad [sic] ♭$\begin{smallmatrix}6\\5\\3\end{smallmatrix}$ on the extream flat ["perfect" is incorrect] 4th below it.

h) "A sharp 7th marked where the Bass lies still makes a $\begin{smallmatrix}8\\6\\3\end{smallmatrix}$ ♯ to the note above it and a 5th 7th [3th ?] and sharp 3d [8th] to the Note below it."

25. ["P. 100" is incorrect. The correct page is 110.]

26. [The *Trias manca* is a chord with a major third and a diminished fifth (i.e., b–d♯–f) above the same root, resulting in a diminished third between the two upper notes.]

27. How quickly the theory of the *Modi moderni* and their transpositions completely replaced the old scales in the public consciousness after they had once been established can be observed in Werckmeister's *Harmonologia musica* (1702) [p. 55]: " I am not condemning those who do not perhaps know the modes (namely, the old modes). I speak only to those who so shamefully despise the theory and who know nothing about it. The earlier musicians have made far too many difficulties, such as those to be seen in Glareano, who wrote a huge volume about the *modis musicis*. Those who, after all, have a preference for antiquity can read those authors. We shall discuss the twelve modes to some extent here because our choral-lieder and now and again other musical works conform to them. In our day two modes are indeed sufficient."

[Page 59]: "But whoever maintains that the old modes are too difficult must at least make use of two modes, such as the *Ionicum* and *Dorium,* to which the Mixolydius and the *Aeolius* have the closest relationship, and be able to furnish harmony for them. Whoever will correctly treat the old choral literature and accurately prepare its *Praeambulum* must necessarily have a correct knowledge of all twelve modes." This is presumably the first attempt to preserve the antiquated church modes from complete destruction.

In other respects, it was a long time before the transpositions of the modern modes also found their correct orthography in theory. While as early as 1702 Werckmeister was correctly writing b sharp and e sharp, L. Mizler in 1739 was still erecting scales according to the ancient customs of the German tablatures, such as (p. 66) C♯, D♯, F (!), F♯, G♯, B♭ (!), c (!), c♯; and D♯ (!), F, G, G♯ (!), B♭, c, d, d♯ (!), and so on. Werckmeister (*Musikalische Temperatur* [2nd ed.], 1691) of course, correctly distinguishes sharp and flat notes. However, he still calls the latter, *moll,* i.e., *e moll*

=e♭, *a moll* = a♭. The note *as* is not our a-flat, but a-sharp (*ais*). But *a dur* is not our a-sharp, but rather, a means the pure major third of f (just as *cis* = the third of a).

The conclusive rule for naming the flats by adding an E♭ to the alphabetical letters apparently can be attributed to J. G. Walther in his *Musikalischen Lexikon* (1732). The article, "Es," [E♭] reads: "It is reasonable that the letter e be designated with a flat in order to distinguish it from the correct function of d♯. The e with two flats can be called e double flat. (!) (See the articles "As," "Ais," "Eis," and so on, which, of course, do not yet normally function according to our present usage.) This is clearly the atmosphere of the art of Bach. Even the problem of naming the double sharps (see the article "Fis durum") and double flats is clarified. First, Sorge (*Vorgemach* [1745], p. 354) and later, Marpurg (translation of d'Alembert's *Systematische Anleitung* [1757]) credit the new terminology to Walther. Heinichen speaks out against certain irregularities of the arrangement of the key signature which were being retained as reminiscences of the church modes (i.e., c minor with only two flats [Dorian], and A major with only two sharps [Mixolydian], and so on). In the greatly enlarged second edition of his *Anweisung,* published under the title *Der Generalbass in der Composition* (1728), it states (p. 150, "Anm"): "For example, no one will deny that in the key of E major the major 7th, d♯, is just as normal and essential as is b-natural in the key of C major. Notwithstanding, in practice this d♯ is seldom placed before the *systema modi*; it generally appears before the note itself, since it appears to be an accidental. . . . Other erroneous key signatures like this are still found in our present-day practice, not only the essential major 7th, and the essential minor 6th (minor mode) but other modes which should have key signatures with ♯, ♮, ♭. . . . We will not discuss here the foreign reliques of the *modorum musicorum*." The organist, Charles Masson (*Nouveau traité des règles pour la composition de la musique* [1st ed., 1694]) was the first among the French to set up the modern keys (p. 9, 3rd ed., 1705): "The ancients used the term *mode,* but most of the moderns are using the term *ton,* [key] in place of mode because the various types of ecclesiastical chants are called *ton.* But in short, in order to facilitate the means of getting more quickly to composition, I will point out only two modes, the major and the minor. Since these two modes lie sometimes high and sometimes low, they comprise all those modes known to antiquity, and even the eight *tons* sung in church, except some which are irregular. It is not difficult to distinguish the major third from the minor, because the major mode proceeds by the major third from the final note up to the mediant. Each of the two modes have three notes which are called the essential tones (tonic, mediant, dominant). The major mode is, in general, appropriate for joyful songs, while the minor mode is more appropriate for serious or sad subjects." The new keys established by Masson are limited to the tones of the basic scale (in addition to B♭) as the *Finalis* with their key signatures.

a) Major modes.

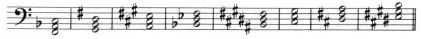

b) Minor modes (all of them have the Dorian key signature, except A minor).

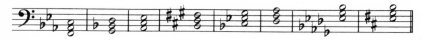

Strange to say, B♭ minor is missing while E♭ minor is listed! The incompleteness (only sixteen instead of twenty-four scales) supports the probability that

Werckmeister was a real pioneer. The first edition of Sebastien de Brossard's *Dictionnaire de musique* (1703) gives the twenty-four modern keys already complete (p. 49): "This manner of setting up and explaining the twelve church modes was tolerable when only the notes of the diatonic scale were used, but since the octave has been divided into twelve chromatic half-steps the distinction of the authentic and plagal modes has been completely rejected. One can sensibly see that the plagal mode was not a true mode at all, that it was nothing more than an extension of the authentic mode, and that all modes had to be authentic. . . . All modes must have three tones that one could say are essential [as in Masson: *Finalle, Dominante, Mediante*]. . . . In short, the mediant is that which divides the interval between the dominant and tonic into two thirds, and also makes what one calls the 'triad,' or the *Trio harmonique* . . . and inasmuch as there are twelve chromatic diatonic tones within the octave there is no note upon which one cannot make naturally or chromatically a major third. Therefore, there are twelve major modes. And as there is no tone upon which one cannot also make a minor third, there are also twelve minor modes." According to Brossard (*ibid.*) the dominant is essentially nothing more than the old *Repercussion* of the church modes (Riemann, *Studien z. Gesch. d. Notenschrift,* p. 87). Moreover, Brossard himself definitely designates the sixth of the plagal mode the *Dominante* (in the second mode, f; in the fourth, c; in the sixth, a; in the eighth, b).

28. ["Chapter XIII" is incorrect; Chapter XII is correct.]

29. [The term *Hauptakkord* as used by Sorge refers to the diatonic triads of the major and minor scales.]

30. The questionable contribution of replacing the numerous individual rules, which for various reasons forbade many interval progressions, with one clearly stated general prohibition of covered fifths and octaves (movement of two voices in similar motion to a perfect octave, or fifth), must be attributed, it seems, to the Nuremberg *Kapellmeister* Johann Andreas Herbst, whose *Musica poetica siva Compendium melopoeticum* (1643), pp. 17–18, explains this rule in the following passage: "Actually, movement from one perfect consonance to another is prohibited, except in contrary motion, because in the leap of a fifth there is created a suspicion of parallel fifths or parallel octaves, which then must be avoided. The following example clearly shows these intervals:

a) Suspected parallel fifths

b) Suspected parallel octaves

The reason why the movement from an imperfect to a perfect consonance without contrary motion is prohibited, even when observing the semitone [according to the old rule in successions 3 > 1,3 < 5, 6 < 8, and so on, one of the two voices must move by half-step; see *Geschichte der Musiktheorie* (2d ed.), p. 385], is that in this progression the same errors appear and suspicion of parallel octaves and fifths is created, just as in the first case, as shown in the following example.

a) Suspected parallel octaves

10   8   10   9 8 8   6   8   6   7 8 8

b) Suspected parallel fifths

3   5   3   4 5 5   6   5   6   5 5

Werckmeister's [1] (*Hodegus curiosus* [1687]) position regarding "covered" fifths and octaves corresponds to that of Herbst. However, he is not yet acquainted with the term *covered* [*verdeckt*] (p. 88): "Our intention is, therefore, to learn briefly, as a music lover, how to avoid the hidden (!) *Vitia* and discolored octaves and fifths . . . (e.g.,

b ⌢ g   or   a' ⌢ d'
g ⌢ c   f ⌢ d).

Although parallel fifths and octaves are not actually present, one knows that Nature moves *gradation* [stepwise] and adds the *sonons in mente* [sounds in the mind] which are concealed in the middle, so that *ad terminum ultimum* [at the end] which aims at *simplicitatem* [for simplicity] the concealed and forbidden progression can be perceived

e ⌒ g as much as e   fg
c ⌒ g   cdefg etc.)."

In conclusion, the notable performance of Lorenz Mizler (*Neu eröffnete musikalische Bibliothek* [1736 ff.] I. 1. p. 20) is included, namely, the exhibition of covered fifths and octaves *a parte post* (!). To prohibit the movement of fifths and octaves in similar motion to any other interval which, for the same reason should be incorrect, would rob the composer entirely of his freedom, if it were taken seriously:

a)   b)   c)   d)

5 3 5 4 5 4 3   8   6   8   8 7 6   5   3   5   5 4 3   5   5 4 3 3

"For at a) g ⌣ b is also a covered fifth, because the space from c to g contains an e,
c ⌣ g
forming a fifth with b" (here, the last remnant of the schoolmaster's threadbare
logic leaves him in the lurch since the reference to the e shows no parallel fifths, as
shown by the numbers written beneath. Mizler would have to demonstrate parallel
fifths as shown at d) [parallel fifths g ⌣ a]. We have the literal translation from
c ⌣ d
Fux's *Gradus ad Parnassum* (1725) to thank for the terms *open* and *covered*.
Regarding the movement:

he remarks (p. 49): "Eo casu duae quintae continenter se sequunter, quarum una ex-
pressa seu aperta altera vero coperta seu abscondita est." ("[In this case one may not
do it] because two fifths follow each other immediately, of which one is apparent or
open, the other, however, concealed or hidden, [and would stand out].") (As an additional curiosity Mizler remarks in his translation of Fux's *Gradus* that often a
diminished fifth is permitted before a perfect fifth, but the inverse progression is
forbidden. It seems that Mizler was completely confused inasmuch as he understood
the second fifth, below to be "the preceeding one"):

31. See page 160. Compare the aforementioned place to Werckmeister's
Harmonologia musica (1702), p. 5: "As soon as a number appears above it, that note
is no longer the root of the harmony. It is a borrowed, or false fundamental."

32. Telemann's *Nouveaux quatuors en six suites à une flûte traversière, un violon,
une basse de viole, ou violoncel et basse continue* (Paris, engraved by Den. Vincent)
for the composer, M. Vater, M. Boivin and Le Clerc. Appearing on the back side of
the title page is an advertisement: "The diminished fifth, 𝄍, here is figured quite
differently. The composer proposes two ways of marking the fifth: (1) the natural
way according to the key signature,

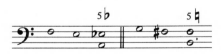

or when the ♭ and ♮ are affecting a modulation;

and (2) by the distinguishing mark of a bow above the figure: 5̑ 5̑♭ 5̑♮. Examples of
the first fifths usually demand the sixth for accompanying, while the others, on the
contrary, demand the octave:

Also, compare the tables in the preface of Telemann's "Musikalisches Lob Gottes" (1744) printed by J. Wolf, *Handbuch der Notationskunde* II: 321. (H. Riemann, *Geschichte der Musiktheorie im IX.–XIX. Jahrhundert,* 2d ed. [1920], pp. 468–469.)

33. [According to F. T. Arnold (*The Art of Accompaniment from a Thorough-Bass,* p. 269), David Kellner's (Keller) *Treulicher Unterricht* was published in 1732, not 1734.]

CHAPTER IX

Musical Logic

*I*F ONE ASKS what the task of a theory of an art consists of, the answer can only be that it must investigate the natural laws which consciously or unconsciously rule the creation of the art and present them in a system of logically coherent rules. Theory in an art still in its infancy is not easy. Moreover, the task grows naturally but enormously with the complexities brought about by the increasing means and magnitudes of conceptions. Since creative power and the disposition for conceptual analysis are seldom found in the same individual, the imagination of the creative artist with his intuitive comprehension of natural laws generally has a very great advantage over theory. For only with great effort can theory push its suspension bridges of prehensible reality forward foot by foot toward the world of the creative arts.

No other art can show a continually progressive development like that found in music. Yet, its most important means of expression (polyphony) evolved only after perhaps thousands of years of long laborious strivings. Because theory was completely new, this would have created strange problems for antiquity. One would think that the basic essence of monodic music, having existed for millenniums, would have been deciphered by the theorists of antiquity, but this was not the case. Both the entire development of polyphonic music from its crudest beginnings to its most sublime conceptions, and a second analysis of harmony appearing in multiple melody were needed in order to disclose completely the theoretical essence of monody. For even the simple one-line melodies as they exist in the preserved monuments of antiquity rest upon a harmonic foundation.[1]

A presentiment of the circumstances was already dawning upon the Greek theorists, as is undoubtedly demonstrated by their scale theories and especially by Aristotle's (or pseudo-Aristotle's) emphasis on the meaning of the *mese* (*Problem* XIX. 20 and 36). Of course, the principle of tonality, or the relationship of the notes of a melody to a fundamental note with respect to which all other notes maintain a definite meaning, has recently been impressively and significantly defined by F. J. Fétis in his *Traité de l'harmonie* (1844), and, according to him, in his lectures on musical esthetics as early as 1832. He was, however, guided by statements of the theorists of antiquity and of the Middle Ages who had alluded to, if not clearly expressed, tonality. Finally, on the threshold of modern times the principle appeared in the foreground when the significance of the unity of the consonant chord was recognized.

In conclusion, Fétis had easy work in his formulation. Basically, Fétis's conclusive contribution was only the word itself, and perhaps a broadening of the meaning of the concept (including modulation). But even this is questionable. The ancients were well acquainted with modulation introduced by a chromatically altered tone. The new tone signified a transposition of the entire system, as is shown by their highly developed transposition scales and the written comments of theorists concerning their connections. In addition, the age of the church modes, which, Fétis says, had known no indispensible modulations from one tonality to another (up to the end of the sixteenth century!!), had from the beginning at least one means of transposition at their disposal (♭ and ♮). Also, it is not yet clearly concluded that progressions such as the transition from the Dorian into the Mixolydian or Phrygian was not an actual change of tonality, i.e., a modulation. The closing section on tones other than the *Finalis* definitely indicated, more often than not, a change of tonality. In Fétis's further contrivances he sees the renunciation of all tonal unity on a large scale as the future ideal of harmonic movement. Indeed, he concocts a graduated scale of tonality which progresses from the *Ordre unitonique* through the *Ordre transitoire* and the *Ordre pluritonique,* to the *Ordre omnitonique*—the latter being a harebrained view of the harmonic chaos of continual enharmonic-chromatic modulation.[2] He thereby expresses himself in a most peculiar way (p. 191) : "In order that one be not mislead, the principles and rules I am going to disclose are entirely new avenues of tonality open to composers. It is the final limits of art from the harmonic aspect." (Also, compare Kirnberger's sensible remarks signifying a very strong defense against Fétis's views [*Kunst des reinen Satzes* I: 132–133]. He discusses enharmonic modulation, transitional dissolutions, and the resulting continuous successions of dissonances "which have been much in use, especially since the time of [Benedetto] Marcello," but which have again more recently digressed.)

As an expression of the gradually arising awareness of the harmonic nature of all types of music there first appeared the concept of the *Finales* and *Sociales* of the church modes, which also formed the main points for cadences at the unison in early polyphony. Then there was the gradual

development of polyphonic cadences in which the so-called harmonic instinct was perceived for the first time. But for an even longer time, the inner
passages of sections separated by cadences do not appear to have been subject to any harmonic rule or principle.[3] After Walter Odington's presentation of the consonant chord concept, and especially since Zarlino's
emphatic antithesis of major and minor harmony, the knowledge that entire groups of chord formations have the same harmonic meaning grew
rapidly. At first this knowledge was obscured through the mechanical
nature of the thoroughbass, which combined wholly heterogeneous tonal
combinations into new categories. On the other hand these mechanical
combinations performed an immeasurable service. Although at first only a
rather vague generalization of the complicated idea of tonal representation
was revealed, the clarification of this idea brought to maturity the real
theory of harmony—the theory of the tonal functions of chords, and with
it the theory of the harmonic significance of melodic tones (tone-
representation). Scales no longer seemed accidental but were necessary successions of tones (Sorge). The principle of cadence formations extended
more and more from the closes of sections into the order of harmonic succession within them and finally developed into a complete theory of the
inherent logic of harmonic succession, a theory of the natural laws of harmonic movement. Sympathetic tones, having come more and more to the
attention of theorists since Descartes, Mersenne, and Athanasius Kircher
(*Musurgia universalis* [1650]), appeared as the first indications of nature.
This is not the limited consonant theory of the ancients which excluded
thirds and sixths. Rather, it concerns much more—the true, expanded
theory based on the *Numerus senarius,* and of course, its twofold application of string lengths (descending series of natural relationships—undertones—minor harmony), and the number of vibrations (ascending
series—overtones—major harmony). In addition further confirmation
came from Joseph Sauveur's method of natural formation of *Klänge*
from the series of harmonic overtones (*Memoires* in the History of the
Royal Academy of Science [1700]), which Jean Philippe Rameau used
as the basis of his harmonic system (*Traité de l'harmonie réduite à ses
principes naturels,* 1722). The final proof was shown by several theorists:
Guiseppe Tartini (*Trattato di musica secondo la vera scienza dell'armonia*
[1754]; the discovery, however, according to his second publication,
De'principi dell'armonia musicale [1767], took place in the year 1714) ;[*4]
Franzose Romieu (*Sitzungsberichte der Ges. der Wissenschaften zu
Montpellier* [1751] [he claims the discovery was made in the year 1743], as
reviewed by Jean-Adam Serre, *Essais sur les principes de l'harmonie*
[1753]) ; and the German, Sorge (*Vorgemach,* p. 12). All three discovered

at approximately the same time and apparently independently the phenomenon of combination tones as a further manifestation of the natural
relationship of tones to one another. And so it seems that the modern
concept of the relationship of tones was developed in a short time,
giving the entirely new theory a special character, so far as it was moving
away from the purely practical figured-bass theory.

Rameau assumed the initiative for the new handling of harmonic
theory—the theory of the meaning of harmony for compositional logic.[5]
He remains famous for this, even though his system can in no way be considered definitive. The main weakness of Rameau's first work, the *Traité de
l'harmonie* (1722), lies in his disregard for the duality of tonal relationships, which had already been proved by Zarlino, Salinas, and others.
Rameau knew Zarlino's writings well and quoted from them repeatedly.
However, in the very first pages of the *Traité* he bluntly sets himself in opposition to Zarlino and attempts with new means to attack the authority of
the "Prince of modern musicians." *[6] He reproaches Zarlino for his inconsistency because Zarlino in one place derives the sixth through the inversion of the third, then in another place by combining the fourth and
third.*[7] He also reproves Zarlino's writings on the handling of dissonance
for being confused and unsupportable.*[8] Above all, however, he troubles
himself over Zarlino's founding of harmonic dualism, which he attacks on
pages 18–20 and to which he later returns several times—presumably with
the uneasy awareness that his own one-sided derivation of the entire harmonic essence from the phenomenon of the overtone series does not give a
satisfactory explanation for minor harmony. He repeats Mersenne's assertions (see p. 191 and n. 12, Chapter X) that the harmonic series as constructed by Zarlino does not correspond to the natural series. Then he attempts to ridicule Zarlino with the remark that instead of being satisfied
with the discovery of the overtone series, he reverses it and overburdens us
with an analogically inverted series.*[9]

We will not continue with Rameau's first attempt to explain the scientific basis of harmonic theory. It is beyond question that Rameau was an
excellent, highly gifted composer, but he was only a mediocre mathematician and physicist, and as a logician was in no way outstanding. As far as
his reasons for limiting the consonant concept to the numerical relationships of 1–6 are concerned, he could do no better than to bring forth a
wordy translation of Descartes's findings, the chief part of which he
misunderstands or omits (Cartesii, *Compendium musicae,* [Frankfurt,
1645], p. 11):[10]

I can again divide the line AB into 4, 5 or 6 parts. Further than that, however,
the division cannot proceed. The ear would not be keen enough to distinguish

greater [*sic,* smaller] differences of pitch without effort (Descartes, *Compendium of Music,* p. 17).

Rameau's *Traité,* page 4, states: "I can again divide the line AB into 4, 5, or 6 parts, but no further, because the ear has not the capacity to hear beyond that." [11] He does not even seem to suspect that the problem of holding the consonant concept to the number 6 had been earnestly pondered by excellent theorists long before his time. Neither does he understand that Descartes had reflected on the smaller differences in pitch resulting through farther divisions of tones in contrast to the tones determined by divisions up to the number 6 (see Salinas's investigations, this study, pp. 110–112).

The manner in which Rameau manipulates the minor triad[12] to coordinate it with the major triad compares poorly with Zarlino's skillful, logical treatment of the antithesis of major and minor, for only the major triad is produced by the first six overtones.*[13] Of course, Rameau later realized this, and he returned to the undertone series as a basis for minor harmony after the manner of Zarlino. Rameau's *Génération harmonique* (1737) has the following honest admission in the preface:[14]

Whatever precautions I might have taken in my other books against common practice and authority, I was not able to prevent myself from subscribing to them in certain cases where my principles were not sufficiently clear to me, as for example, in the rules of the mode in its very origin (!) . . . but being more attentive than before, and more on the alert than ever against my first ideas. . . .

Nevertheless, he consistently refuses to use as a basis for consonance those proportions or progressions which he considers important only to music theory; for, although they coincide with the ratios of the sympathetic tones, they cannot by themselves be regarded as principles. His book brings forward a number of new proposals *(Propositions)* which greatly astonish the physicists and physiologists of today. It seems that the two physicists, de Mairan and de Gamaches, especially the former (p. 3 and other places) have helped Rameau with the explicit wording of these sentences for they are precisely and clearly written in the field of tonal psychology and are not found again earlier or later in Rameau's writings. The following sentences are of special interest (pp. 4–7) :[15]

5th Proposition: Not only does a sonorous body placed in motion transmit its vibrations to the particles of air capable of the same vibrations, but also to all other particles commensurable with the first. These different particles react in their turn upon this body as well as on all those which surround it. They thereby draw different sounds from the different aliquot parts of the first body and in this way produce sounds of higher pitch than those of its tonality. They also disturb all those surrounding which are capable of the same vibrations, and they sometimes also resound (!?).

7th Proposition: The most commensurable sounds are those which convey their vibrations most easily and powerfully. . . . It therefore follows that the effect of the greatest common measure between sonorous bodies which convey their vibrations by the medium of the air must be more powerful than all those of other aliquot parts since this greatest common measure is the most commensurable.

12th Proposition: What one has said of sonorous bodies must equally pertain to the fibers which cover the end of the conch of the ear. We might say these fibers are the sonorous bodies to which the air transmits its vibrations and by which the sensations of sound and harmony are carried to the brain.

These propositions not only refer to the acoustical phenomenon as a higher generality of the tones which show the amalgamation of commensurable vibrations (C. Stumpf), but they also refer to an anlysis of sounds through an apparatus of sympathetic fibers in the narrow end of the cochlea (Corti). There is also a suggestion (p. 17) that the great number and intensity of the beats reveal dissonant intervals and that perfect consonances are recognized by the lack of beats, just as if it had been translated from Helmholtz's *Lehre von der Tonempfindungen*:[16]

Thus, what the sounds are not able to place by themselves upon the ear, the air supplements first by stressing their great discordance through the frequency and rapidity of its beats, then marking their concordance by the cessation of these beats.

In 1749 Rameau presented the academy with a memoir explaining minor chord consonance through sympathetic vibration of strings corresponding to the twelfth and seventeenth below (see the *Extrait des Registres de l'Académie Royale des Sciences,* Vol. X, Dec., 1749, in the appendix of Rameau's *Démonstration du principe de l'harmonie* [1750]). He correctly states that this is nothing new (p. iii: "Moreover, these two experiments were known. See Mersenne and Wallis."). However, since these strings corresponding to the undertones do not vibrate in their tonality but only in segments (strengthening the vibrating fundamental note), Rameau sees only an indication of nature, not a natural basis for the phenomenon. D'Alembert holds the same opinion as Rameau (*Eléments de musique théorique et pratique suivant les principes de Mr. Rameau* [1752]), saying that the minor chord is not so directly given by nature as is the major chord (in Marpurg's translation, p. 16).

However, the significance of Rameau's system does not rest upon these somewhat spasmodic and importunable references to the acoustical phenomenon, but much more on the fact that he attempted above all to create a theory of the meaning of chords for the logic of composition.

The first presentation of the *centre harmonique,* i.e., the unifying point to which all tones of the chord are related and through which are able to preserve their meaning,[17] is an achievement of great significance for theory, even though it was only correctly formulated by him for the major chord. The heart of the theory of the logic of harmonic succession, which has since been developed, lies in the claim that in the perfect cadence from the dominant chord to the tonic "the fifth as it were appears to return to its source."[18] Rameau is well known for the importance of this observation.

One of Rameau's outstanding theoretical accomplishments is his explanation of the deceptive cadence (*Cadence rompue*) : a close that is interrupted by an unexpected note (the sixth above the tonic). In other words, the final chord of the deceptive cadence retains the meaning of the tonic chord, and its third can therefore be doubled any time, since it is actually the fundamental of the tonic chord.[19]

In the *Traité de l'harmonie* (1722) the concepts *Note tonique* (tonic), *Dominante* (fifth of the tonic), *Mediante* (third of the tonic), and *Note sensible* (leading tone) still appear equally important, and the roll of the subdominant is only foreshadowed (except for a *Cadence irregulière* of the six-five chord on the fourth degree).[20] However, in the *Nouveau système de musique théorique* [1726], the three pillars of tonal harmony are established with their names (pp. 60–61 and other pages) :

> *Son principal* (tonic, with its triad)
> *Dominante* (including the natural seventh chord)
> *Sousdominante* (including the six-five chord).

Rameau deserves full credit for the concept and the name of the subdominant chord. Because his joy over the acquistion of this new knowledge is so great, he completely forgets that it is a contradiction of his earlier opinions. He now sees quite clearly that the subdominant with added sixth is no less significant than the dominant with its seventh. Both are equally representative along with the tonic for the tonal logic of the existing harmonic foundation.[21]

As far I know Rameau is also the first writer to state that melody is derived from harmony (*Nouveau système de musique théorique,* preface, p. vi: "La melodie nait de l'harmonie").[22] The major scale consists entirely of only the three primary notes 1, 3, and 9, and their harmonies:[23]

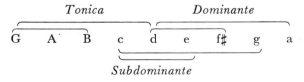

But Rameau knows full well the modulating power of the "characteristic dissonances" (permit me to use this term briefly, which I have introduced for a full analysis of Rameau's statements). The tonic becomes subdominant by adding the sixth to the triad;[24] it becomes dominant with the addition of the minor seventh.[25] Unfortunately, I cannot discuss in detail Rameau's system in its entirety. A whole book would be required for such a presentation. Many separate statements found scattered throughout his numerous works prove that Rameau the musician stands above Rameau the theorist. In a continuous struggle between attempts to stringently carry out his asserted principles and his superior musical instinct, he at times makes statements that must remain for all time as resolute truths. The following observations are examples: the strong beat generally carries the substantial harmonies;[26] harmony that enters on a weak beat and is repeated on the strong beat effects a syncopation;[27] a cadence can never retain dissonance on the final chord without ceasing to be a cadence.[28]

Rameau, unscrupulously and without any reasonable explanation, transferred to the minor mode those chords which unfortunately originate from his principles of the major mode. Therefore, the minor mode also possesses its dominant with seventh and subdominant with sixth (a–c–e tonic, d–f–a–b subdominant, e–g♯–b–d dominant).

According to Mizler (*Anfangsgründe des Generalbasses* [1739], p. 67), the different forms of the ascending and descending minor scale "were first presented by the French." Since neither Brossard nor Masson discuss the subject, it appears that Rameau was the first to present the two forms, for they are clearly shown on page 246 of the *Traité* (1722) :

Rameau observes that "one can never go wrong in following these progressions throughout all the minor keys." The rules for deriving the minor scale from the major scale are very practically conceived:[29] "The ascending minor scale is distinguished from the major only through the minor third; the descending minor, however, relinquishes the leading tone *(Note sensible)* in addition to lowering the sixth scale degree." From the *Nouveau système,* p. 39:[30] "The descending minor scale uses the same notes as the [relative] major scale." Rameau does not attempt to prove the logical necessity of having two forms.

Rameau's incursions into the theory of the meaning of harmonies, as we have seen, lead immediately to the most remarkable and significant results. It is quite understandable that he was not completely successful or satisfied. However, according to his own clarification, Rameau did not primarily view these statements as his most important task. His designs were much greater: to be able to derive the complete essence of harmony from one primary source, namely, the element of successive thirds for chordal construction:

Two thirds of different sizes (one major and one minor) joined together yield the Harmonie parfaite (major or minor). An additional minor third (!) yields the seventh chord, the first dissonance and that which according to whose analogy all others must be understood. All chords which show other relationships than these must be considered as derived and must by inverting their notes be traced back to chords constructed on successive thirds. If three thirds do not suffice, then a fourth, even a fifth should be used, which, however, cannot be placed above, but must be placed beneath (chords by supposition).

This is essentially the system of Rameau the constructive theorist—a system which although not impractical, is, nevertheless, a very plain and dull theory. It was not even really new, for it was implied in the beginning of the figured bass and was gradually developed in the practice of the cembalists (for which I have cited evidence) to the point that the only new thing was an intelligible presentation in the form of a short thesis. But these theories of Rameau found immediate acceptance everywhere, especially because such ideas had been for a long time, so to say, in the air. But the really new theory of the meaning of harmony was understood by only a few. Placing the subdominant beside the dominant was, of course, also regarded as a practical innovation. Yet, the process of introducing names to the individual scale steps continued, so that in C major the d under the mediant e was named *submediante,* and the a above the dominant g was named the *Superdominante* [Rousseau, *Dictionnaire de musique,* 1767]. Now, each scale step had its own name:

c *Tonica (Note tonique, Son principal)*
d *Submediante*
e *Mediante*
f *Subdominante*
g *Dominante*
a *Superdominante*
b *Subsemitonium mode (Note sensible)*

Rameau's impressive presentation of the three pillars of harmony, of course, had to return into obscurity.

Subdominante	— Tonica —	Dominante
(fifth below	I	fifth above)

The only contemporary who comprehended these basic concepts in addition to the stacked-third theory was Friedrich Daube,[31] court musician of the prince of Württemburg. His small, unpretentious book entitled *Generalbass in drey Accorden,* published in 1756, runs against Rameau's designs and conflicts with the newly developed system of successive thirds. Daube's three chords, or, as they are designated in the text, *Hauptakkorde,* are (p. 14):

1. The chord of the key-note, upon which each piece is composed (triad).
2. The chord of the fourth degree (six-five chord).
3. The chord of the fifth degree (seventh chord).

These three chords contain within them all chords found in the figured bass, consonant as well as dissonant. According to my knowledge no one else has up to this time discovered these basic truths, examined them, put them into practical use, and set them forth in a musical science. All earlier publications testify of the knowledge of many chords and figures. . . . A look at the tables of Heinichen [Heinichen], Fux, Mattheson, and others is enough to make one shudder.

But Daube is far from claiming all the credit, as his preface shows on page xiii:

It was absolutely necessary to reduce the overwhelming number of rules in composition. This work has been accomplished, especially by the *Kappelmeister* Fux with his four rules (see pp. 249–252) and Heinichen, Gasparini,*[32] and Rameau (!) through the discovery of the natural progression of tones. It is remarkable that all three of these men hit upon the same ideas, each believing that he had been the first to discover them.

(Indications follow that Heinichen and Mattheson had written in opposition to solmization and the excessive use of counterpoint, and Heinichen had clarified the relationship of tones. He says nothing special concerning Rameau, apparently because his new theory which was exciting the musical world just at that time needed no special attention.)

Daube presents the six-five chord on the fourth degree as a primary chord more clearly than Rameau does and discusses its possible inversions. He is, therefore, as far advanced as Rameau, who was always casting side glances at the seventh chord on the second degree as being fundamental (in order to substantiate his first principle, the stacking of thirds).

All other chordal structures appearing in the harmony of the key are explained by Daube as follows:

(p. 15) By the anticipation (*anticipatio*) or the suspension (*retardatio*) . . . yet, even this, if it were placed in its regular position, could assert its foundation on the three primary chords. . . . This is also true when the chromatic intervals (altered chords) are removed (!!).

(p. 9) (1) If an interval in a chord is changed and another takes its place; (2) by continuous ties frequently found in church works, masses, and other such pieces, in chamber style, and in duets in operatic style.

(Also, in the preface, p. xxi) When one or two notes in the upper voices are tied, the tied part loses its own supporting harmony and takes in its place the harmony of the following tone; or the tied part will then be considered a passing tone. This rule is also applicable to the bass part. If a note remains held, the upper notes can pass on to the next harmony, which really belongs to the following fundamental, or bass note [prepared dissonance].

(3) When the upper voices move, or the bass moves in half notes (that is, of course, in movements twice as slow) ascending or descending [essential passing tones] as is often seen in all three styles (opera, chamber, and church).

In modulating (p. 23) Daube clearly demands a change of meaning of the three primary chords into other harmonies (therefore, a change of function):

As often as the tonality modulates, or the melody passes into another tonality, the three chords of the new tonality must be presented; and those of the preceding are no longer used, unless the melody is to return to that key.

Daube does not differentiate between major and minor keys. In reference to modulation, however, he verifies the following: "For many years there has been the custom that in minor keys the first modulation must be to the third scale degree (relative major), while in major the modulation must first be to the fifth degree (dominant)." He attempts to show the aesthetic reasons for this custom.

It is quite evident that Daube is more consistent than Rameau in accomplishing an entirely new theory of the meaning of harmony, actually succeeding with the use of only a few fundamental principles. With good reason Daube does not discuss Rameau's attempt to establish a definite rule for the fundamental bass progression (i.e., the succession of the basic notes of each chord). Here also, Rameau the "constructive" theorist has played a trick on Rameau the perceptive composer, for the rules of the *Basse fondamentale* have apparently grown out of the unfortunate idea of the stacked thirds. Resulting from a constrained interpretation of Zarlino's statement (cited on p. 259) over the nature of the bass voice (which seems

indeed strange in view of his rude opposition to Zarlino), Rameau deter-
mines that the only permissible steps for the fundamental bass are thirds
and fifths and their inversions (sixths and fourths). Therefore, the progression of a second is excluded from the fundamental bass principle. For
the exceptional cases of the indisputable stepwise bass progression (of the
deceptive cadence) he even goes so far as to take recourse in the allusion
that the second is actually an inverted seventh ($=$ 3 third !!).*33 For the
frequent direct succession of the subdominant to dominant, the first chord
must accommodate the potentiality of a six-five chord (!) which is to be understood as an inversion of a seventh chord (*double emploi*: F 6/5 is a
primary chord [root position] when C follows but is a seventh chord [D7]
when G follows).

In addition to Rameau and d'Alembert, others who base their theories on
the "arithmetic series" first proved by Zarlino are Levens (*Abrégé des
règles de l'harmonie* [1743]), Charles-Henri Blainville (*Essai sur un
troisième mode* [1751]), Baillière de Laisement (*Théorie de la musique*
[1764]), Jamard (*Recherches sur la théorie de la musique* [1769]), and
above all, Tartini. Blainville also recognizes the basic significance of the
pure minor scale which occupied such a prominent position in the monody
of antiquity and the Middle Ages, for it is the exact opposite of the major
scale:*34

c   d   e⌢f   g   a   b⌢c
e   d   c⌢b   a   g   f⌢e

Tartini perceives, as does Rameau, that the scale is composed of the
stepwise succession of the notes of the three harmonies found on the first,
fourth, and fifth degrees. Since he does not accept the *Basse fondamentale*
theory, he sees no reason for not permitting the two dominants to follow
one another in direct succession. (He does not employ their names.) Instead,
he adds to Rameau's *Cadence parfaite* and *Cadence irrégulière* a third kind
of cadence (p. 103) which uses both dominants (mixed cadence):

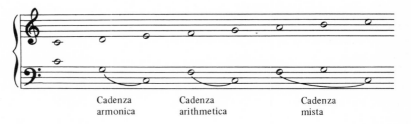

Cadenza   Cadenza   Cadenza
armonica   arithmetica mista

Unfortunately, Tartini does not discuss the minor mode in detail. The following ideas are guilty of being rather irrelevant and of little value to us. They are also of secondary importance and infringe upon the practical value of his work, taking up a large part of the space in his two theoretical treatises, *Trattato di musica secondo la vera scienza dell'armonia* (1745), and *De' principi dell'armonia musicale contenuto nel diatonico genere* [1767]:

1. The demonstration of combination tones.
2. The attempt to introduce the natural seventh as an independent element in music (!).
3. The achievement of an amalgamation of musical and mathematical relationships.

Tartini is convinced that combination tones are a confirmation of the natural relationship of tones first revealed through the overtone series, and he believes that both phenomena are the same (see my *Studien zur Geschichte der Notenschrift*, pp. 96–102). The attempt to introduce the natural seventh, which requires a special accidental in the notation, is especially noteworthy, since the feasibility of comprehending the natural seventh as such should by no means be overlooked (*Trattato*, pp. 127–128):

(Also compare Helmholtz, *Lehre von den Tonempfindungen* [4th edition], p. 555; E. F. F. Chladni, *Akustik*, p. 28; Marpurg, *Versuch über die musikalische Temperatur*, pp. 52 ff; F. W. Opelt, *Allgemeine Theorie der Musik*, p. 20; and others.) Those who attempt to make distinctions between different thirds and fifths in musical practice are not justified in denying distinctions of the seventh determined tone. Rather, they should very earnestly consider the endeavors of Tartini and Kirnberger.[35] A special place should be considered for the natural seventh within the framework of equal temperament, just as there is one for the distinction between the natural and Pythagorean thirds. Interestingly, Tartini supposed that in the distinction of the natural seventh he had found the Greek enharmonic tone (*Trattato*, p. 144):

chromatic   enharmonic

In spite of his discoveries Tartini did not carry on the theory of the meaning of chords established by Rameau. However, he at least avoided some of Rameau's doctrinal errors, especially that of not disputing the possibility of the direct succession of the two dominants. Rameau's, and respectively, the Italians' application of the scale in the sense of the three basic harmonies soon became common property. We also find them in the writings of Christoph Nichelmann,[36] Sorge (see above, p. 166), D. Kellner,[37] Tartini (see above, pp. 196–197), and others. Unfortunately, the simplification of the essence of harmony thereby provided was again obscured and repressed by the continual prepossessive pursuit of the stacked-thirds concept of chordal construction. This concept was readily grasped on all sides, put into use and passed on, thereby bringing into vogue the wholly unfruitful scheme of placing the triad, seventh chord, even the ninth chord, and so on, on every scale degree. This scheme has prevailed from the conventional thoroughbass books to the present time, for only a few have had the intelligence to deviate from it. However, Rameau himself digresses from it in his works (in spite of his obvious inclination toward the principle of added thirds). Thus, in this wildly multiplying forest of identically constructed, uniformly stacked chords the new theory of the meaning of chords was, so to say, nipped in the bud.

It would be difficult to name the person who initiated the disastrous idea of erecting triads on every scale degree, and which were followed by seventh chords, and so forth. I am inclined to believe that Sorge was responsible for it, since the first part of his *Vorgemach* is concerned exclusively with triads and the accompanying practice of inverted chords. The text on page 34 actually identifies the seven triads:

Of these natural diatonic triads (of the major scale) we now find three *Triades perfectas,* three *Triades imperfectas,* and one *Triadem deficientem* which is the seventh:

Tr. perf.   Tr. impf.   Tr. defic.

. . . After the *Final-Chorde* no chord has more right to be heard than the *Chorda dominans.* The remaining five (!) have equalized themselves so that no classifying will be seen. The *Septima modi* will, of course, with its *Triade deficiente* sound rather harsh, but that cannot be helped.

This certainly varies with the better insight into the nature of the scale that Sorge has shown a few pages previously (see p. 166 above). Evidently, from the first appearance of the figured bass the principle of the harmonic identity of chords constructed from the same notes regardless of their octave position [chordal inversion], first expressed in clear simple progressions, had stolen imperceptibly into the consciousness of all thoroughbass practicioners. A theory which in its beginning had set itself in some way or another in contradiction to this obvious simplification of the harmonic apparatus was not allowed to prevail. The degree to which the clever principle of stacked thirds triumphed over all others can be clearly seen in the article "Accord" in the unfinished music dictionary of Framery and Ginguené ([1791], forming one part of the *Encyclopédie méthodique*). Framery states, after reproducing Rousseau's definition of Rameau's *Accord de la Sixth ajoutée* [added sixth chord] : [38]

This chord presented by Rameau and other authors as a fundamental chord has given place to much discussion, even of disputes, and has caused him much embarrassment in order to conciliate it with that of the simple seventh chord on the second degree of the scale, and of which it is only an inversion. He invented the double employment for it, which was held in ridicule for a long time and finally forgotten. Today this chord is no longer regarded as fundamental, at least in practice. It is scarcely ever employed by the better composers except as an inversion of the seventh chord. . . . We mean to say that it (the added sixth) is absolutely useless, and considering that all chords in their direct order are formed by thirds added one above the other, that one cannot become accustomed to regarding as direct a chord whose fourth note forms a second with the third note and a sixth with the sound given as the fundamental.

In view of the unanimous regarding of the six-five chord as a special characteristic harmony of the fourth degree of the scale brought about almost simultaneously by Daube and a number of other authors, it is indeed depressing that such a banal theory of added thirds could so quickly eclipse the better knowledge.

The highly esteemed works of Marpurg and Kirnberger, which would make one forget the merits of Rameau, mean nothing more to the history of music than the reabsorption and standardization of Rameau's ideas which before had digressed from the main line of theory. Kirnberger's *Kunst des reinen Satzes* (1774–1779) really consists of nothing more than Fux's four rules (see above, p. 120) and Rameau's concept of creating chords by adding thirds.[39] In reference to Marpurg's *Handbuch bey dem Generalbasse und der Composition* (1755–1760) a statement by Fétis is hereby rectified. He states in his sketch of the history of music theory from Rameau (*Traité de l'harmonie* [9th edition, 1844], p. 210) : "In Marpurg's system the addition of thirds below the seventh chord, as is found in Rameau's system, disappears. It is replaced by the addition of two or three thirds above the triad."[40] That is an unusual error for this outstanding Belgian scholar who was unrivaled in his extensive reading and excellent judgment about theoretical works. Marpurg holds remarkably steadfast to Rameau's extraordinary idea of increasing the number of successive thirds beyond three through supposition. For example, he defines the ninth chord in the following manner (p. 69) : "The ninth chord is formed when a third is added beneath a seventh chord." He disputes very violently with Sorge "who, out of vain desire to contradict what is new, teaches in error and thus will derive a ninth chord by placing a third over the seventh chord." (Fétis presumably cited from memory and confused Sorge with Marpurg.) The ninth, eleventh, and thirteenth chords are defined by Marpurg much more than by Rameau as the placing of a third, fifth, or seventh underneath (*Handbuch,* p. 29) :

Sorge therefore appears again as the father of the stacked-third scheme. Kirnberger, as was said, fully realized the great significance of Rameau's attempts to trace the entire harmonic apparatus back to a few well-established formulas. On page 5, Part II, of his *Kunst des reinen Satzes* (1774–1776), he produces the notes of the C major scale, placing under them the fundamental notes of the three harmonies—tonic, dominant, and subdominant.

He remarks thereon :

Let it be understood from this that it is possible to compose a bass to every diatonic song in which nothing is used except the triads of the tonic, upper dominant, and lower dominant. This is, therefore, the first and simplest type of harmonic bass. But it is easily seen that in addition to using these three triads the

triads of other notes of the scale can also be used. We will consider this the second type of bass. In a third type of bass, dominant chords may be formed from
such tones so as to effect a modulation from the main key. Finally, it is possible to
construct two, three, and up to four dominant chords one after the other,
resulting in enharmonic modulations to remote keys.

Of course, this is followed by the warning (p. 17 and further) not to
wander too far from the main key, but no indications are given that such
dominants of foreign keys are actually only chromatic transformations of
notes belonging to the scale. Daube is, therefore, far ahead of Kirnberger in
this respect (see above pp. 168–169). Because of Kirnberger's adroit and
penetrating presentation, the rules of composition as Fux had formulated
them became the universal norm for the following period, and free thinkers
such as Daube and Koch (*Versuch einer Anleitung zur Komposition*
[1782–1793] and *Handbuch bey dem Studium der Harmonie* [1811]) remained unnoticed.

Kirnberger's classification of chords (according to *Kunst des reinen
Satzes* I: 33, and *Die wahren Grundsätze zum Gebrauch der Harmonie,*
[1773], p. 5) is:

1. Consonant, namely, the consonant triads which are either major, minor, or
   diminished (!), and their inversions.

2. Dissonant, with an essential dissonance, i.e., the dissonant essential seventh
   chords with major or minor third and perfect or diminished fifth and their
   inversions:

These two classes represent the essential, or two types (?) of fundamental chords. Kirnberger calls all other harmonic formations nonessential.

3. If all possible suspensions were placed on each chord of the two previous
   classes they would all become nonessential dissonant chords.

Therefore, not only are all seventh chords classified equally, but even the
diminished triad is ranked without qualification among the consonances

(p. 38) : "When the diminished fifth appears in the diminished triad, it is consonant and needs no resolution, as the following example proves." [41]

Here again Sorge refers to the consonant diminished triad![42] Marpurg avoids this error (*Handbuch bey dem Generalbasse und der Composition*) by placing two types of dissonant triads, the diminished and augmented, beside the two classes of consonant chords. He even has a clear feeling for the inappropriateness of the note b being doubled in the triad b–d–f (p. 40). In other respects, however, Marpurg's fundamental chords (triads and seventh chords of all types) coincide with those of Kirnberger. The self-evident result of the equalization of all types of triads and seventh chords (and their inversions) was, and had to be, a suppression of ideas which had shown a sharper distinction among those chords. Of course, these ideas did not completely disappear again; nevertheless, there was reason for apprehension over the names *tonic, dominant,* and *subdominant,* which had been established by Rameau (Kirnberger calls them French). By this means the three harmonies from which the scale is derived were distinguished through special names from all the others. They appeared unequivocally as the more important, and it was inevitable that as primary chords, or *Hauptakkorde,* they should be distinguished from the secondary chords. As far as I know the court composer, Heinrich Christoph Koch of Schwarzburg, best known for his excellent *Musikalisches Lexikon* (1802) (reprinted by A. V. Dommer [1865]), is the first to divide the scalewise consonant triads into essential and nonessential chords (*Handbuch bey dem Studium der Harmonie* [1811]). According to the preface, the book is a complete rewrite of the first part of the *Anleitung zur Composition*) :

> (p. 60) In the major mode the three major triads are on the three primary notes of the key, i.e., on the tonic and its fourth and fifth steps (c–e–g, f–a–c, g–b–d). We will call these three triads of the major mode the three essential triads because the scale is derived from them and receives its character from the major thirds of these same triads. Because the three minor triads d–f–a, e–g–b, and a–c–e can be formed from the tones on the second, third, and sixth steps of the scale, we will distinguish them from the former by naming them the three nonessential traids of this mode.

(p. 61) Because the minor mode arises from the minor triads found on the three primary tones (of which the triad on the dominant, in certain . . . cases must be changed into a major triad [!] whereby the scale will contain a leading tone), the three minor triads a–c–e, d–f–a, and e–g–b (or e–g♯–b) are the essential triads in this mode. On the other hand the major triads which fall on the third, minor sixth, and minor seventh degrees (c–e–g, f–a–c, g–b–d) constitute the nonessential triads of this mode.

Koch expressly directs attention to the disssonant notes in all the dissonant chords:

(p. 71) Since in the harmony the dissonant note of a chord is subjected to that process called the preparation and resolution of dissonance, it is necessary that through the acquired knowledge of dissonant chords we direct our attention especially to the dissonant note in order to learn how to distinguish it from the other tones which belong to the chord.*43

(p. 73) It must also be mentioned beforehand that the dissonant interval (the dissonant tone) of a chord cannot be doubled (!) because either its resolution would cause incorrect octaves or the dissonance in one voice would have to make a progression that is contrary to nature.

Koch also clearly recognizes the dual nature of the six-four chord:

(p. 71) The essential six-four chord must always be consonant because it arises from the inversion of a consonant chord. If on the other hand the sixth and fourth appear together in the harmony as suspended tones (!) in such a way as to delay the fifth and third of the chord, they appear as dissonances and as such belong to a special dissonant chord in the same way as the fourth which singly delays the third.

Koch perceives the obvious dissonance of the diminished triad, and he explains this triad as an incomplete form of the dominant seventh chord:

(p. 84) In the diminished triad b–d–f, b is the major third, and d is the perfect fifth of g, for when the two are sounded together nature elicits the note g. It is therefore evident that the note g is the essential and natural fundamental of the triad b–d–f.44

Our investigation clearly proves that the earliest form assumed by the theory of chords met the needs of the accompanists and was postulated by them. Everything written in distinct opposition to this was, in spite of all honorable recognition, soon forgotten and laid *ad acta*. Zarlino's earlier establishment of dual harmony and Rameau's later attempts to break through the stacked-third schematism are isolated cases. But the most fundamental idea of all harmonic theory is that dissonant chords are only transformations of harmonic chords (see p. 316). Even this idea, which was gradually brought to light, was repeatedly obscured by the schematic figured-bass theory and was in danger of again becoming completely lost. Above all, it is quite obvious that the figured bass is to be blamed because of its mechanical enumeration of the intervals without regard to their exact size. For this reason Rameau ventured to break away from the limitations of the harmonic figures which were so unfavorable to theory and to open the way for a more promising chordal figuration. This is explained in his small publication *Dissertation sur les différentes méthodes d'accompagnement* (1732, 2nd edition, 1742). First he criticizes the thoroughbass notation because of its numerous complicated and yet inadequate figures which cause the number of possible chords to appear very great but does not in any way indicate their relationships. The principal reason for this is that bass notes which are wholly incidental are used throughout as the basis for intervallic determination instead of the real fundamental of the harmony.*45

Unfortunately, Rameau's new symbols are also fastened to the bass voice and accomplish no more than a facilitating of the figured-bass performance. It is only a transformation of the figured bass. I shall show a very simple example of it for comparison. The example, found in Rameau's own text, is from the Adagio of Corelli's Sonate, opus 5 no. 3:

Explanation (pp. 22–24) : The capital letters in parentheses indicate the tonality; the remaining letters, after the manner of the fundamental bass, indicate the root of the harmony. The other symbols mean:

2. The triad on the second scale step above tonic (!).
4. The suspension of the fourth into the dominant chord.
aj. The sixth above tonic (!).
* After 4, the resolution of the fourth into the leading tone; otherwise, the leading tone with its harmony.
: (Dots) indicate that the same figure corresponds to the following tones, or the same fingering (pure finger technique).

One look is sufficient to show the inadequacy of this system of symbols. The example shown above is unfortunately very defective. The novelty is Rameau's attempt to reform the figured-bass symbols. What is useful for the further development of the theory of chordal signification is the naming of inversions according to the fundamental tone, for this eliminates the chord of the sixth and the six-four chord, and so on, from the terminology and the figures. Even if the new figures mean nothing more than a direct introduction of the fundamental bass theory into practice as a practical application*46 and not essentially a reiterated innovation, this theory could, by being brought into practice, attain a lasting influence on the manner of instruction and perhaps—which Rameau did not least of all suppose—on composition. Unfortunately, Rameau's new proposals were never put into practice. Rousseau reports (*Dictionnaire de musique,* article "Accompagnement") : 47

However simple the method may be, however favorable it seemed to be for the practice, it did not succeed. Perhaps they believed that Rameau's figures would only correct one defect in order to substitute another. . . . But against so many reasons for preferring it, were not other objections necessary in order to reject Mr. Rameau's method? It was new; it was proposed by a man superior in genius to all his rivals; that was his condemnation!

I do not regard it my task to list and to excerpt from all the theoretical works. We can only concern ourselves with those which have achieved significance for the historical development of the theory of musical composition, whether it be in the positive (furthering) or negative (retarding) sense. Out of the flood of books in part intended for practice and in part dedicated to the speculative investigation of the secrets of artistic creativity which have come forth during the past century, only a very few more can be taken into consideration.[48] Even such an excellent and thorough work as Padre G. B. Martini's *Esemplare o sia saggio fondamentale practico di contrappunto* (1774–1775) can only be mentioned as a commentary on the rules of counterpoint which had been established for over a century, or even two centuries. The ten rules with which Martini prefaces his collection of contrapuntal examples from the sixteenth century (!) differ from those of Franchinus Gaffurius only in the addition of the absolute prohibition of hidden octaves and fifths (p. xxiii) :[49] "The movement in similar motion from any consonance to a perfect consonance is prohibited." Martini, like Fux, transmitted these achievements of the seventeenth century from Andreas Herbst (see this study, p. 180, n. 30). Of course, he refers to Angelo Berardi (*Il perché musicale* [1693]), but the wording ("there arises suspicion of two octaves and of two fifths")[50] points directly to Herbst. Like Fux, Martini retains the church modes as a basis. He belongs mainly to that reactionary group in the field of music theory who assumes that composition reached its highest point in the Palestrina style and who sees a definite decline in the flourishing of instrumental music. This viewpoint is still represented in our time by E. Grell and his pupils. The best known of these is Heinrich Bellermann, who once more has published a text adhering to the old contrapuntal theory (1862; 2nd edition, 1877). Works of this kind seldom have to do with harmony. It would be foolish to seek in them advancements in the knowledge of the natural laws of tonal relationships. The contrapuntal theory of these late successors of Zarlino is completely at sea regarding the development of the logic of the harmonic movement, which attained its highest perfection in the works of the German classicists, especially Sebastian Bach, the unexcelled, unrivalled master. However, they do convey the teachings of those such as Rameau, Daube, and Koch, who renounce all of the blindly credulous imitations of old rules and who do not merely convey the solution of a few fundamental facts. Kirnberger, of course, could not resist the attempt to accept the challenge of a superior musician and undertook an analysis of the B minor Fugue of *Das Wohltemperierte Klavier*. His threefold attempt to explain the harmonic content of this profound and phenomenal achievement through the meaningless figures of the thoroughbass (*Die wahren Grundsätze zum Gebrauch der Harmonie* p. 55 ff.) is sad evidence of the position of harmonic analysis twenty-three years after Bach's death. No master understood so clearly as Bach the simple fundamentals of three functions of tonal harmony, the key to which was given by Rameau. But instead of reducing the many and varied ornamentations and embellishments to these basic fundamentals, Kirnberger serves us a thick, solid harmonic mass and supposes that by means of an abbreviated notation of the figured bass he has presented an intelligent explanation. Of course, Rameau himself could perhaps have written a fugue almost equal to those of Bach, as well as give a penetrating explanation of it. But in order to understand completely the complications of these artistic entwinements more effective work of the type first undertaken by Rameau is required. Even today we should not be so bold as to assume that the problem has been solved.

We have observed that Rameau's ideas for a reform of the chord symbols were frustrated because of the failure of his contemporaries to understand them (or because of their one-sided enthusiasm for his other assertions). They were, however, taken up more successfully by Gottfried Weber (*Versuch einer geordneten Theorie der Tonsetzkunst* [1817–1821]), distinguished musician and state procurator of the grand duke of Hesse. The reasons for his success was not that his symbols facilitated the accompaniment from a figured bass as did Rameau's, for in the meantime the thoroughbass had become entirely antiquated. The reasons are theoretical and pedagogical. His symbols for the seven fundamental harmonies (?!) are shown below (2nd edition, p. 124) :

1. A capital letter designates the major triad: C = c–e–g.
2. A small letter designates the minor triad: c = c–e♭–g.
3. A small letter with ° designates the diminished triad: °c = c–e♭–g♭.
4. A 7 beside the capital letter denotes a major triad with minor seventh: C7 = c–e–g–b♭.
5. A 7 beside a small letter denotes a minor triad with minor seventh: c7 = c–e♭–g–b♭.
6. A 7 beside a small letter with ° denotes a diminished triad with minor seventh: °c7 = c–e♭–g♭–b♭.
7. A stroked 7 by a capital letter means a major triad with major seventh: C7̸ = c–e–g–b.

NB. These symbols are of equal validity for any position of these chords.

In contrast to Rameau's proposals for new chord symbols, the most remarkable advancement is the distinction between the major and minor triad. This would be necessary because the symbols are no longer determined, as they were in Rameau's case, by a bass voice with accidentals written above it. Rather, the independent formulation of chords is supplied without the necessity of a given bass voice. In other respects Weber's new symbols are based on Rameau's scheme of added thirds and remain more adherent to it than Rameau's do (!). All seven of Weber's fundamental harmonies are constructed on thirds. Weber considers all other possible chord formations as arising accidentally through passing tones, chromatic alterations, syncopations, and so on. But the diminished triad remains a fundamental chord in Weber's system as a strange vestige of the traditional view. Weber himself realizes this (I: 250):

Many musical teachers also call the diminished triad dissonant. . . . If this is admitted, the definition must be altered thus: every tone is dissonant except the fundamental, its third (major or minor), and perfect fifth.

How far Weber has progressed from merely determining the intervals of chords to a theory of the meaning of chords is shown in detailed statements, such as Volume I, page 243, where he stresses that chords may have more than one meaning:

1. May be considered a °b as well as G7, the latter in first inversion with omitted root (!).

2. Either °b7 or G7 with omitted root and added major ninth.

3. May be either Bb7 or Bb with the note a considered a passing tone, or g7 in first inversion with the note a as a passing tone to g.

4. The fundamental harmony is either °e7 with an arbitrarily raised third, or an E7, with lowered fifth.

It is strange and unfortunate that with Weber's strong musical sensitivity and clear intellect he did not adhere to Rameau's explanation of the 6/5 on the fourth step of the major scale and the third placed beneath the triad on the fourth step of the minor scale: *51

a)   b)

At a) the note d and at b) the note b are dissonant additions to the triads. Of course, one should not forget that between Rameau and Weber the schematism of stacked thirds was developed to the most absurd consequence through Abt Vogler, and more especially his student, Justin Heinrich Knecht (*Elementarwerk der Harmonie* [1792–1798]). This caused a complete reversal of Rameau's attempt to simplify the harmonic apparatus, and an unpenetrable mass of all possible chords was artificially created. The genuine classical monument of this theoretical aberration is the "continued enumeration of chords" found in the appendix to Part II of Knecht's *Elementarwerk* (2nd edition, pp. 248–262). There are 3,600 chords from musical practice listed, e.g., 132 seventh chords as original chords, which are specified as:

12 minor pleasing seventh chords of the fifth degree of the major and minor scales.
12 minor less-pleasing seventh chords of the seventh degree of the major scale.
12 minor defective seventh chords of the second degree of the minor scale.
12 diminished sad-sounding seventh chords of the raised seventh degree of the major scale.
12 minor rather displeasing (!) seventh chords of the second degree of the major scale.
12 minor very unpleasant (!) seventh chords of the third and sixth degrees of the major scale.
12 major extremely bad sounding (!) seventh chords of the first and fourth degrees of the major scale.
12 minor harsh-sounding seventh chords of the fifth degree of the major scale.
12 doubly diminished seventh chords of the raised fourth degree of the minor scale.
12 harsh diminished seventh chords of the second degree of the minor scale.
12 major very harsh-sounding seventh chords of the third degree of the minor scale.

In addition to these the following chords are also circumstantially specified:

72 ninth chords as original chords.
84 ninth-seventh chords as original chords.
72 eleventh chords as original chords.
72 eleventh-ninth chords as original chords.
24 eleventh-seventh chords as original chords.
60 eleventh-ninth-seventh chords as original chords.
36 thirteenth chords as original chords.
60 thirteenth-eleventh chords as original chords.
36 thirteenth-seventh chords as original chords.

36 thirteenth-eleventh-seventh chords as original chords.
36 thirteenth-eleventh-ninth-seventh chords as original chords.

All these with their inversions are called original chords (!), each with its exquisite title as e.g., the twelve "minor-major-minor-sad-sounding eleventh-ninth-seventh-six-five chord" [no. 118, table 75, fig. 2 at a]!!!

Only after one has seen this shocking abuse of the added third and inversion schematism will he completely understand the merits of such works as those of Koch and Weber. (Knecht's *Elementarwerk* attained great esteem.)

Weber's innovation was quickly accepted. Even before the completion of the work, i.e., before the publication of Parts III and IV, Johann Gottlob Werner (*Versuch einer kurzen und deutlichen Darstellung der Harmonielehre* [1818]) and Friedrich Schneider (*Elementarbuch der Harmonie und Tonsetzkunst* [1820]) eagerly made use of Weber's simplified terminology, and Schneider immediately accepted Weber's new chordal notation. Weber was the first to designate chords with Roman numerals (large for major and small for minor chords) and to indicate tonality with alphabetical letters in anteposition (which change with modulation). These designations, now found in harmony texts in all countries, were first established in this form by Weber for chordal analysis in Part II of his work, and not by Schneider. Although this innovation is not perhaps sufficient for all situations, I must point out that it did initiate a creative means of harmonic analysis for future development (II: 38):

We will hereafter make use of a method of designating all the various harmonies of a key that is still more general . . . and is not like that limited to a particular key, but is applicable to every key; that is to say, instead of employing the German letters we will use the Roman numerals to denote the degrees of the scale on which chords have their fundamental tones; and in the place of the large letters, we will use small numerals, and we will mark these numerals with the characters 7, $\mathcal{7}$, and °, just as we did the German letters.

(p. 41) We can, however, unite the advantages of both modes of designation, by prefixing a large or small Italic letter to the Roman numeral, as an index of the key, by which means everything becomes perfectly definite. Thus, e.g., the designation C: IV $\mathcal{7}$ would carry the following definite meaning: the large fourfold chord on the fourth degree of the large [major] scale of C, consequently the harmony F $\mathcal{7}$ as IV$\mathcal{7}$ of C = large.[52]

Weber expressly states (II: 60, and other places) that he has hereby created a means of indicating the double meaning of chords. By denoting the shift of meaning away from that which chords have in one tonality to that which they hold in another, the essence of modulation is clearly set forth, for example:

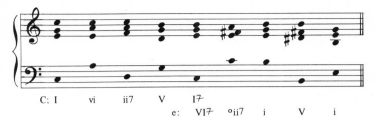

C: I   vi   ii7   V   I7̶

                            e: VI7̶   °ii7   i   V   i

Nevertheless, Weber's new system of chordal designation is incomplete from the position of the thoroughbass insofar as it generally denotes only the "fundamental chords." This, of course, could have easily been remedied by the application of the numbers 2, 4, 6, 9, and so on, as well as the stroked 5, or the 5 with a flat, to designate passing tones, alterations, suspensions, and others. Apparently, Weber's intention was to designate only "essential" formations, while all "nonessential" formations were to be characterized by the lack of markings. This is unobjectionable as long as these chord symbols, not being further developed, are used only for analytical purposes, but they are not adequate as figures in lessons for students.

The augmented triad, intentionally omitted by Weber because he did not consider it to be an essential harmony, had, nevertheless, grown into a highly valued chord in the thoroughbass system. Therefore, Ernst Friedrich Richter (*Lehrbuch der Harmonie* [1853]) added to Weber's labels an apostrophe (or a cross) to the capital letter to mark the augmented triad:

$$C' \text{ or } C+ = c\text{–}e\text{–}g^{\sharp}$$

He thereby created the possibility of figures for two more types of seventh chords:

$$C'7̶ = c\text{–}e\text{–}g^{\sharp}\text{–}b^{\flat}$$
$$C'7 = c\text{–}e\text{–}g^{\sharp}\text{–}b$$

Weber also discusses the diminished seventh chord and designates it an incomplete minor ninth chord (with omittted root). By adding °7 to denote the diminished seventh it could also be designated

$$°C° 7 = c\text{–}e^{\flat}\text{–}g^{\flat}\text{–}b^{\flat\flat}$$

(called by Weber an A♭7, ignoring the added ninth), but the different possibilities are now exhausted.

The development and universal employment of Weber's chordal notation was prevented by its obvious inner inconsistencies. It was already an
inconsistency to place the diminished triad alongside the major and minor
triads as a third kind of original chord from which other formations could
be derived. Yet, the text recognizes the essential nature of the chord.
(Doubtlessly, the dimminished triad on the second degree of the minor
scale, that Weber found so undefinable and irregular in meaning, prevented him once and for all from designating it an incomplete dominant
seventh chord. He could have learned the correct explanation from
Rameau's works.)

Further progress beyond the initial distinction between primary and
secondary chords, which had taken place since Rameau, was first made
possible through the clarification of the theory of *Klang*-representation—
the harmonic meaning of the single tone. The consequential complete
distinction between the primary and secondary harmonies was possible
only after it was realized that a feigning consonant chord[53] could have
a dissonant harmonic meaning, i.e., when it does not function as the
chord it seemingly represents. The first presentation of a feigning consonance is probably C. H. Koch's explanation, given above (p. 203), of
the six-four chord as a double suspension. Proof was found by Moritz
Hauptmann (*Die Natur der Harmonik und der Metrik*, p. 45), not through
musical logic and aesthetics, but rather on the basis of acoustical tonal ratios, that the feigning minor triad on the second degree of the major scale
has too small a fifth:

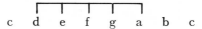

It must therefore be regarded as a type of diminished triad[54] whose consonance cannot be acknowledged (the ratio of the fifth of the dominant, d,
to the third of the subdominant [a] is 27:40, or 54:80 instead of 54:81
[= 2:3]).

Helmholtz's one-sided derivation of tonal relationships in which
Klänge are formed only from overtones (in his *Lehre von den
Tonempfindungen* [1863]) is obviously the weak point of the Helmholtz
system because it cannot show the minor triad to be a perfect consonance.
However, it reveals for the first time a feasible and correct way of interpreting the minor chord under certain circumstances, which should be
of great significance to the further development of the meaning of harmony, although of course, not as Helmholtz would have interpreted it
(4th edition, p. 478) :

In the minor chord c—e♭ + g, the g is a constituent of the compound tones

[*Klänge*] of both c and e♭. Neither e♭ nor c occurs in either of the other two compound tones c, g. Hence it is clear that g at least is a dependent tone. But, on the other hand this minor chord can be regarded either as a compound tone of c with an added e♭ or as a compound tone of e♭ with an added c. Both views are entertained at different times, but the first usually prevails. If we regard the chord as the compound tone of c, we find g for its third partial, while the foreign tone e♭ only occupies the place of the weak fifth partial e. But if we regarded the chord as a compound tone of e♭, although the weak fifth partial g would be properly represented, the stronger third partial, which ought to be b♭ is replaced by the foreign tone c. Hence in modern music we usually find the minor chord c − e♭ + g treated as if its root or fundamental bass were c, so that the chord appears as a somewhat altered and obscured compound tone of c. But the chord also occurs in the position e̅♭ + g − c (or better still as e̅♭ + g − c̅)[55] even in the key of B♭ major, as a substitute for the chord of the subdominant e♭. Rameau then calls it the chord of the great Sixth [in English "added Sixth"], and, more correctly than most modern theoreticians, regards e♭ as its fundamental bass.

When it is important to guide the ear in selecting one or other of these two meanings of the minor chord, the root intended may be emphasized by giving it a low position or by throwing several voices upon it.[56]

This remarkable prediction contains the entire theoretical program of Helmholtz with its many merits and gross defects. The main defect is that Helmholtz did not really produce an explanation for the minor chord. The use of a note deflected nearly a half step instead of one exacted into the consonant chord by nature is an atrocity within a system based on pure tuning and which asserts the inadequacy of our twelve-tone temperament. (The *chroma* 24:25 is, of course, only a little more than a third part of a whole tone 8:9, but, in our tempered music in which one interval is enlarged and another diminished, it amounts to approximately a half tone.) Strange to say, no one has yet noticed that Helmholtz has here been caught in his own snare. Pure tuning (see above, p. 212) has the special advantage of showing more clearly and decidedly than equal temperment the dissimilarities of the tones of the major and minor chords. Consequently, in just intonation the error against nature committed by inserting a foreign tone instead of the natural third must therefore be completely exposed. The whole point and value of just tuning rests on giving the exact sizes of intervals as they should be given. Therefore, a purely tuned minor chord would without any contradiction have to appear as a dissonance. Every musician would raise a protest if this were really true, but it is not.

It was not long, however, before Helmholtz's main error was rectified since only three years later A. von Oettingen's *Harmoniesystem in dualer Entwicklung* (1866) proved that the disturbance of consonance is almost entirely the same for both major and minor.[57] A glance below reveals how the nearest overtones of each of the three notes of the triad collide with the chord tones themselves:

One might be convinced that neither the major nor the minor triad can be considered consonant if he were to question the quality which results when the overtones of one chord constituent is at the interval of a second with those of other chord members. Also, Oettingen especially pointed out that the two strongest derived tones, the common overtone (the phonic overtone) and the main combination tone (the tonic fundamental), have equal positions in the major and minor chords:

However, Oettingen does not entirely free himself from the idea that consonance must be explained and proved through the phenomenon of overtones. He seeks the sign of unity of the minor triad in the union of its elements in the first common overtone ("phonic," i.e., generated from all three):

Oettingen therefore uses a physiological basis to establish a series of harmonic undertones. This is nothing more than a series of tones which have in common the beginning note (prime) as an overtone:

Oettingen thereby gives Hauptmann's explanation of the minor chord, as the antithesis of the major chord, a scientific foundation. However, he points out at the same time that Rameau (or d'Alembert) is really the father of this new interpretation (he did not know that the establishment of the undertone series reaches back even to Zarlino).

Thus, Oettingen maintains both types of unifying relationships—that of overtones having a common fundamental (major) and that of the fundamentals having a common overtone (minor)—as being equal in authority and strength. Yet, he also surprisingly but incontestably states that from the opposite point of view both major and minor chords appear dissonant (p. 45).

The major chord is tonically consonant (in reference to the tone of which all three notes are overtones) and phonically dissonant (in reference to the tone of which all three tones are undertones). The minor chord is phonically consonant and tonically dissonant.

This sentence is the first positive result of the *Klang* dualism imputed to the minor triad through Helmholtz (c–e♭–g = C *Klang* [c–g], and E♭ *Klang* [e♭–g]), and it is the first mention of looking at the major triad from the viewpoint of the minor triad, and the minor triad from the major viewpoint. From him dates the possibility of an exhaustive definition of the so-called secondary triads of the mode (Koch's nonessential triads) in contrast to the primary harmonies tonic, dominant, and subdominant.

Inasmuch as Rameau has pointed out that in the subdominant 6/5 chord and in the dominant seventh chord there is simultaneous representation of both dominants, and Hauptmann has suggested that in the "diminished" triad (b–d–f and d–f–a in C major) both dominants are demonstrable, it has also become quite evident that other chord formations can be considered as simultaneously representing two primary harmonies. Strange to say, Hauptmann did not come to this conclusion. A fate similar to Rameau's befell his system. As Rameau's ideas for musical logic were stifled by the construction of chords by added thirds, so were Hauptmann's by the similar but practical and schematic presentation of the relationship of chords through common tones. This unfortunate idea caused Hauptmann to cast his basic concepts aside and produce a chain of near-related chords (read vertically) :

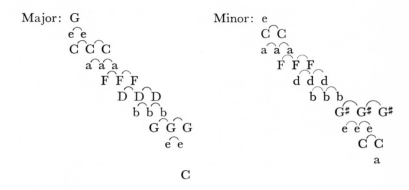

Turn and twist Hauptmann's system as you will, this harmonic series must be deduced as the most perfect and most natural. Hauptmann's fundamental principle states (p. 21) "There are three directly intelligible intervals:

I. The octave
II. The perfect fifth
III. The (major) third

They are unchangeable." But the interval b–f is certainly not a perfect fifth. Nevertheless, the seventh chord G–b–D/F (p. 76) is, according to him, "the sounding together of two triads joined by a common interval" (i.e., two common tones), viz., b–D/F appear therewith in the series of triads! (p. 78) :

> Only those triads having a harmonic unity, i.e., a common interval, can be sounded simultaneously: that is, only two triads which are related in two notes. For the passage into the nearest is the only immediately intelligible progression. The passage from c–e–G to F–a–C which leads to the position C–F–a is a compound one and consists of the progressions C–e–G . . . C–e–a. Both progressions can happen at once.[58]

Here again Hauptmann has digressed far from Koch's nonessential triads and the natural harmonization of the scale by the Italian practitioners (the rule of the octave).

We will not detain ourselves unnecessarily with these new deviations from the true way. Neither should we dwell on those which were incurred through extensions of the theory of *Klang*-representation involving further changes by Helmholtz. We need mention only briefly that Ottokar

Hostinsky in his *Die Lehre von den musikalischen Klängen* (1879) raised the *Klang* duality of the minor chord to a *Klang* triplicity (p. 88) :

While the intervals of the major triad, c–e–g (c–g, c–e, e–g), collectively belong to the tonic C triad and represent it, the minor triad C–e♭–g is composed of three intervals, each of which belongs to a different *Klang*:

c–g from the C *Klang*
e♭–g from the E♭ *Klang*
c–e♭ from the A♭ *Klang*

. . . But in spite of the perfect consonance of the minor chord consisting of three consonant intervals which is not called into question (!!) there is, nevertheless, no uniform meaning of the *Klang*.

This is the end of logic, vanquished by the one-sided establishment of consonance through the phenomenon of overtones.

The incentive for freeing music theory from its dependence on acoustics came from Oettingen (*Harmoniesystem,* p. 42). He believed that "a deeper psychological significance must be recognized for the principle of the relationship of *Klänge* on the basis of pure overtones" and, therefore, saw (p. 46) "the principle of the relationship of *Klänge* generalized, not depending upon the actual existence of overtones for their existence." Carl Stumpf (*Tonpsychologie,* 2 vols. [1883, 1890]) went further in this direction by stating that it is possible for chords having ratios of major or minor to amalgamate to the uniform representation of *Klänge* as psychological facts, which cannot be further explained. In the acoustical phenomenon he accepted only those facts concerning the compatibility of vibrations which are necessary to show the ratios of sounding bodies. I must refrain from delving further into his exposition and limit myself to expressing the conviction that this new turning away of music theory from the one-sided reference to the acoustical phenomenon is a great advancement. The transformation of the actually produced tonal combinations into *Klang*-representation is a psychological occurrence which naturally is in closest contact with them—even dependent upon them, but not without limitation. It has long been known that we cannot be forced to understand series of intervals which are produced through pure intonation. But we prefer to hear tempered tuning than illogical tonal successions of pure tuning, in spite of its false temperment. It was with this awareness that the theory of the meaning of chords finally acquired a firm basis and won complete freedom for further development.

We need no longer require that tonal ratios be the basis for consonance. As a further supposition we may assume that single tones sounded simultaneously may be effectively fused into the unified representation of a *Klang*. For not only are tones able to represent a *Klang,* but they actually do according to their connection. Thus, the concept of the feigning consonance appears alongside the concept of consonance.*59 The possibility of hearing a major chord in the minor sense, or a minor chord in the major sense, thereby gains a very high aesthetic significance.60 On the whole, however, instead of the simple substantiality of intervals, many different meanings of the tonal complex appear (a fourth can be heard as a third [in 4–3 suspensions] and a fifth as a sixth [with suspension of the fifth] and so forth).

Since my dissertation ("Ueber das musikalische Hören") was published in 1873, I have dedicated a number of detailed books to the perfection of the theory of the meaning of chords. I shall therefore show in only a few sentences the order this theory must take:

1. We always hear tones as representatives of *Klänge,* i.e., consonant chords, of which there are only two kinds, namely major (over-*Klänge*) and minor (under-*Klänge*).61

2. Chordal progressions (also melodies, since they exhibit the principle of chordal progression in its simplest form) are heard much as one hears the relationship of chords to a main *Klang* (Rameau's *Centre harmonique,* the tonic) against which these chords, being harmonically related, are made intelligible. The two primary harmonies in question are those which were discovered long ago by musicians but were first theoretically established by Rameau. They are the dominant (the closest related *Klang* by an ascending fifth) and the subdominant (the closest related *Klang* by a descending fifth), for with these a purely diatonic melody can be rendered.62

3. It is possible to comprehend two kinds of *Klang*-representation at the same time. However, one *Klang* is always more prominent, and the representation of the other appears as a disturbance of the consonance of the primary *Klang,* as dissonance (not haphazardly, for it is evaluated differently according to the relationship of the second to the primary *Klang*). Such a duality of *Klang*-representation is also comprehensible in such cases where tonal relationships [triads] can be interpreted in the sense of another (third) *Klang.* For example, each of the secondary triads of the key represent simultaneously two of the three primary harmonies, one primary harmony being comprehended as the main content (consonance), the other, the foreign addition (dissonance) (for example, a–c–e in C major is either a dissonant form of the tonic [with sixth instead of the fifth] or a form of the subdominant [with its leading tone substituting for the prime]). In addition to the three primary harmonies, all other

possible and intelligible chord formations originate through such dissonant formations without abandoning the key (viz., without changing the
key center, the tonic).[63]

4. Modulation is nothing more than a new interpretation of the chords
from the meaning they have in the key being left, to that which they hold
in the new key. Therefore, it is, above all, a shifting of the significance of
tonic to a new chord.[64]

These four tenets actually circumscribe the entire extent of harmonic
theory. As far as my own intellectual accomplishments go, I can claim
nothing more than to have organized them in a concise manner and to
have shown that all appearances of the practical nature of harmony can be
explained in them. However, in order to put this newly acquired but effective simplification of theory into practice, the new Rameau-Weber chordal designations must be improved. But this is only the smallest part of
my work, since Oettingen and Otto Tiersch have paved the way for me.
Oettingen restored Weber's method of denoting chords with capital and
small letters, in which much of the thoroughbass theory is still concealed
(large letters for the major, and small letters for the minor third of the
same root). However, he retained only the small letters but added to these
the symbols + and °, which designate the notes as roots of over-*Klänge*
and under-*Klänge* respectively:

$$c+ = \overrightarrow{c\text{--}e\text{--}g} \ (\text{over-}Klang \text{ of C})$$
$$°g = \underleftarrow{c\text{--}e^{\flat}\text{--}g} \ (\text{under-}Klang \text{ of g})$$

The designation of the dissonant additions to the pure harmonies made
the use of numbers like those used in the thoroughbass for the second,
fourth, sixth, seventh, and so on, indispensable. It also seemed desirable
to be able to indicate the position of the third or the fifth in the bass. Thus,
Otto Tiersch's different application of Arabic and Roman numerals for
exhibiting the various meanings of the prime, third, and fifth in major and
minor chords gave me the impulse to apply these two forms of numbers in
a similar way. Hauptmann's antithesis of major and minor is indicated
below (*Die Natur der Harmonik und der Metrik*, pp. 34–35):

I — — — — — — — — II	II — — — — — — — — I
C e G	F a♭ C
I — — — III	III — — — I

Tiersch set up the following (*System und Methode der Harmonielehre*
[1868], p. 79):[65]

	2		II		2			II
C		e	G		c	e♭		G
	3		III			3		III

He marks with a 2 or 3 the note determined downward by the interval of a
fifth or third, respectively, and with a II or III the note determined upward
by the same interval.

I chose the Arabic numerals used in the thoroughbass for the more familiar
and more frequently used intervals, determined upward (major), and for
the intervals newly brought into practice and determined downward
(minor), I used Roman numerals. The two numeral systems are necessary
because of the possibility that the symbols + or ° may be omitted as soon
as any number indicates that the harmony is major or minor. Furthermore, I left out the +, i.e., the major chord can be plainly understood by a
letter without any further additions. As early as my first attempt
(*Musikalische Syntaxis* [1877]), I indicated the omission of the chord root
by means of a stroke. I should like to illustrate by a few examples the
changes in thoroughbass notation through Rameau, Weber, Oettingen,
and myself (instead of the actual note of the thoroughbass I have used the
corresponding Latin capital letter, presuming that the key is C major) :

Thoroughbass	Rameau	Weber	Oettingen	Riemann		
C	c	C	c+	c		
6	c	C	c+	c	more	c
E					precise	3
G_4^6	c	C	c+	c	"	c
						5
G₇	g⁷ (?)	G⁷	...	g⁷		
B_5^6	g⁷	G⁷	...	g⁷	"	g⁷
						3
D_3^6	g⁷	G⁷	...	g⁷	"	g⁷
						3
F₂	g⁷	G⁷	...	g		
					7	
D₇	f aj.	d⁷	...	f⁶ or		aⱽᴵ
C₇	c⁷ (?)	C₇	...	c⁷< or		bⱽᴵᴵ>
G₄ 3	g₄ 3	...	...	$_6^4$ 3		
C	...	...	...	c⁵> or g♯ⱽ>, also		
				e⁶> or eⱽᴵ<		
A	a	a	°e	°e		
B₇	b⁷ (d aj.?)	°b⁷ (g⁷)	...	aⱽᴵᴵ (or g⁹)		
B₇b	b⁷⁹ᵇ (?)	°b°⁷ (g⁷)	...	g⁹> (or ℂᴵˣ<)		
F_2^6	$_6^7$ (?) ₆7	G+⁷	...	g₆⁷<		
$D♯_3^6$	g⁵ᵇ (?)	(oG⁷?)	...	g⁵> (or f ⱽᴵᴵ_ⱽ<)		

I intended to show more precisely the position of the chord in the key and to clarify the essence of modulation in the figures; in short, to make it possible to express in the figures themselves everything that theory has to explain, and thereby to bring Rameau's ideas to a certain conclusion. To accomplish this I was induced to carry out a generalization—to devise a type of designation that would be separate from any particular key and that could be applicable to all keys. It would be similar to that of Weber's but would include all harmonic structures, nonessential as well as essential. In order that this method of designation might have an immediate international acceptance I chose symbols for the primary figures that most nearly correspond to those of the three primary harmonies in general use: [66]

Weber's scale degrees

	Riemann's symbols	Weber's	Riemann's
I	T = Major tonic	i	°T = minor tonic
IV	S = Major Subdominant	iv	°S = minor subdominant
V	D = Major Dominant	v	°D = minor dominant

I have placed the secondary harmonies beside those primary harmonies from which they are derived (!) either as socalled parallel *Klänge* which occur when the sixth instead of the fifth appears in the chord, or as leading-tone-change *Klänge* which arise through the appearance of the leading tone[67] in place of the chord root. The former is designated by a p added to the T, S, or D. The latter was first symbolized by a stroke through the letter with a 2> or II> beside it indicating the leading tone, but this was later changed (English edition of *Vereinfachte Harmonielehre* [1895]) by means of a > or a < through the letter (> indicates the leading tone of the minor root from above;[68] the symbol, <, indicates the leading tone of the major chord root) :

a) Parallel *Klänge*

Weber Riemann

vi Tp = Tonic parallel (in C-major: a–c–e)

ii Sp = Subdominant parallel (in C-major: d–f–a)

iii Dp = Dominant parallel (in C-major: e–g–b)

Weber Riemann

III °Tp = Minor tonic parallel (in a-minor: c–e–g)

VI °Sp = Minor subdominant parallel (in a-minor: f–a–c)

VII °Dp = Minor dominant parallel (in a-minor: g–d–b)[69]

b) Leading-tone-change *Klänge*

iii $\maltese$ = Leading tone of major   VI $\maltese$ = L. of minor tonic
  tonic (in C-major: e–g–b)   (in a-minor: f–a–c)

vi $\maltese$ = L. of subdominant   II $\maltese$ = L. of minor subdominant
  (in C-major: a–c–e)   (in a-minor: b♭–d–f)

vii $\maltese$ = L. of dominant   VII $\maltese$ = L. of minor dominant
  (in C-major: b–d–f$^{\sharp}$)   (in a-minor: g–b–d)[70]

An example will demonstrate how these symbols will clarify the process
of modulation:

By differentiating between the primary harmonies (to which the °S in
major and the D+ in minor also belong) and the feigning consonant secondary harmonies which are derived from them, a clearer formulation for
determining the doubling of chord tones has also become possible. Of
course, by simply adhering to basic principles, doubling of the third is in
general too striking and is therefore to be avoided. The doubling of a
third in a primary harmony is good only when one of the two voices
moves stepwise in contrary motion, but even this is generally not true for
the major dominant (D+) and minor subdominant(°S) in either major or
minor. On the other hand, doubling the third in parallel *Klänge* and
leading-tone-change chords (!) is unobjectional, even in similar motion (!).
From this new viewpoint the disagreeable question of "covered octaves"
is done away with. (I shall pass over additional statements to avoid ex-
tensiveness, especially regarding the doubling of the fifth).

If I do not really think my own works should go unmentioned, it
should not be taken for vanity. For twenty-five years I have worked
diligently to develop the natural laws of harmonic succession. (My
published dissertation carries the title *Musikalische Logik,* and in spite of
some youthful awkwardness it was written with an eye toward this goal.)
I have studied the theorists of all ages as far as they were attainable and
have dug up many pieces of gold, which seemed to me worth the effort of

recoining. I have also received much satisfaction from subsequent ideas which came to me independently, only to find them aforementioned by others (but again forgotten). In such cases it would be foolish to lay great importance on these new assertions which were made without assistance. But I hold as highly significant the proof that ideas which contain a truth continually return until they can no longer be kept down. Therefore, this history, especially the third book, may be regarded as an account of the origin of my ideas on the theory of music. Except for a few unimportant details the many ideas which appear to be new in my book have proved to have a long-established existence. Thus, the position I hold rests on an unshakable foundation.

APPENDIX

FOOTNOTE 4: (Page 36): "Nell anno 1714 giovine di anni 22 incirca scopre fortunatemente sul Violino questo fenomeno in Ancona dove non pochi ricordevoli testimonj sopravvivono ancora. Lo comunica fin de quel tempo senza riserva e mistero ai Professori di Violino. Lo fa regola fondamentale de perfetto accordo per i Giovani della sua scuola nell'anno 1728 incominciata in Padova."

FOOTNOTE 6: (Page 18): ". . . nous devons nous attacher principalement à cet Auteur, qui a servi de modele a sa posterité, auquel on nous renvoye toujours à l'egard de la pratique, qui est encore l'Oracle de quelques Musiciens et que Monsieur de Brossard même appelle le Prince des Musiciens modernes."

FOOTNOTE 7: (Page 14): "Zarlin après avoir remarqué dans ses Dèmonstrations Harmoniques (Rag. 2°. def. X) que les Sixtes sont renversées des Tierces, dit dans ses Institutions qu'elles sont composées d'une Quarte et d'une Tierce, ce qui fait perdre de vue sa premiere propostion."

FOOTNOTE 8: (Page 20): ". . . s'il parle des Dissonances c'est sans aucun fondement et le principe se trouve confondu partout dans ses Démonstrations, dans ses Regles et dans ses Exemples."

FOOTNOTE 9: Zarlin après avoir remarqué que la Musique est subordonée à l'Arithmétique, que l'unité qui est le principe des nombres nous represente le corps sonore, dont on tire la preuve du rapport des sons, et que l'Unisson est le principe des Consonances; Zarlin dis-je, oublie tout cela dans ses Démonstrations et dans ses regles loin d'y suivre le principe qu'il vient de declarer plus il pénètre plus il s'en eloigne, et s'il ne peut s'empescher de nous le laisser appercevoir dans une corde entiere dont il propose la division et qui est ce corps sonore, dont nous venons de parler, il efface cet objet de notre idée par une nouvelle comparaison qu'il fait en particulier de chaque longueur qui resulte de cetter division, en y confondant pour lors la corde entiere, qui bien loin d'y servir de principe devient au contraire dépendante de ce qui en dependait auparavant. . . . sans prevoir que le rapport, que ces nombres ont entr'eux suffit pour nous donner l'intelligence la plus parfaite que l'on puisse souhaiter de l'Harmonie, et qu'il ne s'agit pour en venir à la preueve, que d'attacher une nouvelle idée a ces nombres, en disant que puisque la Musique est subordonée a l'Arithmetique et si la progression Harmonique doit aller en diminuant il n'y a qu'a a'imaginer que les nombres qui marquent la multiplication de l'unite dans l'Arithmetique marquent au contraire dans l'Harmonie la division de cette unite en autant de parties égales qu'ils contiennent d'unités de sorte que tel qui ne s'attache qu'a la proprieté des nombres ne trouve rien ici que de simple et de naturel dans la musique et il en fait la preuve aussi facilement de cette facon que de l'autre: mais pour n'avoir pas volu hazarder cette supposition, Zarlin aime mieux fatiguer nôtre esprit par une seconde operation, ou il renverse non seulement la progression naturelle des nombres mais encore tout ce bel ordre d'Harmonie."

FOOTNOTE 13: (*Traité*, p. 36): "L'accord parfait mineur pourrait etre demontré comme majeur, puisqu' il est composé de même et qu' il donne par son renversement les mêmes accords que le majeur nous a donné, n'y ayant de difference que dans la disposition des tierces dont la quinte est formée, la tierce qui a été majeure d'un côté étant mineure de l'autre ainsi que les sixtes qui en proviennent."

FOOTNOTE 17: (*Traité*, p. 127): "Le principe de l'Harmonie ne subsiste pas seulement dans l'Accord parfait dont se forme celuy de Septième, mais encore plus précisément dans se son grave de ces deux Accords, qui est pour ainsi dire le Centre harmonique auquel tous les autres sous doivent se rapporter. . . . Ce n'est pas assez de s'appercevoir que tous les Accords et leurs differentes proprietez tirent leur origine du Parfait de celuy de la Septieme; il fait remarquer de plus, que toutes le proprietez de ceux cy dependent absolument de ce centre harmonique et de sa progression: les Intervalles dont ils sont composez ne sont tels que par rapport a ce centre."

FOOTNOTE 18: (Page 129): "Lorsque nous entendons une Cadence finale formée de cette progression, ou il semble que la Quinte retourne à sa source en passant à l'un des Sons de l'Octave dont elle est engendrée (car monter de Quarte ou descendre de Quinte s'est icy la meme chose), il n'y a pas de doute qu'on ne soit principalement attaché aux proprietez de cette cadence pour en tirer quelques avantages; en quoy nous sommes d'autant mieux fondé que cette premiere progression de principe suffit seule pour mettre le comble à nos Règles."

FOOTNOTE 19: (Page 63): "Remarquez que lorsque la parti A sert de Basse:

on entend dans les Accords l'Octave de la Tierce preferablement à celle de la Basse, parce que cetter Tierce suppose pour lors le veritable son fondamental, dont la replique ne peut déplaire, au lieu que dans une suite d'Harmonie parfaite l'Octave de la Tierce préferée a celle du son fondamental deviendrait defectueuse. Ce n'est pas a dire qu'on ne puisse mettre icy l'Octave de la Basse au lieu de celle de la Tierce mais il faut etre auparavant bien assuré de ce que l'on fait, parce que cette octave ne peut guere s'y fair entendre sans tomber dans des fautes grossieres."

FOOTNOTE 20: (Page 64): "C'est le propre de la quatrième Note de porter un accord grande-sixte et de celui de la Note tonique de porter le parfait."

(Preceding this): "Cette dissonance que nous ajouterons icy ne sera point-elle contre le Son fondamental? ce sera une Sixte qui est consonante mais qui formera dissonance avec la Quinte de ce Son fondamental; et s'il semble que nous nous contredisons en cette occasion vu que nous avons avancé que la septieme etait la source de toutes les dissonances, l'on verra neonmoins que l'Accord dissonant form' de cette Sixte ajoutée n'est autre que celuy de la grande Sixte renversé de la Septième."

(Supp., p. 3): "Cependant il doit etre regard ici comme Original."

(*Traité*, p. 41): "Addition d'une tierce mineure au dessous de l'Accord parfait mineur":

FOOTNOTE 21: (*Nouveau système*, p. 62): "Nous ne connaissons que la Dominante et la Sousdominante pour Sons fondamenteaux dans la Modualtion d'un Son principal donné, qui d'ailleurs ne peut subsister comme tel qu'avec son harmonie pure et parfaite."

(Preceding this): "Aussi ne voit-on pas icy la Dominante se reunir a l'harmonie de la Sousdominante mais on voit sa Quinte D prendre sa place et la répresenter pour ainsi dire."

FOOTNOTE 22: (*Traité de l'harmonie*, p. 138): "Il semble d'abord que l'Harmonie provienne de la Melodie, en ce que la Melodie que chaque voix produit Harmonie par leur union; mais il a fallu déterminer auparavant une route à chacune des voix, pour qu'elles pussent s'accorder ensemble."

FOOTNOTE 23: (*Nouveau système*, p. 32): "Tout ce systeme n'est composé que des Sons fondamentaux 1. 3. 9. et de leurs Accords."

FOOTNOTE 24: (*Nouveau système*, p. 69): "Le Son C supposé Principal devient sousdominante à G par la Sixte majeure A ajoutée a son accord parfait et cette Sixte A fait pressentir pour lors la Modulation du son principal G."

(*Génération harmonique* [1732], p. 178): "Voulez-vous changer de Mode, passez d'une Tonique à telle autre qu'il vous plaire, soit tout d'un coup par les routes dictées soit en rendent Dominante ou Sousdominante la Tonique que vous quittez, soit enfin Dominante tonique la note ou vous passez apres cette Tonique, n'y aiant pour cet effet qu'a substituer la Tierce majeure à la mineure que cette dernière Note ou vous passez aurait dû naturellement porter dans le Mode que vous quittez."

FOOTNOTE 25: (*Nouveau système*, p. 60): "La Septième n'a plutôt été entendue que nous sentons en nous le desire d'entendre la tierce H du Son principal G. . . . Remarquez ensuite que dans l'Accord de Septiéme la reunion des deux Sons fondamentaux D (Dominante) et C (Sousdominante), qui servent au progrès du Principal

G et qui semblent en effet s'y reunir, pour rendre encore plus sensible la conclusion que chacun d'eux peut announcer en particulier lorsqu'ils passent au Son principal."

FOOTNOTE 26: (*Traité*, p. 134): "L'Harmonie ne se fait sentir ordinairement que dans le premier instant de chaque temps de la meaure, bien que l'on piusse partager quelquefois un temps en deux egaux ou pour lors elle se fait sentir dans le premier instant de chaque moitie de ce temps."

FOOTNOTE 27: (*Nouveau système*, p. 79): "On ne doit jamais faire syncoper l'Harmonie, c'est à dire qu'une Note de la Basse fondamentale dont la valeur n'aura pas commencé dans le premier Temps d'une Mesure ne doit pas etre continuée successivement dans la Mesure suivante, excepté cependant qu'on n'y soit force par la construction du Chant."

FOOTNOTE 28: (*Traité*, p. 117): "Si une Cadence es evitée par l'addition d'une Dissonance à l'Accord parfait qui la termine . . . vu qu'il ne s'y agit plus d'une Cadence."

FOOTNOTE 32: (Rameau, *Dissertation sur les différentes méthodes de l'accompagnement* [1732], p. 8): "C'est effectivement dans cette règle de l'octave que les Accords sont determinez relativement au rang qu'occupent les Notes de la Basse dans un Ton donne."

FOOTNOTE 33: "En effet on n'entend jamais de cadences finales ou de conclusions de chants, que cette progression (de quinte descendante) n'en soit le premier objet . . . et ce que nous disons de la Quinte doit s'entendre aussi de la Quarte (ascendante) qui la represente toujours . . . ensuite pour tenir l'auditeur dans une suspension agréable comme la Quinte est composée de deux tierces l'on peut faire proceder la Basse par une ou plusiers tierces, reservant toutes les cadences à la Quite seule et à la Quarte qui la représente, de sorte que toute la progression de la Basse fondamentale doit être renfermée dans ces consonances. Et si la dissonance nous oblige quelquefois a ne faire monter cette Basse que d'un Ton ou d'un semi-Ton, outre que cela provient d'une licence introduite par la cadence rompue . . . l'on peut remarquer que ce Ton ou ce semi-Ton, en montant et non pas en descendant sont renversez de la Septième qui se fait entendre pour lors entre ces deux sons qui forment ou Ton ou semi-Ton."

FOOTNOTE 34: (J. J. Rousseau, *Dictionnaire de musique* [1782] "Système, p. 308): "On me permettra de remarquer en passant, que l'inverse de deux modes . . . ne se borne pas à l'Accord fondamental qui les constitue mais qu'on peut l'entendre à toute la suite d'un Chant et d'une Harmonie qui notée en sens direct dans le Mode majeur, lorsqu'on renverse le papier et qu'on met des clefs à la fin des lignes devenues le commencement présente à rebours une autre suite de Chant et d'Harmonie en Mode mineur, exactement inverse de la première, ou les Basses deviennent les Dèssus et vice versa. C'est ici la clef de la manière de composer ces doubles Canons . . . M. Serre . . . lequel a très-bien expose dans son livre (*Essais sur les principes de l'harmonie* [1753] cette curiosité harmonique, annonce une Symphonie de cette espèce, composé par M. De Morambert, qui avait du la faire graver: c'était mieux fait assurément que de la faire exécuter. Une composition de cette nature doit être meilleure a présenter aux yeux qu'aux oreilles."

FOOTNOTE 43: (Rameau, *Traité*, p. 97): "Article premier du principe de la dissonance: lequel des deux sons d'un Intervalle doit être pris pour dissonant et pour lequel de ces deux sons la règle de préparer et de sauver la dissonance a été etablie."

(Rameau, *Code de musique pratique*, p. 71): "Déjà non seulement la note sensible et la Sixte majeure ajoutée ne doivent point être preparées, mais encore toute dissonance qui accompagne la note sensible, n'exige nullement cette précaution."

(Page 133): "Si la Dissonance majeure s'engendre de la Tierce majeure naturelle à l'Accord parfait, cela suffit pour nous prouver qu'elle n'exige aucune autre precaution que celle de monter d'un semi-Ton, comme c'est le propre de cette Tierce majeure; de sorte que si l'on n'est point obligé de la préparer, nous pouvons dire que c'est encore en sa faveur que la Dissonance mineure profite du même avantage dans les progressions fixées à la Basse fondamentale."

FOOTNOTE 45: (Page 2): "Quoi-qu'il n'y ait qu'un seul Accord consonant, on l'a cependant toujours distingué en trois: scavoir en Accord parfait ou naturel, en Accord de Sixte, et en Accord de Sixte-Quarte . . . et pour indiquer à l'Accompagnateur lequel de ces Accords il doit pratiquer, on s'est toujours servi de cinq Singes ou Chriffre scavoir d'un 8, d'un 5, d'un 3, d'un 6 et d'un 6/4, outre qu'il est encore decidé que partout où il n'y a point de Chiffres, l'Accord parfait est supposé. Quoi-qu'il n'y ait non plus qu'un seul accord dissonant on l'a cependant toujours distingué en plusieures de sorte qu'à mesure que l'expérience en a fait sentir les différentes Combinaisons et les différens rapports relativement à difféerentes Notes d'une Basse arbitraire on en a fait autant d'Accords différens."

FOOTNOTE 46: (Page 62): "Cette metode qui est directement tirée de la Basse Fondamentale, nous la rend d'une maniere si simple qu'il n'y a pas moyen d l'y meconnaitre."

FOOTNOTE 51: (Rameau, *Génération harmonique* [1732], p. 142): "Mais si l'on y ajoute la Dissonance nécessaire pour en rendre le Mode plus determiné, au lieu d'un (son) on en trouvera trois communs:

ainsi RE comme Dominante recevant la Septième UT, et LA comme Sousdominante recevant la Sixte majeure FA*."

FOOTNOTE 59: (Rameau, *Traité de l'harmonie*, p. 232): "Lorsque l'on ne compose qu'à deux ou à trois parties l'on ne fait entendre souvent que les consonances d'un accord où la dissonance a lieu, de sorte que si l'on n'a pas egard à la progression de la basse et si l'on ne connait pas le Ton dans lequel on est, toutes nos règles deviennent inutiles, . . . puisque ces accords dissonants contiennent toujours au moins deux consonances qui sont la tierce et la quinte . . . de sorte que l'on passe souvent d'un accord dissonant à un autre sans le connaitre."

NOTES

1. [See pp. 39–40.]

2. "Qu'on ne s'y trompe pas, le principe et les formules que je viens de faire connaitre sont la voie d'un monde nouveau de faits de Tonalite ouverte aux artistes: c'est le dernier terme de l'art sous le rapport harmonique."

3. [See pp. 42–43.]

4. (Page 36): "In the year 1714, while a youth of about twenty-two years, he fortunately discovered this phenomenon on the violin in the city of Ancona where a number of witnesses who remember this are still living. From that very time he communicated this fact without any reservation or mystery to all professors of the violin. He made it a *fundamental rule of perfect harmony* for the students in his school which he began in Padua in the year 1728."

5. [See pp. 18–20.]

6. (Page 18): "We should adhere principally to that author who has been a model to his posterity, to whom we always turn in regards to practice, who is still the oracle of some musicians, and who Monsieur de Brossard even calls the 'Prince of modern musicians.' "

7. "Zarlino, after having remarked in his *Dimostrazioni harmoniche* (Rag. 2°. def. X) that sixths are inverted thirds, states in his *Istituzioni* [but this is the earlier work!] that they are comprised of a fourth and a third, having lost sight of his first proposition." (p. 14).

8. "He has no basis for what he says concerning dissonanace, and his principles are scattered throughout his demonstrations, rules, and examples" (p. 20).

9. "Zarlino points out that music is subordinate to arithmetic; that unity, the source of numbers, represents the sounding body; and that the unison is the source of consonance. But he forgets all this in his demonstrations and rules. Far from following his declared principles the deeper he goes the further away he gets from them. Although he cannot prevent this principle from being perceived in the entire chord of which he proposes the division, and which is the sounding body about which we have just spoken, he obliterates this idea by a new comparison he makes from each length which results from this division. The entire string is confused with the division and, far from serving as the source, becomes, on the contrary, dependent on that which apparently would depend on it. . . . He fails to see that the relationship between these numbers is sufficient in order to give us the most perfect understanding possible of harmony. His new ideas cannot be proved by attaching them to numbers or by saying that music is subordinate to arithmetic. He cannot say that since the harmonic progression gradually decreases one has only to imagine that the numbers which mark the multiplication of unity in arithmetic mark to the contrary in harmony the division of this unity into so many equal parts. Thus, it cannot be concluded that the property of numbers can be duplicated in music, for there is nothing so simple and natural in music, and this can be proved just as easily in this manner as in any other. But not wanting to risk this supposition Zarlino prefers to tire our minds with a second process, wherein he not only inverses the natural progression of the numbers, but also the entire beautiful order of harmony as well."

10. "Rursus possum dividere lineam A B in 4or partes vel in 5e vel 6, nec ulterius fit divisio: quia scilicet aurium imbecillitas sine labore majores [*sic,* minores] sonorum differentias no posset distinguiere."

11. "Je puis encore diviser la ligne A B en 4, en 5 ou en 6 parties, pas d'avantage, parce que la capacité des oreilles ne s'etend pas au-de-là."

12. [See this study, p. 9.]

13. Rameau, *Traité*, p. 36: "The minor triad can be demonstrated as major (!), since it is formed in the same way, and since it gives in its inversion the same (?) chords that the major gives us, having as the only difference the disposition of the thirds (!) which together make up the fifth. One of the thirds is major, and the other is minor, which is also true for the sixths." This treatment of the position of the two thirds as being completely irrelevant (see also Rameau, *Nouveau système théorique*, p. 6) spoils the value of referring to the overtone series as the basis for major consonance.

14. "Quelques précautions que j'aie prises dans mes autres livres contre l'usage et l'autorité, je n'ai pû cependant m'empêcher d'y souscrire en certains cas ou mon principe ne m'éclaircissait pas d'assex près, comme dans les bornes du Mode, dans son origine meme . . . mais plus attentif qu'au-paravant et plus en garde que jamais contre mes premières idées. . . ."

15. "Ve propositon. Un corps sonore mis en mouvement communique ses vibrations non seulement aux particules de l'Air capables des mêmes vibrations, mais encore, à toutes les autres particules commensurables aux premières; et ces différentes particules réagissent a leur tour sur ce même Corps aussi bien que sur tous ceux qui l'environment, tirent non seulement différens Sons des différentes parties aliquotes de ce premier Corps et par là lui font rendre des sons plus aigus que celui de sa totalité; mais elles agitent encore tous ceux d'alentour qui sont capables des mêmes vibrations et les font quelquefois meme resonner."

"VIIe proposition. Les sons les plus commensurables sont ceux qui se communiquent leurs vibrations le plus aisément et le plus fortement . . . d'ont il suit, que l'effet de la plus grande commune mensure entre les corps sonores qui se communiquent leurs vibrations par l'entremise de l'air doit l'emporter sur celui de toute autre partie aliquote puisque cette plus grande commune mensure est la plus commensurable."

"XII proposition. Ce qu'on a dit des corps sonores doit s'entendre également des Fibres qui tapissent le fond de la Conque de l'Oreille: ces Fibres sont autant de corps sonores auxquels l'Air transmet ses vibrations et d'ou le sentiment des sons et de l'harmonie est porté jusqu'a l'Ame."

16. "De sorte que ce que les Sons ne peuvent ici par eux-mêmes sur l'Oreille, l'Air y supplée en marquent c'abord leur grande Discordance par la fréquence et la precipitation de ses battements et en marquant ensuite leur Concordnance par la cessation de ces battements."

17. (Rameau, *Traité*, p. 127): "The principle of harmony subsists not only in the perfect triad and the seventh chord which is formed from it, but still more in the lowest sound of these two chords, which is to say, the harmonic center to which all the other sounds must be related. . . . It is not enough to perceive that all of the chords and their different proportions originate in the triad and the chord of the seventh. It must also be noted that the properties of these two chords absolutely depend on the harmonic center and its progression. The intervals constituting them are only those that relate to this harmonic center."

18. (Page 129): "When we hear a final cadence formed by the progression where it appears that the fifth is returning to its source in moving to one of the tones of the

octave from which it is generated (for the ascending fourth or descending fifth amounts to the same thing), there is no doubt that one is struck by the properties of this cadence for several reasons. In this we are further justified because this first progression from the source is alone sufficient in order to satisfy our rules."

19. (Page 63): "Notice that when Part A is used as the bass (namely, the progression from the dominant to the sixth of the tonic which is assigned to the soprano with supposition of the fundamental bass) for the first presentation of the deceptive cadence, one hears in the chords (the final chords in both cases) the octave of the third preferably to that of the bass:

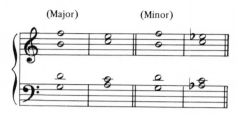

(Major)   (Minor)

This occurs because the third assumes the real fundamental sound, which its replica cannot displease, although, in a succession of triads the octave of the third in preference to the fundamental would become defective. This does not mean that the bass cannot be doubled in lieu of the third, but one must be previously assured of what is going on because the octave can scarcely be heard without falling into the greatest of errors."

20. (Page 64): "The fourth scale step appropriately bears the *grande Sixte* chord, and the tonic bears the triad." Preceding this: "Is not this added dissonance contrary to the fundamental sound? The sixth is consonant, but it is dissonant to the fifth of its root. Now, if it appears that we are contradicting ourselves with the proposition that the seventh chord is the source of all dissonance, it can be shown that the dissonant chord formed by this added sixth is nothing other than the '*grand Sixte*' inverted from the seventh chord." Rameau was not born to be a dogmatist. He was very much taken with his first principle of reducing all harmonic formations to the triad and the seventh chord (pp. 34 and 39). Here, his musical consciousness conflicts with his theoretical authority, and the latter naturally comes off the loser. The revisions in the supplement of Chapter 7, Book 2 of the *Traité,* wherein he declares that, in this case (namely, on the fourth degree of the key) the six-five chord must be regarded as fundamental and not as an inversion, shows how much Rameau was cogitating these new theories (Supp., p. 3): "Still, it must be regarded as original." In a similar manner, dictated by a strong musical sensitivity, but indicating a certain contradiction within the system, there is the explanation of the chord e–g–bb–d in d minor as originating through the addition of a third beneath the minor triad (*Traité,* p. 41: "the addition of a minor third below the minor triad").

This is the complete explanation which consequently aided the breakthough of the principle of major and minor antithesis in harmony.

21. (*Nouveau système*, p. 62): "We recognize only the dominant and sub-dominant as fundamental sounds in the modulation of a given principal sound, which, moreover, cannot subsist as such with its harmony pure and perfect." Preceding this: "Besides, one does not view the dominant joined to the subdominant harmony: but one sees its fifth, D, take its place and represent it, so to say." Here, we have the clearly stated concept of *Klang*-representation.

22. This is expressed in more detail in the *Traité de l'harmonie*, p. 138: "It may seem at first that harmony proceeds from melody since melodies produced by separate voices become harmony through their union. But the route of each of the voices has been previously determined so they can harmonize" and so on. [Also, see this study, p. 19.]

23. (*Nouveau système*, p. 32): "The entire system is comprised only of the fundamental notes 1, 3, 9, and their chords."

24. (*Nouveau système*, p. 69): "The supposed tonic, C, becomes subdominant to G by adding the major sixth, A, to its triad, and this sixth, A, gives the suggestion of a modulation to G." A similar statement is found in the *Génération harmonique* (1732), p. 178: "If you wish to change keys, pass from one tonic to another of your choice either suddenly by one of the described methods, or changing the tonic you are leaving into a dominant or subdominant, or finally, making the note to where you pass after this same tonic a *Dominante tonique* [dominant seventh], of course, substituting the major third for the minor third. This last note upon which you arrive must naturally be found in the key from which you are leaving."

25. (*Nouveau système*, p. 60): "The seventh (C above the triad D–F♯–A) has been understood only when we feel in us the desire of hearing the third (B) of the fundamental, G, . . . Notice then, that in the chord of the seventh the joining of the two fundamental sounds D (dominant) and C (subdominant), which occurs in the progression from the fundamental G, seems to be, in fact, a reunion in order to again make more reasonable the conclusion that each of them can individually declare when they are returning to the fundamental sound" (compare similar statements on p. 89).

26. (*Traité*, p. 134): "Ordinarily, we are conscious of harmony for only the first instance of each beat of the measure. Sometimes, however, the beat can be divided into two equal parts where it can then be felt for the first instance of each half of the beat." (He further indicates that tones can appear in the first instance of harmony which do not belong to the chord itself ["not at all a member of the harmony"], but are only embellishments of it, or figurations ["for good taste in singing"].)

27. (*Nouveau système*, p. 79): "One must never syncopate the harmony. This is to say that the note of the fundamental bass whose value does not begin on the first beat of the measure must not be continued successively into the following measure, unless it is forced to by the construction of the song." (His point in question is not the prohibition; rather, it concerns the stressing of the unusualness of the phenomenon.)

28. (*Traité,,* p. 117): "If a cadence is evaded by the addition of a dissonance to the terminating chord . . . it no longer functions as a cadence." This also applies to the

deceptive cadence already explained by Rameau as the provisional consonant [feigning consonant] form of the closing chord and to a half cadence such as G–D⁷, no longer qualifying as a half cadence because of the 7. Moreover, Rameau does not yet recognize the half cadence of the tonic to dominant.

29. (*Traité*, p. 246): "La progression du Ton mineur n'est différente du majeur en montant que dans la Tierce qui est mineure d'un cote et majeure d l'autre; mais en descendant il faut rendre le ♭ mol a la note Si [in D minor] et oter le Dieze de la Notte sensible Ut."

30. "Les Sons diatoniques de système mineur pris en descendant sont les memes que ceux du système majeur."

31. [See this study, pp. 20–21.]

32. In Gasparini's *L'armonico pratico al cimbalo* one may search in vain for theoretical discussions, which in Daube's opinion is justified. But the practical examples reveal a full consciousness of harmonic clarity. The distinct, perfected harmony of the Corelli epoch is manifest in every group of notes. Certainly, Fétis correctly stated that the *Regula dell'ottava* was gradually developed by the seventeenth-century Italian cembalists. The *Regula dell'ottava* consists of nothing more than harmonizing the scale with the three primary triads. Consider the following (Gasparini, *L'armonico pratico,* p. 55):

Heinichen's bass shows, of course, a much richer formation (triads on all scale degrees, and a mixture of four-part secondary harmonies). It does not emphasize in the same degree the tendency toward a harmonic simplification as found among the Italians. There is, however, a complete tonal clarity, and the unquestionable German inclination toward a fuller harmonic development is apparent, i.e. (*Anweisung* [1711], p. 61):

Compared to Mattheson's basses this is certainly much closer to Italian simplicity. Rameau expressly declares that the *Regle dell'octave* is the first attempt to establish a foothold beyond the individual bass note within the key (*Dissertation sur la différentes méthodes de l'accompagnement* [1732], p. 8): "It is by the effective rule of the octave that chords are determined relative to the series of bass notes in a given key." Rameau feels that Delaire in his *Traité d'accompagnement* (1700) did not at first set up the rule of the octave, but only in a similar sense made the chordal progressions dependent upon the direction of the bass line, only later (ca. 1725) taking it up again after Campion in the meantime had made it famous (*Traité d'accompagnement et de composition selon la règle de l'octaves* [1716]). Fétis, by the way, corrects the date of Delaire's work to 1690.

33. "In fact, one never hears of final cadences or of song closes that do not have this progression (the descending fifth) as its primary goal. . . , and what we are saying of the fifth must also include the fourth (ascending) which always represents it. . . . Then, in order to keep the listener in pleasant suspense, as the fifth comprises two thirds, the bass can proceed by one or several thirds, reserving all the cadences for the fifth alone and the fourth which represents it. Thus, every progression of the fundamental bass must be confined to these consonances. And if the dissonance compels the bass at times to ascend only one step or a half step other than that proceeding from the license introduced by the deceptive cadence . . . it might be observed that this ascending, but not descending (!), step or half step is an inversion of the seventh (!), which is heard then between the two sounds forming the tone or semitone.

34. J. J. Rousseau makes the following remark in his detailed analysis of Tartini's system (*Dictionnaire de musique* [1782], "Système," p. 308): "Permit me to remark in passing that reversing the two modes . . . is not restricted to the fundamental chord constituting them. They can be extended to all successions in a song and of harmony, as seen in a direct sense in the major mode when the paper is turned upside down and when a clef is placed at the end of the lines, making it the beginning. This inversion presents another succession of song and harmony in the minor mode exactly the opposite of the first, or the bass becomes the top and visa versa. This is the key to the way of composing double canons. . . . M. Serre, who has so ably exposed this harmonic curiosity in his book (*Essais sur les principes de l'harmonie* [1753]), mentions a symphony composed in this manner by M. de. Morambert, who was to have had it engraved. This was better than having it performed (!). A composition of this type is more acceptable to the eyes than to the ears." Here is found already the harmonic reflected image of A. von Oettingen (*Harmoniesystem in dualer Entwicklung* [1866]) and a well-aimed criticism of the excessive pursuit of analogies! [The year 1782 is not given in *Musik in Geschichte und Gegenwart* for Rousseau's *Dictionnaire de musique*. The dates and places listed are Geneva, 1767; Paris, 1768; Amsterdam, 1768; and Geneva, 1781.]

35. Kirnberger's idea of giving the name *i* to the tone determined as the natural seventh above c is practically worthless since the insertion of an eighth step into the basic scale is impossible. Tartini's further modification of the accidentals (in which we have a ♭, ♯, ♮, ♭♭, x) is perfectly sufficient and a new name is not necessary.

36. [Christoph Nichelmann], *Die Melodie nach ihrem Wesen sowohl als nach ihren Eigenschaften* [1755], p. 48): "All possible series of simple tones can be resolved again into the natural chord and in the original progressions which spring from it, an indication that they have their origin in this same chord. And if a large part, even the largest part, of the musical construction were reduced to its simplest structure and resolved into the original fundamental progressions, it would hardly consist of more than the continual movement of the tonic to its upper and lower fifth and the return from these progressions to the tonic."

37. [David Kellner], *Treulicher Unterricht im General-Bass* (1732). The author is

not named in the first edition. The preface to the second edition (by G. P. Telemann) names him "Herr Kellner," the title shortening it to D. K. The necessary figures for the ascending and descending major and minor scales are (pp. 30–34):

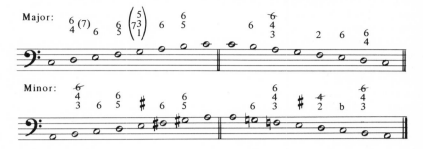

This arrangement is presumably based on the Italian practice. Kellner does not appear to be acquainted with Rameau's works. The idea of erecting a triad on every scale step is foreign to him. As a peculiarity he records that many prefer the triad on the sixth degree in major. Fétis unjustly mentions this work as being unsignificant. It is, of course, a practical work, but was highly esteemed in his time.

38. "Cet accord, que Rameau et d'autres auteurs ont présenté comme un accord fondamental, a donné lieu à beaucoup de discussions, de querelles même et lui a causé beaucoup d'embarras pour le concilier avec celui de la septième simple qui se fait sur la seconde note du ton, et dont il n'est que le renversement; il lui a fait imaginer le double emploi, qu'on a longtemps tourné en ridicule et qu'on a fini par oublier. Aujourd'hui cet accord parait n'être plus admis comme fondamental, au moins dans la pratique; il n'est plus guère employé par les meilleurs auteurs que comme renversement de l'accord de septième. . . . Nous dirons seulement ici qu'elle (la sixte ajoutée) est absolument inutile et qu'en considerant que tous les accords dans leur ordre direct sont formés des tierces ajoutees les unes sur les autres, on peut s'accoutumer a regarder comme direct un accord dont le quatrieme son fait seconde avec le troisieme et sixte avec le son donné pour fondamental."

39. It should be mentioned that Volume II of [Kirnberger] *Kunst des reinen Satzes*, Part I, Section IV, Chapter III, contains a number of appropriate remarks about the construction of periods (sections and divisions) (pp. 137–153), "Vom Rhythmus." Particularly noteworthy is Kirnberger's remark about the possibility of a synchronism of the end and of the new beginning (p. 139, an example from J. S. Bach's D minor Concerto). Also, he does not at all subscribe to the opinion that sections beginning with a full measure must continue on in the same way (p. 149): "If the first division begins with a down-beat, the following can begin with an upbeat. But if the piece begins with an upbeat, the following must also properly begin with an upbeat," and so on. He is also cognizant of other contradictory endings and discusses them critically (p. 150). Just how original are Kirnberger's remarks defining the motive cannot be investigated here, since I have undertaken the study of phrasing elsewhere, as well as earlier in this book. I remember that J. A. P. Schulz's article, "Vortrag," in [Johann Georg] Sulzer's *Allgemaine Theorie der schönen Künste* (1772), is written earlier, and that Schulz generally has a considerable interest in Kirnberger's works (the *Wahren Grundsätze zum Gebrauch der Harmonie* is Schulz's work, according to E. L. Gerber [*Neues Lexikon* IV: 146]). [Part I of

Kirnberger's *Die Kunst des reinen Satzes in der Musik* (1771–1779) was first published in 1771. The year 1774 given by Riemann is the year of the second printing of Part I. Part II was published in three issues from 1776–1779.]

40. "Dans le système de Marpurg l'addition de Tierces au-dessous des accords de septième, qu'on trouve dans celui de Rameau, disparaît; elle est remplacée par des additions de deux on de trois tierces au-dessus des accords parfaits."

41. That this example does not prove it has been made clear to everyone since Fétis has pointed out that in a sequence harmony does not follow its natural and logical progressions. It is, rather, a logical succession of chords that is mechanically imitated stepwise through the scale (*Traité de l'harmonie*, p. 253). This custom, especially the succession of fourths and fifths moving stepwise in the bass, originated in the stepwise series of bass notes figured alike (*Marche de basse, Progression*), so frequent in the earlier thoroughbasses:

Its influence is also easy to trace in Rameau's theory of the normal fundamental bass progression. Even later, Simon Sechter (*Die Grundsätze der musikalischen Komposition* [1853–1854]) sees in the progression of the subdominant triad to the leading-tone diminished triad a normal and typical harmonic movement!

42. [Sorge's name is completely out of context here since the quotation and example are from Kirnberger.]

43. But compare this to Rameau's *Traité*, p. 97: "First Article of the Principle of Dissonance: One of the two tones of an interval must be comprehended as dissonant, and for this tone the rule has been established for preparing and understanding dissonance." Rameau finds the source of all dissonance in the seventh—a tenet whose maintenance forces him into a medley of subterfuges [double emploi and others]. It should be observed that through Rameau an entirely new concept in the theory of dissonance was introduced, namely the independent dissonance, originating neither through syncopation nor through other types of melodic decoration (passing tones, auxiliary tones). Fétis errs in attributing the inception of this concept to Sorge (*Traité de l'harmonie*, p. 218). Of course, Sorge states expressly that in addition to the prepared (syncopated) dissonance and the passing dissonance on the weak beat there is a third type in the new music "which does not appear to be tied, yet must even so be resolved" (p. 337). Times change, and the modern practice sufficiently proves that it is not unnatural to use the seventh freely and without ties, from which are derived a variety of sevenths in composition such as 6/5, 4/3, 4/2, and so on. But Rameau maintains the same views in the *Traité de l'harmonie* (1722) as he does in the *Code de musique pratique,* appearing in 1760. In the latter he remarks (p. 71): "Not only does the leading tone (the 'major dissonance') and the added sixth not have to be prepared, but neither does any dissonance accompanying the leading tone require this precaution." (!) Also, further (p. 133): "If the major dissonance is generated from the natural major third of the triad, this suffices to show that no further precaution is needed other than to have it ascend a half step, as is proper for this major third. Again, we might say that it is favorable for the minor

dissonance (the minor seventh), since it does not at all have to be prepared, to profit from the same advantage in the progressions determined by the figured bass."

44. This explanation goes back to Rameau, whose "*Accords par emprunt*" (*Traité*, pp. 43 and 79 ff.) Likewise have for a fundamental note one not found in the chord.

45. (Page 2): "Although there is only one consonant chord, yet three have always been distinguished: the perfect or natural triad, the chord of the sixth, and the six-four chord . . . and in order to indicate to the accompanist which chord to play, five signs or figures have always been used, to wit: 1, 5, 3, 6, and 6/4, apart from the fact that wheresoever figures are lacking the perfect triad is still assumed. Although there is only one dissonant chord (namely, the seventh chord), nevertheless several types have always been distinguished, so that as soon as experience with them has made musicians aware of the different combinations and connections relating to different notes of an arbitrary bass, as many different chords have been invented."

46. (Page 62): "This method, directly taken from the fundamental bass, is laid out in such a simple manner that no one can fail to recognize it."

47. "Quelque simple que soit cette methode quelque favorable qu'elle paroisse pour la pratique, elle n'a point en du cours; peut-être a-t-on cru que les chiffres de M. Rameau ne corrigeaient un defaut que pour en substituer un autre. . . . Mais contre tant de raisons de préférénce n'a-t-il point fallu d'autres objections encore pour faire rejetter la methode de M. Rameau? Elle était nouvelle, elle était proposée par un homme superieur en genie a tous ses rivaux: viola sa condamnation!"

48. Even the renowned work of the *Kapellmeister* of St. Antonio in Padua, Francesco Antonio Vallotti (*Della scienza teorica e pratica della moderna musica* [1779]), cannot be given any particular consideration because it contributes nothing. The only subjects treated in detail are the calculation of intervals—of course, in the manner of Rameau—and the antithesis of the harmonic and arithmetic series (!). The only thing worthy of mention is the attempt to derive the entire scale from the overtone series of one tone (p. 93). Vallotti quite correctly rejects the values 1/7, 1/11, and 1/13, and all further primaries as *inconcinni* ("because, in fact, they do not belong in our modern music") and uses instead the second order of overtones, i.e., 1/9, 1/15, 1/27, and 1/45:

$$\frac{1}{24} \quad \frac{1}{27} \quad \frac{1}{30} \quad \frac{1}{32} \quad \frac{1}{36} \quad \frac{1}{40} \quad \frac{1}{45} \quad \frac{1}{48}$$

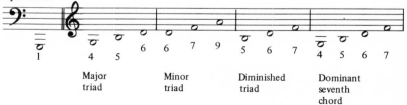

Of course, the root of the series (C) can no longer be understood as tonic. Evidently, he does not have the proper theoretical interest to consider the principle of tonality and the function of harmony. Charles Simon Catel proceeds correctly in his *Traité d'harmonie* (1800), at least when he finds all the essential chords and all the dissonances in the overtones up to the number 17 (!) which can be introduced without preparation:

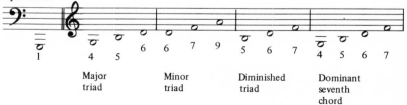

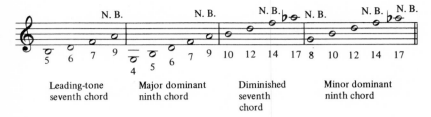

| Leading-tone seventh chord | Major dominant ninth chord | Diminished seventh chord | Minor dominant ninth chord |

See Fétis's rejection of this derivation, *Traité de l'harmonie*, p. 244. [According to *Die Musik in Geschichte und Gegenwart*, Catel's *Traité d'harmonie* appeared in 1802.]

49. "Vien proibito il passagio di qualumque Consonanza ad una Consonanza perfetta per moto retto."

50. "Nasce il sospetto delle due ottave e delle due quinto."

51. I find the expressed antithesis of the dominant seventh chord of the major mode and of the subdominant-six-five chord of the relative minor mode in Rameau's *Génération Harmonique* (1737), p. 142: "But if one adds here the dissonance needed to determine the mode more closely, in lieu of one tone there will be three tones in common:

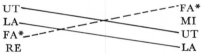

Thus, RE as dominant (in G major) receives the seventh, UT. LA as the subdominant (in E minor) receives the major sixth, FA."

52. Gottfried Weber, *Theory of Musical Composition*, trans. James F. Warner (Boston: O. Ditson & Co., 1851), pp. 288–290.

53. [See this study, pp. 63–67.]

54. If the dissonant triad having as its root the third of the upper dominant, i.e., in C major, b–D/F, can be called a diminished triad, then the same term can be used to designate the triad on the fifth of the upper dominant, D/F–a, since D–a is, according to the foregoing statement, as small a fifth as b–F. Both chords have a dual basis: the under and upper dominants, F and G. Likewise, in the [C] minor mode there are the triads b–D/F, and D/F–a♭.

55. In the first edition Helmholtz had written E♭–g–c [= e♭–g–c] instead of E♭–g–C [e♭–g–c], which was corrected by Oettingen (*Harmoniesystem*, p. 43). The emendations in brackets are taken from Oettingen's corrections.

56. Hermann Helmholtz, *On the Sensations of Tone*, trans. John Alexander Ellis, 6th ed. (New York: Peter Smith, 1948), 294–295.

57. [See this study, pp. 14–17.]

58. Moritz Hauptmann, *The Nature of Harmony and Meter*, p. 57. [Also, see above, pp. 12–14.]

59. It is more than probable that Rameau already understood the concept of the feigning consonant. Unfortunately, he omitted any detailed expressions like those in his meditations on "secondary harmonies." Yet, I find on page 232 of the *Traité de*

l'harmonie the following extraordinary passage: "In a composition for only two or three voices often only the consonances of a chord are heard where the dissonance takes place, so that if one has not looked at the bass progression, and if one does not recognize the key of the piece all of the rules become useless. . . . Since these dissonant chords still contain at least two consonances, the third and the fifth . . . so that in progressions one often passes from one dissonant chord to another without knowing it."

60. [See p. 66.]

61. [See pp. 52–60.]

62. [See pp. 60–63.]

63. [See pp. 63–67.]

64. [See pp. 67–69.]

65. [The Arabian numerals 2 and 3 denote a perfect fifth and major third, respectively, above the given bass. The II and III indicate the perfect fifth and major third, respectively, below the given bass. The symbols shown above can better be explained by an example of each:

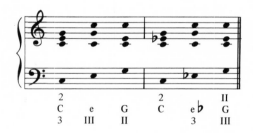

66. These symbols were used in my *Vereinfachten Harmonielehre* (1893).

67. [The term *leading tone* in this case refers to the tone one step below the root of each of the three primary tones.]

68. [Riemann calls the fifth of the minor triad the root because he conceives minor harmony downward. Therefore, its "leading tone" is one step above the root. For example, in the triad a–c–e, e is the root. In the leading-tone-change chord the root e is replaced by its leading tone f.]

69. [This chord is misspelled; it should read g–b–d.]

70. [This example is incorrect. It should read:

Weber's Riemann's

III   ♮ = L. of minor dominant

(in a-minor: c–e–g).]

Bibliography

Abraham, Lars Ulrich. *Der Generalbass in Schaffen des Michael Praetorius und seine Harmonischen Voraussetzungen.* Berlin: Merseberger, 1961.

Achtelik, Joseph. *Der Naturklang als Wurzel allen Harmonien; Eine ästhetische Musiktheorie.* Leipzig: C. F. Kahnt, 1922.

Agazzari, Agostino. "Discorso del sonare sopra il basso con tutti li stromenti." In *Sacrarum cantionum.* Vol. 2, Opus 5. Venice, 1608.

Aichinger, Gregor. *Cantiones ecclesiasticae 3 et 4 voc. cum basso generali et continuo ad usum organistarum.* Dillingen, 1607.

Albert, Heinrich. *Ander Theil der Arien oder Melodeien etlicher Theils geistlicher, Theils weltlicher, zu gutten Sitten und Lust dienender Lieder.* . . . Konigsberg, 1640.

d'Alembert, Jean le Rond. *Eléments de musique théorique et pratique suivant les principes de M. Rameau.* Paris, 1752. Reprint. New York: Broude Brothers, 1966.

Ambros, August Wilhelm. *Geschichte der Musik* 4 vols. Breslau and Leipzig, 1862–1878.

Apel, Willi. *Harvard Dictionary of Music.* 2d ed., rev. Cambridge, Mass.: Harvard University Press, Belknap Press, 1969.

――――. *Accidenten und Tonalität in den Musikdenkmälern des 15. und 16. Jahrhunderts.* 2d ed. Baden-Baden: Valentin Körner, 1972.

Arnold, Frank Thomas. *The Art of Accompaniment from a Thorough-Bass as Practiced in the XVIIth and XVIIIth Centuries.* London: Oxford University Press, 1931.

Artusi, Giovanni Maria. *L'Arte del contrapunto ridotta intavola.* 2 vols. Venice, 1586–1589. Reprint of 1598 edition. Hildesheim: Georg Olms, 1967.

――――. *L'Artusi overo delle imperfettioni della moderna musica.* 2 vols. Venice, 1600–1603.

Baillière de Laisement, Charles-Louis-Denis. *Théorie de la musique par M. Baillière.* Paris, 1764.

Baini, Giuseppe. *Memorie storico-critiche della vita e delle opere di Giovanni Pierluigi da Palestrina.* 2 vols. Rome, 1828.

Baker's Biographical Dictionary of Music and Musicians. Edited by Nicolas Slonimsky. 5th ed., rev. New York: G. Schirmer, 1958.

Banchieri, Adriano. *Concerti ecclesiastici a 8 voci.* Venice, 1595.

240   RIEMANN'S HISTORY OF HARMONIC THEORY

———. *Ecclesiastiche sinfonie dette canzoni in aria francese, a 4 voc., Opere 16.* Venice, 1607.

———. *Conclusioni del suoni dell'organo.* 2d ed. Bologna, 1609.

———. *La Cartella musicale.* 2d ed. Venice, 1610.

Barbour, Murray James. *Tuning and Temperament, a Historical Survey.* East Lansing: Michigan State College Press, 1951.

Baresel, Alfred. *Jazz-Harmonielehre.* Trossingen: M. Hohner, 1953.

Baryphonus, Heinrich [Pipegrop]. *Pleiades musicae.* Halberstadt, 1615.

Beach, David. "A Schenker Bibliography." *Journal of Music Theory* 13, no. 1 (Spring 1969): 2–37.

Bellermann, Johann Gottfried Heinrich. *Der Kontrapunkt oder Anleitung zur Stimmführung in der musikalische Komposition.* [1862]. 2d ed. Berlin: J. Springer, 1877.

Berardi, Angelo. *Il perché musicale.* Bologna, 1693.

Bernardi, Steffano. *Porta musicale per la quala il principiante con facile brevità all'-acquisto delle perfette regole del contrapunto vien introdetto. . . .* Verona, 1615.

Bimberg, Siegfried. "Zur Festigung des Funktions begriffs in der Musik." In *Wissenschaftliche Zeitschrift der Universität Halle* 3, 1954.

Blainville, Charles-Henri. *Essay sur un troisième mode.* Paris, 1751.

Bononcini, Giovanni Maria. *Musico prattico che brevemente dimostra il modo di guingere alla perfetta cognizione di tutte quelle cose. . . .* Op. 8. Bologna, 1673.

Boyvin, Jean. *Traité abrégé de l'accompagnement pour l'orgue et le clavessin.* Amsterdam, 1700.

Brossard, Sebastien de. *Dictionnaire de musique contenant une explication des termes grecs, italiens, et français les plus usités dans la musique.* Christoph Ballard, 1703.

Buelow, George J. *Thorough-Bass Accompaniment According to Johann David Heinichen.* Berkeley: University of Calfornia Press, 1966.

Bukofzer, Manfred. *Music in the Baroque Era.* New York: W. W. Norton & Co., 1947.

Bumcke, Gustav. *Harmonielehre.* 2 vols. Berlin: Saturn, 1921.

Calvisius, Sethus. *Compendium musicae practicae pro incipientibus.* Leipzig, 1594.

———. *Exercitationes musicae duae.* Leipzig, 1600.

———. *Exercitatio musica tertia.* Leipzig, 1609.

Campion, François. *Traité d'accompagnement et de composition selon la règle des octaves.* Paris, 1716.

Capellen, Georg. *Fortschrittliche Harmonie- und Melodielehre.* Leipzig: C. F. Kahnt Nachfolger, 1908.

Caramuel de Lobkowitz. *Arte nueva de musica.* 1644.

Catel, Charles Simon. *Traité d'harmonie.* Paris, 1802.

Caus, Salomon de. *Institution harmonique.* Frankfurt, 1615.

Chladni, Ernst Florens Friedrich. *Die Akustik.* Leipzig, 1802.

Christ, William; DeLone, Richard; Kliewer, Vernon; Rowell, Lewis; and Thomson, William. *Materials and Structure of Music.* 2 vols. Englewood Cliffs, N.J.: Prentice-Hall, 1966–1967.

Coperario, John. *Rules How to Compose.* [Unpublished, c. 1610.] Edited by Manfred Bukofzer. Los Angeles: E. Gottlieb, 1952.

Dahlhaus, Carl. "War Zarlino Dualist?" *Die Musikforschung* 10 (1957): 286–290.

———. "Ueber den Begriff der tonalen Funktion." In *Beiträge zur Musiktheorie des 19. Jahrhunderts*. Edited by Martin Vogel. Regensburg: Gustav Bosse, 1966.

———. *Untersuchungen Ueber die Entstehung der harmonischen Tonalität*. Kassel: Bärenreiter, 1968.

Daniels, Arthur Michael. "The De Musica Libri VII of Francisco de Salinas." Ph.D. dissertation, University of Southern California, 1962.

———. "Microtonality and Mean-tone Temperament in the Harmonic System of Francisco Salinas." *Journal of Music Theory* 9, no.1 (Spring 1965) : 2–51.

Daube, Johann Friedrich. *Generalbass in drey Accorden*. Leipzig: Johann Benjamin Andra, 1756.

Delair, Etienne Denis. *Traité de'accompagnement pour le théorbe et le clavessin, qui comprend toutes les règles nécessaires pour accompagner sur ces deux instruments.* . . . Paris, 1690.

Denecke, Heinz Ludwig. "Die Kompositionslehre Hugo Riemanns, historisch und systematisch dargestellt." Inaugral Dissertation. Kiel: Dissertationsdruckerei von Robert Kleinert in Quakenbrück, 1937.

Descartes, René. *Compendium musicae*. 1618. Translated by Walter Robert as *Compendium of Music*. Rome: American Institute of Musicology, 1961.

Distler, Hugo. *Funktionelle Harmonielehre*. Kassel und Basel: Bärenreiter, 1940.

Egan, John Bernard. "Marin Mersenne: 'traité de l'harmonie universelle' (1627); Critical translation of the second book." Ph.D. dissertation, Indiana University, 1962.

Eidenbenz, Richard. "Dur- und Moll-Problem und Erweiterung der Tonalität." Ph.D. dissertation, Zurich, 1927.

Erpf, Hermann. *Studien zur Harmonie- und Klangtechnik der neueren Musik*. Leipzig: Breitkopf und Härtel, 1927.

Euler, Leonhardt. *Tentamen Novae Theoriae Musicae*. St. Petersburg, 1739.

Federhofer, Hellmut. "Die Funktionstheorie Hugo Riemanns und die Schichtenlehre Heinrich Schenkers." In *Bericht über den Internationalen Musikwissenschaftlichen Kongress, Wien, Mozartjahr 1956*. Edited by Erich Schenk, pp. 183–190. Graz: H. Böhlaus Nachfolger, 1956.

Ferris, Joan. "The Evolution of Rameau's Harmonic Theories." *Journal of Music Theory* 3, no. 1 (1959) : 231–256.

Fétis, François Joseph. *Esquisse de l'histoire de l'harmonie, considérée comme art et comme science systematique*. Paris: Bourgogne et Martinet, 1840.

———. *Traité complet de la théorie et de la pratique de l'harmonie* [1844]. 2d ed. Paris: Braudwe, 1853.

———. *Biographie universelle*. 8 vols. Paris, 1860–1865. Reprint. 8 vols. plus 2 supplements. Brussels: Joseph Adam, 1963.

Fogliano, Lodovico. *Musica Theorica*. Venice, 1529.

Forte, Allen. "Schenker's Conception of Musical Structure." *Journal of Music Theory* 3, no. 1 (April 1959) : 1–30.

Framery, Nicolas Etienne. *Encyclopédie méthodique*. 2 vols. Paris: Framery et Ginguend, 1791.

Frezza dalle Grotte, Giuseppe. *Il Cantore ecclesiastico per istruzione de' religiosi minori conventuali*. Padua, 1698.

Fux, Johann Joseph. *Gradus ad Parnassum; sive manuductio ad compositionem musicae reqularem, methode nova*. Vienna: Joanis Petri Van Ghelen, 1725.

Reprint. New York: Broude Brothers, 1966. Translated by Alfred Mann as *Steps to Parnassus*. New York: Norton and Co., 1943.

Gaffurius, Franchinus. *Practica musicae*. Milan, 1496. Translated and edited with musical transcriptions by Irvin Young as *The Practica Musica of Franchinus Gafurius*. Madison, Milwaukee: University of Wisconsin Press, 1969.

Gasparini, Francesco. *L'armonico pratico al cimbalo*. 1708. Translated by Frank S. Stillings as *The Practical Harmonist at the Harpsichord*. Edited by David L. Burrows. New Haven: Yale University Press, 1968.

Gevaert, Francois August. *Traité d'harmonie théorique et pratique*. 2 vols. Paris and Brussels, 1905–1907.

Gerber, Ernst Ludwig. *Neues historische-biographisches Lexikon der Tonkünstler*. 4 vols. Leipzig, 1812–1814. Reprint. Edited by Othmar Wessely. Graz, Austria: Akademische Druck- und Verlagsanstalt, 1966.

Gerbert (von Hornau), Martin. *De cantu et musica sacra a prima eccles iae aetate usque ad praesens tempus*. 2 vols. St. Blasien, 1774.

Glarean, Heinrich Loriti. *Dodecachordon* [1547]. Translated with commentary by Clement A. Miller. Rome: American Institute of Musicology, 1965.

Gombosi, Otto Johannes. *Tonarten und Stimmungen der Antiken Musik*. Copenhagen: Ejnar Munksgaard, 1939.

Grabner, Hermann. *Die Funktionstheorie Hugo Riemanns und ihre Bedeutung für die Praktische Analyse*. Munich: Otto Halbreiter, 1923.

———. *Handbuch der Harmonielehre; Praktische Anleitung zum funktionellen Tonsatz*. 2 vols. Berlin: Max Hesse, 1944.

Groves Dictionary of Music and Musicians. Edited by Eric Blom. 10 vols. 5th ed. New York: St. Martin's Press, 1966.

Gruber, Albion. "Mersenne and Evolving Tonal Theory." *Journal of Music Theory* 14, no. 1 (Spring 1970): 37–67.

Handschin, Jacques. *Der Toncharakter, eine Einführung in die Tonpsychologie*. Zurich: Atlantis, 1948.

Hauptmann, Moritz. *Die Natur der Harmonik und der Metrik*. [1853.] 2d ed. Berlin: Breitkopf und Härtel, 1873. Translated by W. E. Heathcote as *The Nature of Harmony and Meter*. London: Swan Sonnenschen and Co., 1888.

Heiden, Bernhard. "Hindemith's 'System'—A New Approach." *Modern Music* 14 (January-February 1942): 102–107.

Heinichen, Johann David. *Neu erfundene und gründliche Anweisung . . . zu vollkommener Erlernung des Generalbasses*. Hamburg: B. Schillers, 1711.

———. *Der Generalbass in der Composition, oder Neue und gründliche Anweisung*. . . . Dresden: Privately published, 1728. Reprint. Hildesheim and New York: Georg Olms, 1969.

Helmholtz, Hermann von. *Die Lehre von den Tonempfindungen als physiologische Grundlage für die Theorie der Musik*. Brunswick, 1863. Translated, thoroughly revised and corrected, rendered conformable to the 4th (and last) German ed. of 1877 by John Alexander Ellis as *On the Sensations of Tone as a Physiological Basis for the Theory of Music*. 6th ed. New York: Peter Smith, 1948.

Henderson, Isobel. "Ancient Greek Music." In *New Oxford History of Music*. Edited by Egon Wellesz. 5 vols. London and New York: Oxford University Press, 1954–1973.

Herbst, Johann Andreas. *Musica poetica siva Compendium melopoeticum*. Nuremberg, 1643.

Hindemith, Paul. *The Craft of Musical Composition*. Book 1, *Theoretical Part*. Translated by Arthur Mendel. London: Associated Music Publishers, 1942.

Hitzler, Daniel. *Newe musica oder Singkunst*. Tübingen, 1628.

Holder, William. *A Treatise of the Natural Grounds and Principles of Harmony*. London: J. Heptinstall, 1694. Reprint. New York: Broude Brothers, 1967.

Hostinsky, Otakar. *Die Lehre von den musikalischen Klängen*. Prague: H. Dominicus, 1879.

Imig, Renate. *Systeme der Funktionsbezeichnung in den Harmonielehren seit Hugo Riemann*. Düsseldorf: Gesellschaft zur Förderung der systematischen Musikwissenschaft, 1970.

Jacobi, Erwin Reuben. "Harmonic Theory in England after the Time of Rameau." *Journal of Music Theory* 1, no. 2 (November 1957): 126–146.

———. *Die Entwicklung der Musiktheorie in England nach der Zeit von Jean-Philippe Rameau*. Baden-Baden: Valentin Koerner, 1971.

Jamard. *Recherches sur la théorie de la musique*. Paris, 1769.

Jeppeson, Knud. "Zur Kritik der Klassichen Harmonielehre." In *Bericht über den International Musikwissenschaftlichen Kongress, Bonn, 1970*. Kassel and Basel: Bärenreiter, 1970.

Jocabus of Liège. *Speculum musicae*. 7 vols. [ca. 1330.] Reprint. Vols. I, VI, VII in *Scriptores de musica medii aevi*. Edited by E. de Coussemaker. Vol. 1. Paris, 1864. Reprint. Milan: Bollettino bibliografico musicale, 1931.

Johannes de Muris. *Ars discantus secundum Johannes de Muris*. In *Scriptores de musica medii aevi*. Edited by E. de Coussemaker. Vol. 3. Paris, 1864. Reprint. Milan: Bollettino bibliografico musicale, 1931.

Jonas, Oswald. *Das Wesen des musikalischen Kunstwerks; eine Einführung in die Lehre Heinrich Schenkers*. Vienna: Saturn, 1934.

———. "Heinrich Schenker." *Die Musik in Geschichte und Gegenwart*. Edited by Friedrich Blume. Kassel and Basel: Barenreiter, 1949.

Jorgenson, Dale Alfred. "A History of Theories of the Minor Triad." Ph.D. dissertation, Indiana University, 1957.

Karg-Elert, Sigfrid. *Polaristische Klang- und Tonalitätslehre*. Leipzig: Leuckhart, 1931.

Katz, Adele T. "Heinrich Schenker's Method of Analysis." *Music Quarterly* 21 (1935): 311.

———. *Challenge to Music Tradition: A New Concept of Tonality*. London: Putnam and Co., 1945.

Kauder, Hugo. *Entwurf einer neuen Melodie- und Harmonielehre*. Vienna: Universal-edition, 1932.

Kaun, Hugo. *Harmonie- und Modulationslehre*. Leipzig: J. H. Zimmermann, 1915.

Keane, Sister Michaela Maria. *The Theoretical Writings of Jean-Philippe Rameau*. Washington, D.C.: Catholic University of America Press, 1961.

Keller [or Kellner], David. *Treulicher Unterricht im General-Bass*. Hamburg, 1732.

Keller, Gottfried. *Rules for Playing a Thorow-bass; with variety of Proper Lessons, Fuges, and Examples. . . . Also Directions for Tuning an Harpsichord or Spinnet*. Added to William Holder, *A Treatise of the Natural grounds and principles of Harmony*. London: Raphael Georg, 1731. Reprint. New York: Broude Brothers, 1967.

Keller, Wilhelm. *Handbuch der Tonsatzlehre.* 2 vols. Regensburg: Gustav Bosse, 1957–1959.

————. "Heinrich Schenkers Harmonielehre." In *Beiträge zur Musiktheorie des 19. Jahrhunderts.* Edited by Martin Vogel. Regensburg: Gustav Bosse, 1966.

Kiesewetter, Raphael Georg. *Die Musik der Araber.* Leipzig: Breitkopf und Härtel, 1842.

Kircher, Athanasius. *Musurgia universalis sive ars magna consoni et dissoni.* 2 vols. Rome, 1650. Reprint. Hildesheim: Georg Olms, 1970.

Kirnberger, Johann Phillip. *Die Kunst des reinen Satzes in der Musik.* 2 parts. Berlin, 1771–1779.

————. *Die wahren Grundsätze zum Gebrauch der Harmonie.* Berlin, 1773.

Kirsch, Ernst. *Wesen und Aufbau der Lehre von den harmonischen Funktionen, ein Beitrag zur Theorie der Relationen der musikalischen Harmonie.* Leipzig: Breitkopf und Härtel, 1928.

Kitson, Charles Herbert. *Elementary Harmony.* Oxford: The Clarendon Press, 1920.

Klatte, Wilhelm. *Grundlagen des mehrstimmigen Satzes.* Berlin: N. Simrock, 1922.

Knecht, Justin Heinrich. *Gemeinnützliches Elementarwerk der Harmonie und des Generalbasses. Das ist: wahre Art, die Begleitungskunst . . . zu lehren und zu lernen . . . zum Gebrauche für Lehrer, Anfänger und Geübtere.* 4 parts. Augsburg and Stuttgart, 1792–1798.

Koch, Heinrich Christoph. *Versuch einer Anleitung zur Composition.* 3 vols. Leipzig: A. F. Böhme, 1782–1793.

————. *Handbuch bey dem Studium der Harmonie.* Leipzig: J. F. Hartknoch, 1811.

————. *Musikalisches Lexikon, welches die theoretische und praktische, encyclopädisch bearbeitet, alle alten und neuen kunstwörter erklärt, und die alten und neuen instrumente beschreiben, enthält.* Frankfurt am Main: A. Harman, 1802. Reprint. Hildesheim: Georg Olms, 1964.

Krehbiel, James Woodrow. "Harmonic Principles of Jean-Philippe Rameau and his contemporaries." Ph.D. dissertation, Indiana University, 1964.

Kurth, Ernst. *Die Voraussetzungen der Theoretischen Harmonik.* Bern: M. Drechsel, 1913.

————. *Grundlagen des linearen Kontrapunkts, Einführung in Stil und Technik von Bach's melodischer Polyphonie.* Bern: M. Drechsel, 1917.

————. *Romantische Harmonik und ihre Krise in Wagners "Tristan."* Berlin, 1923. Reprint. Hildesheim: Georg Olms, 1968.

————. *Musikpsychologie.* Berlin, 1931. Reprint. Hildesheim: Georg Olms, 1969.

León Tello, Francisco José. *Estudios de historia de la teoría musical.* Madrid: Consejo Superior de Investigaciones Científicas, Instituto Español de Musicología, 1962.

Levens. *Abrégé des règles de l'harmonie, pour aprendre la composition, avec un nouveau projet sur un systeme de musique sans temperment, ne cordes mobile.* Bordeaux: J. Chappuis, 1743.

Lippius, Johann. *Synopsis musicae novae omnino verae atque methodicae universae.* Argentoratum (Strasbourg), 1612.

Lobkowitz, Caramuel de. *Arte nueva di musica.* Rome, 1669.

Locke, Matthew. *Melothesia with a Choice Collection of Lessons for the Harpsichord.* London, 1673.

Louis, Rudolf, and Thuille, Ludwig. *Harmonielehre.* 4th ed. Stuttgart: Carl Grüninger, 1913.

Lowinsky, Edward Elias. *Tonality and Atonality in Sixteenth-Century Music.* Berkeley and Los Angeles: University of California Press, 1962.

Ludwig, Hellmut. *Marin Mersenne und seine Musiklehre.* Halle an der Saale and Berlin: Buchhandlung des Waisenhauses, 1935. Reprint. Hildesheim: Georg Olms, 1971.

Mahmud, Qutb al-Din al-Shirazi. "Durrat al-taj." Manuscript. London, British Museum Library, Persian Add. 7694.

Mäler, Wilhelm. *Beitrag zur Harmonielehre.* Leipzig: Lückhardt, 1931.

Mann, Michael. "Schenker's Contribution to Music Theory." *Music Review* 10 (February 1949): 3–26.

Marchettus von Padua. *Lucidarium in arte musicae planae.* [1274.] In *Scriptores de musica medii aevi.* Edited by E. de Coussemaker. Vol. 3. Paris, 1864. Reprint. Milan: Bollettino bibliografico musicale, 1931.

Marpurg, Friedrich Wilhelm. *Handbuch bey dem Generalbasse und der Composition mit zwo- drey- vier- funf- sechs- sieben- acht und mehren stimmen, für anfänger und geübtere.* 4 vols. Berlin: G. A. Lange, 1755–1760.

———. *Versuch über die musikalische Temperatur.* Breslau: J. F. Korn, 1776.

Marschner, Franz. *Die Klangschrift, ein Beitrag zur einheitlichen Gestaltung der Harmonielehre.* Vienna, 1894.

Martini, Padre Giovanni Battistti. *Esemplare o sia saggio fondamentale pratico di contrappunto sopre il canto fermo.* 2 vols. Bologna: Lelio della Volpe, 1774–1775. Reprint. Ridgewood, N.J.: Gregg Press, 1965.

Masson, Charles. *Nouveau traité des règles pour la composition de la musique par lequel on apprend à faire facilement un chant sur des paroles; a composer à 2, à 3, et à 4 parties.* [Paris, 1694.] 3rd ed., rev. Brussels, 1705.

Matthaei, Conrad. *Kurtzer, doch ausführlicher Bericht von den Modis musicis.* Königsberg, 1652.

Mattheson, Johann. *Das neu-eröffnete Orchestre.* Hamburg: B. Schillers, 1713.

———. *Das beschützte Orchestre.* Hamburg, 1717.

———. *Grosse General-Bass-Schule; Oder exemplarischen Organisten-Probe.* Hamburg, 1731.

———. *Kleine General-Bass-Schule.* Hamburg, 1735.

———. *Der Vollkommene Capellmeister, Das ist Gründliche Anzeige aller derjenigen Sachen, die einer wissen . . . muss, der einer Capelle . . . vorstehen will.* Hamburg, 1739.

Mekeel, Joyce. "The Harmonic Theories of Kirnberger and Marpurg." *Journal of Music Theory* 4, no. 2 (November 1960): 169–193.

Mersenne, Marin. *Harmonie universelle contenant la théorie et la pratique de la musique.* 19 books. Paris: S. Cramoisy, 1636–1637. Seven books translated by Roger E. Chapman as *Harmonie universelle, the Books on Instruments.* The Hague: Martinus Nijhoff, 1957.

Mitchell, William J. "Schenker's Approach to Detail." *Musicology* 1, no. 1 (1946): 117–128.

Mizler, Lorenz Christoph. *Neu eröffnete musikalische Bibliothek, Oder gründliche Nachricht nebst unpartheyischen Urtheil von musikalischen Schriften und Bühern.* 4 vols. Leipzig: Mizler, 1736–1754.

———. *Die Anfangsgründe des Generalbasses, nach mathematischer Lehrart abgehandelt.* Leipzig, 1739.

Morley, Thomas. *A Plaine and Easie Introduction to Practicall Musicke*. London: P. Short, 1597.

Moser, Hans Joachim. "Funktionslehre." In *Musiklexikon*. Edited by Hans Joachim Moser. 4th ed. Hamburg: Hans Sikorski, 1955.

Münnich, Richard. "Von Entwicklung der Riemannschen Harmonielehre und ihrem Verhältnis zu Oettingen und Stumpf." In *Riemann-Festschrift; Gesammelte Studien, Hugo Riemann zum sechzigsten Geburtstage überreicht von Freunden und Schülern*. Leipzig: Max Hesse, 1909. Reprint. Tutzing: Hans Schneider, 1965.

Muris, Johannes de. "Ars contrapuncti secundem Johannem de Muris." In *Scriptores de musica medii aevi*. Edited by E. de Coussemaker. Paris, 1864. Reprint. Milan: Bollettino bibliografico musicale, 1931.

Musik in Geschichte und Gegenwart, Die. Edited by Friedrich Blume. 15 vols. Kassel and Basel: Bärenreiter, 1949–.

Neumann, Friedrich. *Synthetische Harmonielehre*. Leipzig: Breitkopf und Härtel, 1951.

New Oxford History of Music. Edited by Egon Wellez. 5 vols. London and New York: Oxford University Press, 1954–1973.

Nichelmann, Christoph. *Die Melodie nach ihrem Wesen sowohl als nach ihren Eigenschaften*. Danzig, 1755.

Niedt, Friedrich Erhardt. *Musikalische Handleitung*. Hamburg, 1700. [2d ed. 1710].

Nivers, Guillaume-Gabriel. *La gamme du Si; Nouvelle méthode*. Paris, 1646.

Odington, Walter. *De speculatione musicae*. In *Scriptores de musica medii aevi*. Edited by E. de Coussemaker. Vol. 1. Paris, 1864. Reprint. Milan: Bollettino bibliografico musicale, 1931.

Oettingen, Arthur von. *Harmoniesystem in dualer Entwicklung*. Leipzig: W. Glaser, 1866.

Oeuvres des Descartes. Published under the direction of the Ministere de l'Instruction publique. Vol. 1, *Correspondance*. Paris: Charles Adam and Paul Tannery, 1897–1909.

Opelt, Friedrich Wilhelm. *Allgemeine Theorie der Musik auf den Rhythmus der Klangwellenpulse gegründet and durch neue Versinnlichungsmittel erläutern*. Leipzig, 1852.

Ortiz, Diego. *Tratado de glosas sobre clausulas y otros generos de puntos en la musica de violones nueuamente puestos en luz*. 1553.

Piston, Walter. *Harmony*. 3rd ed. New York: Norton, 1962.

Planchart, Alejandro. "A Study of the Theories of Giuseppi Tartini." *Journal of Music Theory* 4, no. 1 (April 1960): 32–61.

Playford, John. *An Introduction to the Skill of Musick*, to which is added *The Art of Discant, or Composing Musick in Parts*, by Thomas Campion. 8th ed. London: W. Godbid, 1679.

Pontio, Don Pietro. *Dialogo . . . ove si tratta della theoria e prattica di musica et anco si mostra la diversità de' contraponti et canoni*. Parma, 1595.

Praetorius, Michael. *Syntagma musicum*. 3 vols. 1614–1620. Reprint. New York: Broude Brothers, 1965.

Puteanus, Erycus. *Modulata Pallas*. 1599.

Rameau, Jean-Philippe. *Traité de l'harmonie réduite à ses principes naturels*. 4 vols. Paris: J. B. C. Ballard, 1722. Reprint. New York: Broude Brothers, 1965.

Translated with an introduction and notes by Philip Gosset as *Treatise on Harmony, Reduced to its Natural Principles.* New York: Dover Publications, 1971.

―――. *Nouveau système de musique théorique.* Paris: J. B. C. Ballard, 1726. Reprint. New York: Broude Brothers, 1965.

―――. *Dissertation sur les différentes méthodes d'accompagnement pour le clevecin ou l'orgue.* Paris, 1732.

―――. *Génération harmonique, ou Traité de musique théorique et pratique.* Paris, 1737. Reprint. New York: Broude Brothers, 1965. Translated with commentary by Deborah Hayes as "Rameau's Theory of Harmonic Generation." Ph.D. dissertation, Stanford University, 1968.

―――. *Démonstration du principe de l'harmonie, servant de base à tout l'art musical théorique et pratique.* Paris: Chez Durand, 1750. Reprint. New York: Broude Brothers, 1965.

―――. *Code de musique pratique ou Méthode pour apprendre la musique.* Paris, 1760.

―――. *The Complete Theoretical Writings of Jean-Philippe Rameau.* Edited by Erwin R. Jacobi. 6 vols. Rome: American Institue of Musicology, 1967–1972.

Ramos de Pareja, Bartolomé, *De Musica practica.* [1482.] Edited by Johannes Wolf. Leipzig: Breitkopf und Härtel, 1901.

Reger, Max. *Beiträge zur Modulationslehre.* 10th ed. Leipzig: C. F. Kahnt Nachfolger, 1917. Translated by John Bernhoff as *Supplement to the Theory of Modulation.* Leipzig: C. F. Kahnt Nachfolger, 1904.

Reese, Gustave. *Music in the Middle Ages.* New York: W. W. Norton & Co., 1940.

―――. *Fourscore Classics of Music Literature; A Guide to Selected Original Sources on Theory and Other Writings on Music Not Available in English, with Descriptive Sketches and Bibiliographical References.* New York: Liberal Arts Press, 1957. Reprint. New York: Da Capo Press, 1970.

Reuter, Fritz. *Praktische Harmonik des 20. Jahrhunderts: Konsonanz- und Dissonanzlehre nach dem System von Sigfrid Karg-Elert mit Aufgaben von Fritz Reuter.* Halle: Mitteldeutscher Verlag, 1952.

Révész, Géza. *Introduction to the Psychology of Music.* Translated by G. I. C. de Courcy. Oklahoma City: University of Oklahoma Press, 1953.

Richter, Ernst Friedrich. *Lehrbuch der Harmonie.* Leipzig, 1853.

Riemann, Karl Wilhelm Julius Hugo. [Hugibert Ries]. "Musikalische Logik." *Neue Zeitschrift für Musik* 28 (1872): 1. Reprinted in Hugo Riemann's *Präludien und Studien.* Vol. 3. Leipzig, 1901. Reprint of the latter (3 vols in 1). Hildesheim: Georg Olms, 1967.

―――. "Ueber das musikalische Hören." Ph.D. dissertation. Leipzig: F. Andras Nachfolger, 1874.

―――. *Musikalische Logik, Hauptzüge der physiologischen und psychologischen Begründung unseres Musiksystems.* [The published dissertation.] Leipzig: C. F. Kahnt, 1874.

―――. "Die objective Existenz der Untertöne in der Schallwelle." *Allgemeine Deutsche Musikzeitung* 5 (1875).

―――. *Musikalische Syntaxis, Grundriss einer harmonischen Satzbildungslehre.* Leipzig: Breitkopf und Härtel, 1877. Reprint. Wiesbaden: Breitkopf und Härtel, 1971.

―――. *Studien zur Geschichte der Notenschrift.* Leipzig: Breitkopf und Härtel, 1878.

————. *Skizze einer neuen Methode der Harmonielehre.* Leipzig, 1880.

————. "Zarlino als harmonischer Dualist." In *Monatshefte für Musikgeschichte* (1881).

————. "Die Natur der Harmonik." In *Sammlung musikalischer Vorträge.* Edited by Paul Graf von Waldersee. Series 4, no. 40 (1882): 157–190. Leipzig: Breitkopf und Härtel. Translated as "The Nature of Harmony," by John Comfort Fillmore and added to his *New Lessons in Harmony.* Philadelphia: T. Presser, 1887.

————. *Systematische Modulationslehre als Grundlage der musikalischen Formenlehre.* Hamburg, 1887.

————. *Katechismus der Musikgeschichte.* [1888.] 2d ed. Leipzig: Max Hesse, 1889.

————. *Katechismus der Harmonie- und Modulationslehre.* [1890.] Leipzig: Max Hesse, 1906.

————. *Katechismus der Akustik (Musikwissenschaft).* Leipzig, 1891.

————. *Vereinfachte Harmonielehre, oder die Lehre von den Tonalen Funktionen der Akkorde.* London: Augener and Co., 1893. Translated by H. Bewerung as *Harmony Simplified.* London: Augener and Co., 1896. Reprint. Ann Arbor: University Microfilms, 1968.

————. *Geschichte der Musiktheorie im IX.–XIX. Jahrhundert.* 3 books in 1. Leipzig: Max Hesse, 1898. Books I and II translated by Raymond Haggh as *History of Music Theory.* Lincoln: University of Nebraska Press, 1962.

————. *Encyclopaedic Dictionary of Music.* Translated by J. S. Shedlock. Philadelphia: Theodore Presser, 1899.

————. "Zur Theorie der Konsonanz und Dissonanz." In *Präludien und Studien.* Vol. 3. Leipzig, 1901. Reprint. (3 vols. in 1). Hildesheim: Georg Olms, 1967.

————. *Grosse Kompositionslehre.* Vol. 1: *Der Homophone Satz.* Berlin, 1902.

————. "Das Problem des harmonischen Dualismus." *Neue Zeitschrift für Musik* 17 (1905): 26. Translated by S. Harrison Lovewell as "Consonance and Dissonance, A Discussion of the Principles of Harmonic Dualism." Typewritten, 1925. Copy in the Boston Public Library, Boston.

————. *Elementarschulbuch der Harmonielehre.* Leipzig, 1906.

————. "Ideen zu einer 'Lehre von den Tonvorstellungen.'" *Jahrbuch der Musikbibliothek Peters* 21/22 (1914/15): 1–26. Reprint. Wiesbaden: Lessing, 1965.

————. "Neue Beiträge zu einer Lehre von den Tonvorstellungen." *Jahrbuch der Musikbibliothek Peters* 23 (1916): 1–21. Reprint. Wiesbaden: Lessing, 1965.

————. *Handbuch der Harmonielehre.* 9th ed. Leipzig: Breitkopf und Härtel, 1921.

Riemann Musik-Lexikon. Edited by Wilibald Gurlitt. 3 vols. 12th ed. Mainz: B. Schotts Söhne, 1959–1967.

Rousseau, Jean Jacques. *Dictionnaire de musique.* Paris: Veuve Duchesne, 1768. Reprint. Hildesheim and New York: Georg Olms, 1969.

Rubeli, Alfred Ulrich. *Das Musiktheoretische System Giuseppe Tartinis.* Winterthur: P. G. Keller, 1958.

Rummenhöller, Peter. "Moritz Hauptmann, der Begründer einer transzendental-dialektischen Musiktheorie." In *Beiträge zur Musiktheorie des 19. Jahrhunderts.* Edited by Martin Vogel. Regensburg: Gustav Bosse, 1966.

————. *Musiktheoretisches Denken im 19. Jahrhundert; Versuch einer Interpretation erkenntnistheoretischer Zeugnisse in der Musiktheorie.* Regensburg: Gustav Bosse, 1967.

Salinas, Francisco. *De musica libri septem*. Salamanca: Mathias Gastius, 1577. Reprint. Kassel and Basel: Barenreiter, 1958.

Salzer, Felix. *Structural Hearing: Tonal Coherence in Music*. 2 vols. 2d ed. New York: C. Boni, 1952.

Sauveur, Joseph. Acoustical Essays in *Histoire de l'Academie Royale des sciences*. Edited by Fontenelle. Paris, 1700–1713.

Schenk, Paul. *Modulationslehre*. Leipzig: n.p., 1954.

———. "Karg-Elerts polaristische Harmonielehre." In *Beiträge zur Musiktheorie des 19. Jahrhunderts*. Edited by Martin Vogel. Regensburg: Gustav Bosse, 1966.

Schenker, Heinrich. *Harmonielehre*. Stuttgart and Berlin: J. G. Cotta, 1906. Translated by Elizabeth Mann Borgese as *Harmony*. Edited and annotated by Oswald Jonas. Chicago: Chicago Press, 1954.

———. *Der freie Satz*. 2d ed. Vienna: Osward Jonas, 1956.

Schneider, Johann Christian Friedrich. *Elementarbuch der Harmonie und Tonsetzkunst; Ein leitfaden beim unterricht und hülfsbuch zum selbststudium der musicalischen composition, von Friedrich Schneider*. [1820.] 2d ed. Leipzig: C. F. Peters, 1827.

Schönberg, Arnold. *Harmonielehre*. Vienna: Universal Edition, 1966.

———. *Structural Functions of Harmony*. 1st rev. ed. Edited by Leonard Stein. New York: Norton & Co., 1969.

Schubert, Dietran. *Satzlehre (Satztechniken der Musik)*. Wolfenbüttel: Möseler, 1960.

Sechter, Simon. *Die Grundsätze der musikalischen Komposition*. 3 vols. Leipzig: Breitkopf und Härtel, 1853–1854.

Seidel, Elmer. "Die Harmonielehre Hugo Riemanns." In *Beiträge zur Musiktheorie des 19. Jahrhunderts*. Edited by Martin Vogel. Regensburg: Gustav Bosse, 1966.

Serre, Jean-Adam. *Essais sur les principes de l'harmonie*. 1753. Reprint. New York: Broude Brothers, 1967.

Shirlaw, Matthew. *The Theory of Harmony; an Inquiry into the Natural Principles of Harmony, with an Examination of the Chief Systems of Harmony from Rameau to the Present Day*. 2d ed. Dekalb, Ill.: Dr. Birchard Coar, 1955. Reprint. New York: Da Capo Press, 1969.

Smith, Charles Samuel. "Leonhard Euler's Tentamen Novae Theoriae Musicae: A Translation and Commentary." Ph.D. dissertation, Indiana University, 1960.

Sorge, Georg Andreas. *Vorgemach der musikalischen Composition*. 3 vols. Lobenstein: Privately published. 1745–1747.

Stevens, Stanley Smith, and Davis, Hallowell. *Hearing, Its Psychology and Physiology*. New York: Wiley and Sons, 1938.

Strunk, William Oliver. *Source Readings in Music History from Classical Antiquity through the Romantic Era*. New York: W. W. Norton & Co., 1950.

Stumpf, Friedrich Carl. *Tonpsychologie*. 2 vols. Leipzig: S. Hirzel, 1883, 1890.

———. *Konsonanz und Dissonanz*. Leipzig: Johann Ambrosius Barth, 1898.

Sulzer, Johann Georg. *Allgemeine Theorie der schönen Künste*. 4 vols. 1772.

Svensson, Sven E. *Harmonilära*. Stockholm: n.p., 1933.

Sweertius, Francisus. *Athenae belgicae*. Antwerp, 1628.

Tartini, Giuseppe. *Trattato di musica secondo la vera scienza dell'armonia*. Padua: G. Manfre, 1754.

———. *De'principi dell'armonia musicale contenuto nel Diatonico Genere*. Padua, 1767. Reprint. New York: Broude Brothers, 1967.

Telemann, Georg Philipp. "Avertissement." In *Nouveaux quatours en six suites à une flûte traversière, un violon, une basse de viole, ou violoncel et basse continue.* Paris, 1730.

Thomson, William E. "The Problem of Tonality in Pre-Baroque and Primitive Music." *Journal of Music Theory* 2, no. 1 (April 1958): 36–46.

Tiersch, Otto. *System und methode der Harmonielehre, gegründe auf fremde und eigene beobachtungen, mit besonderer berücksichtung der neusten physikalisch-physiologioschen untersuchen über Tonempfindungen.* Leipzig: Breitkopf und Härtel, 1868.

Tigrini, Orazio. *Il compendio della musica nel quale brevemente si tratta dell'arte del contrapunto, divisi in 4 libri.* Venice, 1588.

Vallotti, Francesco Antonio. *Della scienza teorica e pratica della moderna musica libro primo.* Padua: G. Manfre, 1779.

Van der Pol, B. "Frequency Demultiplication." *Nature* 120 (September 10, 1927): 363–364.

Viadana, Ludovico. Preface. *Cento concerti ecclesiastici a 1, a 2, a 3 e a 4 voci con il basso continuo per sonar nell'organo.* Venice, 1602.

Vogel, Martin, ed. *Beiträge zur Musiktheorie des 19. Jahrhunderts.* Regensburg: Gustav Bosse, 1966.

Vogel, Martin. "Arthur v. Oettingen und der harmonische Dualismus." In *Beiträge zur Musiktheorie des 19. Jahrhunderts.* Edited by Martin Vogel. Regensburg: Gustav Bosse, 1966.

Walther, Johann Gottfried. *Musicalisches Lexicon.* Leipzig, 1732.

Weber, Gottfried. *Versuch einer geordneten Theorie der Tonsetzkunst, zum Selbstunterricht mit Anmerkungen für Gelehrtere.* 3 vols. Mainz: B. Schott, 1817–1821. Translated by James F. Warner as *Theory of Musical Composition.* Boston: O. Ditson & Co., 1851.

Weigl, Bruno. *Harmonielehre.* 2 vols. Mainz: B. Schotts Söhne, 1925.

Werckmeister, Andreas. *Musicae mathematicae Hodegus curiosus.* Frankfurt and Leipzig, 1686. [2d ed. 1687.]

———. *Musikalische Temperatur.* Frankfurt and Leipzig, 1686/87.

———. *Die Nothwendigsten Anmerckungen und Regeln.* Aschersleben, 1698.

———. *Harmonologia musica, oder kurze Anleitung zur musikalischen Composition.* Frankfurt, 1702.

Werner, Johann Gottlob. *Versuch einer kurzen und deutlichen Darstellung der Harmonielehre, oder Anweisung, richtige Harmoniefolgen und kleine Musiksätze zu erfinden für Anfänger und zum Selbstunterricht.* Leipzig, 1818.

Wienke, G. "Voraussetzungen der 'musikalischen Logik' bei Hugo Riemann; Studien zur Musikästhetik in der 2. Häfte des 19. Jahrhunderts." Ph.D. dissertation, University of Freiburg in Breisgau, 1953.

Wienpahl, Robert W. "English Theorists and Evolving Tonality." *Music and Letters* 36 (1955): 377–393.

———. "Zarlino, the Senario, and Tonality." *Journal of the American Musicological Society* 12, no. 1 (1959): 27–41.

Williams, David Russell. *A Bibiliography of the History of Music Theory.* 2d ed. Fairport, N.Y.: Rochester Music Publishers, 1971.

Zacconi, P. Lodovico. *Prattica di musica.* 2 vols. Venice, 1592–1622.

Zarlino, Gioseffo. *Le Istituzioni harmoniche.* Venice, 1558. Reprint. New York: Broude Brothers, 1965. Part III translated by Guy A. Marco and Claude V.

Palisca as *The Art of Counterpoint*. New Haven and London: Yale University Press, 1968.

————. *Dimostrazioni harmoniche*. Venice, 1571. Reprint. New York: Broude Brothers, 1965.

————. *Sopplimenti musicale*. Venice, 1588. Reprint. Ridgewood, N.J.: Gregg Press, 1966.

————. *De Tutte l'opere del R. M. G. Zarlino da Chioggia*. Venice, 1588/89. Reprint. Hildesheim: Georg Olms, 1968.

Index of Authors and Composers

Abraham, Lars Ulrich, 176
Achtelik, Joseph, 93
Adler, A., 176
Agazzari, Agostino, 154–155
Aichinger, Gregor, 154
Albert, Heinrich, 174
Alchin, Carolyn, 93
Alpharabius (El Farabi), 110
d'Alembert, Jean le Rond, 9, 190, 196
Ambros, August Wilhelm, 176
Anonymus IV, 147
Anseln von Flandern, 148
Apel, Willi, 41 (n. 47), 43–44, 173
Aristotle, 185
Arnold, Frank Thomas, 173–174, 183
Artusi, Giovanni Maria, 113, 157–158
Augustine, Saint, 111

Bach, Johann Sebastien, 121, 151,
    163, 165, 175, 206–207
Baillière de Laisement, Charles-Louis-
    Denis, 196
Baini, Giuseppe, 156–157, 172, 173
Banchieri, Adriano, 148, 149–150
Baresel, Alfred, 93
Bartók, Béla, 71
Baryphonus, Heinrich (Pipegrop), 113
Bellermann, Johann Gottfried
    Heinrich, 121–122, 206
Berardi, Angelo, 206
Bernardi, Stefano, 164
Bianciardi, 172
Bimberg, Siegfried, 90
Blainville, Charles-Henri, 196
Bononcini, Giovanni Maria, 149
Boyvin, Jean, 158
Brossard, Sebastien de, 180, 192, 228
Bumcke, Gustav, 93, 94

Caccini, Giulio, 149, 173
Calvisius, Sethus, 113, 149
Campion, Francois, 17–18, 156, 233
Capellen, Georg, 93–94
Caramuel de Lobkowitz, 148–149
Catel, Charles Simon, 236
Caus, Salomon de, 113, 116
Cavaliere, Emilio de, 149, 153, 173
Chladni, Ernst Florens Friedrich, 197
Christ, William, 93
Coussemaker, Charles Edmond Henri,
    147
Corti, Count, 190
Croce, Giovanni, 174

Dahlhaus, Carl, 7, 62–63
Daube, Johann Friedrich, 17, 20–21,
    22, 168–169, 194–195
Davis, Hallowell, 55
Delair, Etienne Denis, 18, 156, 233
Denecke, Heinz Ludwig, xii, 90, 101
    (n. 46)
Descartes, René, 8, 138–139, 143–144,
    166, 187
Distler, Hugo, 92, 94
Dommer, A. v., 202
Doni, Giovanni Battista, 174

Eidenbenz, Richard, 93, 94
Eitner, Robert, xi
El Farabi, 110
Erpf, Hermann, 89, 90–91, 94
Euler, Leonhardt, 56, 58

Federhofer, Hellmut, 62, 96 (n. 26)
Ferris, Joan, 9 (n. 17), 19 (n. 45)
Fétis, Francois Joseph, xi, 18, 22, 33,
    66, 148, 156, 169, 186, 199–200, 235

Index of Subjects

257

Riemann, 4–5, 41–44, 55–56, 61, 218
Schenker, 94–97
Sorge, 166–169
Tartini, 10–12
Werckmeister, 166, 168
Zarlino, 6–8, 107–110
March de basse, 235 (n. 41)
Mediant. *See* Chords, Mediant
Mehrklang, 90
Melody is derived from harmony, 6,
   19, 21, 33, 191
Merides, 149
Mese, 39–40
Messel theory, 40–41, 109–110
MI contra FA. *See* Tritone
Minor scale. *See* Scale
Minor sixth
   More perfect than the major sixth,
     168
   A replica, 7
Minor-third change, 81
Minor-third step, 82
Minor triad, harmony, and mode
   Derived from the arithmetic series, 3
   Hauptmann, 13–14, 216
   Helmholtz, 212–213
   Hindemith, 97
   Hostinsky, 216–217
   Mattheson, 162–164
   Oettingen, 14–16, 214
   Rameau, 9, 46, 189, 190
   Riemann, 4–5, 30, 39–40, 41–44,
     55–56, 61, 89, 218
   Schenker, 94–97
   Sorge, 166–169
   Tartini, 10–12, 13–14
   Werckmeister, 166, 168
   Zarlino, 6–8, 14, 107–110
Mixolydian seventh, 82
Modes
   Church, 41–44, 71, 95–96, 112–113,
     178 (n. 27)
   Greek Dorian, 16, 39–40
   Hyperdorian, 42
   Major and minor modes. *See* Major
     triad, harmony, and
     mode, *and* Minor triad,
     harmony, and mode
   Phrygian, 43, 44, 71

Modulation
   Daube, 195
   Fétis, 186
   Grabner, 92
   Hauptmann, 68–69
   Hindemith, 99
   Rameau, 192
   Riemann, 47, 67–71, 75, 77, 79, 83,
     85, 89, 96, 99, 222
   Sorge, 167, 219
   Schenker, 96–97, 98–99
   Weber, 210–211
Monody, 150
Motion, similar, contrary, oblique,
   120–123
Multiple tone, 53–54
Musica ficta, 42–44, 122–123, 125

Natural seventh, 169, 197–198
Notation, Medieval, 41–42
Note sensible (leading tone), 191, 193

Octave
   Instrumental doubling of, 157–158
   Revesz' two-component theory, 59
   Riemann and others, 58–59
   Salinas, 111
   Zarlino, 123
Orchestral composition, Origin of, 157
Ordinarakkord, 174 (n. 12)
Ordre unitonique, transitoire,
   pluratonique, and omnitonique, 186
Organ building, 157–158
Over-Klang, 218
Over-third clang, 92
Overtones
   Catel, 236 (n. 48)
   First indication of nature, 187
   Helmholtz, 53
   Hindemith, 97
   Mersenne, 139 (n. 12)
   Oettingen, 14–16, 38, 213–215
   Rameau, 8, 45–46
   Riemann, 3–5, 11, 31, 33–34, 46,
     53–54, 55–56, 69–70
   Tartini, 11, 34
   Sauveur, 187
   Sorge, 166, 167
   Vallotti, 236 (n. 48)

temperament
Tenor voice, representative of the
  mode, 126
Theory, Speculative and practical, 6,
  25, 45, 47, 75, 90, 126, 152, 165, 169,
  185, 206
Theses. *See* Dialectics
Third change, 81
Third step, 81
Thorough-bass. *See* Figured bass
Three-part writing antiquated, 125–126
Three pillars of harmony. *See*
  Chords, Primary
Tonal concepts, 30–31, 85–88, 99–101
Tonality and key
  Fétis, 22, 33, 186–187
  Hauptmann, 12, 68
  Hindemith, 98–99
  Kirnberger, 186
  Mattheson, 162–163
  Oettingen, 14–16
  Rameau, 68, 190–191
  Riemann, 28, 32–33, 35–36, 38, 63,
    67–68, 96
  Schenker, 96–97, 98–99
Tonal relationships, 36, 68–69, 90,
  92–98, 196
Tone-representation, 36, 37–38, 187
Tonic. *See* Chords, Primary
Tonicalization, 99
Tonvorstellungen. *See* Tonal concepts
Transposition, 162, 186

Triad. *See* Chords
Trias harmonica, 174 (n. 12)
Trias harmonica perfecta, minus
  perfecta, deficiens, manca, superflua,
  166–168
Tritone, 117, 164, 168
Tritone change, 82
Tuning and temperament, 37, 40, 70,
  87, 114, 197, 213, 217
Turn of harmony, 80
Two-component theory. *See* Octave,
  Revesz

Under-Klang, 218
Under-third clang, 92
Undertones
  Oettingen, 15, 38, 214–215
  Rameau, 22, 46, 189, 190
  Riemann, 3–4, 11, 30–31, 33–35, 38,
    41, 46, 52–56, 187
  Tartini, 11
  Zarlino (Senarius), 187, 189
Unison, 111, 123, 124
Urlinie, 97
Ursatz, 97

Variation suite, 147
Vorstellung. *See* Tonal concepts

Whole-tone change, 81–82
Whole-tone step, 80, 83